SUZANNE WHEELER

365 DAYS WITH GOD

THE PROMISE BOX: 365 DAYS WITH GOD
Copyright © 2025 by Suzanne Wheeler

All rights reserved. Neither this publication nor any part of this publication may be reproduced or transmitted in any form or by any means, electronic or mechanical, including photocopying, recording or any information storage and retrieval system, without permission in writing from the author.

Unless otherwise indicated, scripture quotations are taken from THE HOLY BIBLE, NEW INTERNATIONAL VERSION®, NIV® Copyright © 1973, 1978, 1984, 2011 by Biblica, Inc.® Used by permission. All rights reserved worldwide. • Scripture quotations marked (NLT) are taken from the Holy Bible, New Living Translation, copyright © 1996, 2004, 2015 by Tyndale House Foundation. Used by permission of Tyndale House Publishers, Inc., Carol Stream, Illinois 60188. All rights reserved. • Scripture quotations marked (CEV) are taken from the Contemporary English Version® Copyright © 1995 American Bible Society. All rights reserved. • Scripture quotations marked (AMP) are taken from The Amplified Bible, Copyright © 2015 by The Lockman Foundation, La Habra, CA 90631. All rights reserved. • Scripture quotations marked (HCSB) are taken from the Holman Christian Standard Bible®, Copyright © 1999, 2000, 2002, 2003, 2009 by Holman Bible Publishers. Used by permission. Holman Christian Standard Bible®, Holman CSB®, and HCSB® are federally registered trademarks of Holman Bible Publishers. • Scripture quotations marked (GW) are taken from GOD'S WORD®. © 1995, 2003, 2013, 2014, 2019, 2020 by God's Word to the Nations Mission Society. Used by permission. • Scripture quotations marked (KJV) are taken from the Holy Bible, King James Version, which is in the public domain. • Scripture quotations marked (WEB) are taken from the World English Bible, which is in the public domain.

ISBN: 978-1-4866-2784-4
eBook ISBN: 978-1-4866-2785-1

Word Alive Press
119 De Baets Street Winnipeg, MB R2J 3R9
www.wordalivepress.ca

Cataloguing in Publication information can be obtained from Library and Archives Canada.

To my husband, Terry.
Your push and support kept me on track to finish this book.

"But these are written that you may believe that Jesus is the Messiah, the Son of God, and that by believing you may have life in his name" (John 20:31).

JANUARY 1

"Forget the former things; do not dwell on the past.
See, I am doing a new thing!" (Isaiah 43:18–19a)

What a racket was heard as people at the cove shot off their guns to welcome in the new year. This was the way it had been done years ago, but these days, fireworks light up the sky and make the loud noise. Isn't it perplexing to think of the passing of time? We can't see the moments until they're upon us, and as soon as we see them, they're gone and already part of the past.

Some of the most commonly used phrases in Newfoundland are: "What time are you leaving?" "What time did you get there?" or "What time did that happen?" People are obsessed with time, almost as much as they are about the weather. We wear watches or electronic devices that tell us the time: time to get up, time to leave, time to eat, time to sleep, time to go home—time, time, time.

But most of us waste time. Sometimes we say that we don't have enough time to get everything done. How much time do we waste in the twenty-four hours of a day? I'm sure I don't have to list examples of time wasters, because as you're reading this, you're already thinking of your own examples. How many of us wish we could get back wasted time and opportunities?

Everyone has the same number of hours in a day. It's not about having time but about setting priorities and making time for the important things. In this new year, do a new thing: make time for God and family, and make time to know others. What matters are relationships that will last for eternity, and the most important of them is your relationship with God.

Father God, thank You for another new year. We look forward to each new moment, knowing that You're present in our living. Strengthen our faith and our heart. Amen.

JANUARY 2

"Let us hold tightly without wavering to the hope we affirm, for God can be trusted to keep his promise" (Hebrews 10:23, NLT).

Nan said, "Can you reach the Promise Box over there on the cupboard? We'll read a promise now before we get up from the table." I reached for the little red box and passed it to my grandmother. She removed a little card; my grandfather removed a card, and then I removed a card. I read the words in my mind before saying them out loud.

I remember that little red box on my grandmother's side table so well. It was a special thing to pick a card and then in turn read the Bible verse. Sunday suppers and sometimes the weekday meals also ended with picking a card from the box. I remember reading the verses slowly and then carefully pronouncing each word. Of course, as a child, I hoped to pick a short verse. Sometimes it seemed that I chose the card with the longest verse.

I still like to read a verse from my promise box. Often the verse is just what I need for the day. One promise reads: "The Lord is my shepherd; I shall not want" (Psalm 23:1, KJV). On the reverse side it says: "The Good Shepherd never leads astray. The Great Shepherd never lacks supply. The Chief Shepherd never loses control." When your faith is weak, your hope small, and you want to retreat from the world, remember this verse. He can be trusted to keep His Word.

As you step through the coming days and year ahead, remember that the Good Shepherd is with you. He will guide you; He will give you what you need, and He is in control no matter what's going on around you.

Father God, thank You for all Your promises I learned and remembered from Nan's promise box. I am grateful for the people in my life who pointed me to You, the Good Shepherd. Amen.

JANUARY 3

"I saw also the Lord sitting upon a throne, high and lifted up, and his train filled the temple ... the whole earth is full of his glory"
(Isaiah 6:1b, 3b, KJV).

I looked out over the ocean today; I saw the water in the distance as it pulled up and launched at the beach, the resulting waves rolling towards the shore. As they neared the beach, they lifted higher for a moment and then flattened out in layers of white. The waves tumbled on the beach and covered everything. The stones moved and made a rumbling noise as the waves rolled them along.

I'm blessed today to be visiting my mom in my hometown. I love to look out over the ocean to see what picture it leaves in my mind. In winter, ice layers cover the shore where the freezing-cold waves have washed the rocks. Some of the water stays frozen there, forming lacy coverings.

The waves are lively and beautiful. Layer after layer, they move towards the land, white foam covering the rocky coastline. When I stand on the beach, witnessing the power of the waves, I know I am in the presence of something wonderful. Every sense is affected—sight, hearing, smell, touch, and taste. I see the grey waves turning to white as they tumble on the rocks. I hear the rumbling sound of the rolling rocks and the crashing waves. I smell the fresh sea air. I touch the cold, wet rocks. I can taste the salt air.

When I read the verse above from Isaiah, I think about the oceans that wrap themselves around the earth. The Lord spreads out His creation, filling the world with the wonderful life all around us. *"The earth is full of his glory."*

Father God, thank You for the beautiful ocean and for all the life that exists on earth. I can't help but be amazed at the wonders You've created. From a thankful heart. Amen.

JANUARY 4

"And I will give to each one a white stone, and on the stone will be engraved a new name that no one understands except the one who receives it" (Revelation 2:17b, NLT).

There was Little Jake, One-Eyed Jake, Back Cove Jake, War Jake, Nina's Jake, and many more.

Like every out-port community in Newfoundland, Chance Cove has its share of nicknames. It seems as though everyone has a nickname. I don't know how these people got their nicknames, but whenever you refer to the person by their nickname, everyone knows who you mean. When several people have the same name, it's easy to get them mixed up; however, there was no mistaking them with those nicknames. Sometimes a nickname refers to something peculiar about the person's physical stature. Sometimes it refers to where they built their house. Sometimes it refers to their character, and sometimes it refers to nothing at all.

These days with the Internet, it's easy to discover the meaning of your given name. Sometimes it's surprising to find out where the names originated and what they mean. Why did your parents give you your name? Were you named after someone, or did they just like it?

God has promised to give us a new name. What do you think it will be? Will it refer to your physical appearance, your character, or something else? What would you like it to mean? How will you ensure that you have a good name?

Father in Heaven, thank You for my name, Suzanne, which means "lily." Lilies thrive in the valleys and harsh conditions. Help me, Lord, to do just that, so that when I get to Heaven, I will have a good name. Amen.

JANUARY 5

"My grace is sufficient for you, for my power is made perfect in weakness" (2 Corinthians 12:9a).

This morning, I awoke early and pulled the covers up around me a little further. The bedroom was cold, and the bed was cozy. This is Friday, and I'm glad; it's been a busy week. I slowly got out of bed (wish I could bound out like some people do) and prepared for the day.

The thermometer outside the kitchen window said −23°C. It was the coldest morning so far this winter, but the sun was shining and there wasn't any wind. I poured milk into a bowl of cereal and sat at the kitchen table. The sound of chirping birds got my attention. I looked through the patio window and saw the evening grosbeaks noisily fighting their way to the sunflower seeds in the feeder. There were yellow finches and juncos there, too. I was amazed that their little bodies didn't freeze right there on the patio rail. What makes such tiny, frail creatures able to withstand this one element of nature? We are much bigger, but we can't withstand the cold as they do.

Once again, I'm reminded that God gives strength when needed to the smallest and weakest of creatures. We're disappointed when we can't accomplish something in our strength. But when we're at our weakest, God's power is best felt and seen.

Dear God, thank You for this lesson from the little birds outside my window. When our own strength is exhausted, You are able to fill us with Your power. Amen.

JANUARY 6

"I have come as a light into the world, that whoever believes in me may not remain in the darkness" (John 12:46, WEB).

From my earliest memories, I remember sleeping in my nan's house. Most times, I slept in the bedroom that overlooked the side yard and the big tree. The bed was soft, and in winter it was covered with quilts and an eiderdown comforter.

I remember too that in the early days, my nan put an oil lamp at the top of the stairs on the upstairs landing. This was our nightlight. She lit the lamp and kept it burning during the night. If anyone had to get up in the middle of the night, they had light to see their way. I'm sure many people remember the little lamp at the top of the stairs.

Many of us have nightlights in our homes. Some nightlights we just turn on when needed, and others have a built-in sensor so that when it's dark, they come on automatically.

These days I keep a little nightlight plugged in on the upstairs landing. It has a sensor and comes on after dark. If I have to get up, it's just enough light to show the hallway and where to turn for the bathroom. It keeps me from stubbing my toe or bumping my head in the darkness.

Just as the nightlight helps me see my way around our home, Jesus is the light in my life. I have a devotional book titled *Just Enough Light for the Step I'm On*, written by Stormie Omartian. Just like this title says, God shows me the way to go one step at a time. When the way seems especially dark and uncertain, He gives me light enough to keep me from stumbling and from looking too far ahead.

Father God, thank You for oil lamps and nightlights. Thank You for sending Jesus to the world and for being my Light in the darkness. Amen.

JANUARY 7

"For who knows a person's thoughts except their own spirit within them? In the same way no one knows the thoughts of God except the Spirit of God" (1 Corinthians 2:11).

Newfoundland waters are known to be a good place to see icebergs. Every spring, tourists flock to our island to get a glimpse or a close-up picture of the majestic ice formations that make their way to our waters from the north. No two icebergs are alike. I've seen numerous sizes and shapes of ice. Some have bands of blue and green colours going through them. Some have flat areas, and some spiral high like a skyscraper. They're beautiful to look at and make magnificent subjects for photographing, but unfortunately, only one-tenth of the gigantic ice flow is above the water and visible to us. Only scuba divers or underwater cameras can see what's below the water.

People's lives are like an iceberg. We only see the one-tenth above the surface. Nine-tenths are below the water and only visible when you look deep beneath the surface.

Sometimes what we think we know about people is wrong or only part of the picture, a small piece of the puzzle. We can look at others' lives, but we only see a small portion. If you really want to know someone, you need to look more deeply and ask the right questions. The Bible tells us in 1 Samuel 16:7 that *"Man does not see what the Lord sees, for man sees what is visible, but the Lord sees the heart"* (HCSB). Only God knows a person's thoughts and heart. If you really want to understand a person, ask God to help you see them as He sees them.

Father God, forgive me when I look at the outside of someone and even judge sometimes by their appearance. I want to be more like You and look deeper into the heart. Amen.

JANUARY 8

"I will give them an undivided heart and put a new spirit in them; I will remove from them their heart of stone and give them a heart of flesh" (Ezekiel 11:19).

Peaches have a hard pit in their centre. Sometimes the pit is jagged and the delicious pulp is attached so tightly that it's hard to get off. There are different kinds of peaches, and some have pits or stones that are easier to remove.

There are two categories of peaches: clingstone peaches and freestone peaches. As you might guess, clingstones have pits that are hard to remove, but freestone peaches have pits that come away easier from the pulp. I definitely prefer the freestone peaches as a snack. I dislike trying to get all the juicy pulp from the clingstone.

I wonder if people are like those peaches? Do some people hold on to their hard hearts more than others? In Ezekiel 36:26 we read: *"And I will give you a new heart, and I will put a new spirit in you. I will take out your stony, stubborn heart and give you a tender, responsive heart"* (NLT).

God requires us to have a responsive heart. He says that He will give us a new heart and a new spirit. We can only be obedient to God with a new heart. Do you have a clingstone heart or a freestone heart?

Father God, I want to be sensitive to Your will. Help me to have a soft and responsive heart so that I can be what You want me to be. Amen.

JANUARY 9

"Or suppose a woman has ten silver coins and loses one. Doesn't she light a lamp, sweep the house and search carefully until she finds it? And when she finds it … says, 'Rejoice with me; I have found my lost coin'" (Luke 15:8–9).

My nan's shop had a wooden step up to the door. Around the bay, everyone calls that step *the bridge*. My townie friend says that a bridge is something with water under it. I told her that I guess the shop step had water under it when it rained!

On my nan's shop bridge were openings between the boards. On days when there wasn't much else to do, I looked through the openings and poked around in the dirt with a stick to see what I could find. Sometimes customers lost money and other small items through those openings. I found lost pennies, nickels, dimes, bottle caps, and things that were interesting but had no value. It was a lot of fun—like hunting for treasure!

When my children were young, we'd visit my husband's relatives on the west coast. My sister-in-law and I took our kids on outings around the Port Au Port area, where we'd dig for fossils in the cliffs on the peninsula. We found fossils of shells, small sea creatures, and other unfamiliar things. It took time and patience to find and then break open the pieces of rock and shale. I loved to search the rocky cliffs, as did the children. It was an adventure, and every little piece was an exciting find.

I remember how fun it was to find a lost coin under the steps of the old shop, just like finding fossils in the earth. Discovering God's salvation is like that—a treasure of great value.

Jesus, my most exciting find today is the knowledge of Your love for me. No other find compares to that. Thank You for loving me so much that You died for me so that I may have everlasting life. Amen.

JANUARY 10

"Join five of the curtains together into one set and the other six into another set. Fold the sixth curtain double at the front of the tent" (Exodus 26:9).

When I read this verse, I thought of folding sheets out of the laundry. I'm sure most of you know what I'm talking about. Fold it in half lengthwise and then keep folding until you get the size that fits in the closet. The fitted sheets are a bit more tangly to fold, and I remember my dad helping Mom fold sheets, especially the fitted ones with the elastic corners.

I also thought about folding clothes. Seems like everyone has their own unique way of folding. People who work in retail clothing stores are taught to fold clothes a certain way. Both of my daughters worked in clothing stores when they were young and learned to fold shirts in a way that displayed them properly. When they were still teenagers, I was amazed to see their dresser drawers filled with neatly folded clothing.

According to several commentaries, the curtains in Exodus were folded to hang in a certain way in the front of the tent of the tabernacle. Just as we use sheets on our beds to protect our other bedding materials, those curtains protected the inner coverings of the Lord's temple. You might ask, "What does this have to do with my life?" Sometimes we skip over obscure verses. But this verse tells us that even simple folding instructions have a meaning and a purpose.

As Christians, we're covered and protected by God's curtain of love, by the truth of His Word, and by the grace of the Lord Jesus: *"The unfolding of Your words gives light"* (Psalm 119:130).

Father God, thank You for revealing the meaning behind these obscure verses. Help me to apply the truths from Your Word to my life. Amen.

JANUARY 11

"A furious squall came up, and the waves broke over the boat, so that it was nearly swamped" (Mark 4:37).

Tap! Tap! Tap! My grandfather tapped the glass on the barometer with his fingers. Pop said, "The glass is down. Could be a storm coming."

The barometer hung in a prominent place on the wall in the dining area. Pop checked the reading on it every day. By interpreting the readings on the dial, he could usually forecast major weather changes. When he expected a storm to strike, he prepared for it.

He went outside to check that everything was secure. He made sure the boat was anchored and the gear tied securely. No one travelled or went out in the boat. The horse was in the barn and the ducks fed. There was enough firewood on hand, oil for the lamps, and food in the pantry. Then he waited for the storm to come and to pass.

Although the barometer shows the possibility of a weather change, some storms are unpredictable. They come on quickly with little or no warning, causing a lot of damage. I'm sure my grandfather experienced storms like this. But even if you know a hurricane is coming, you can still experience the effects of the storm and end up with some damage.

Consider the example in Mark 4, when the storm's waves nearly swamped the disciples' boat. They frantically asked Jesus to rescue them. We will encounter many storms in our lifetime—sickness, tragedy, financial burdens, and relationship breakdown. On whom will you rely for help? The disciples wondered, *"Who then is this, that even the wind and the sea obey Him?"* (Mark 4:41b, AMP). Put your trust in the One who calms the storm.

Father God, You are the One who can still the roaring of the seas and the turmoil of nations. Please be with us during our storms and provide all the help and protection we need. Amen.

JANUARY 12

"So, the sisters sent word to Jesus, 'Lord, the one you love is sick'"
(John 11:3).

I have four sisters. We don't live close together, but we chat daily. When a sister sends a word by a message, a text, an email or a direct call, you can be sure I respond.

I've received calls with a similar message to the one above: "The one you love is sick." The people we share most in common, of course, are our parents. But my sisters could be calling sometime about a friend, a child, a cousin, an aunt, or an uncle.

I can imagine how Jesus felt when He received the message from Mary and Martha that Lazarus was sick. I've had those calls from my sisters. When I hear about a sick family member or close friend at death's door, I make plans to be there immediately. As soon as I hear, I'm already packing a bag in my mind. If I delay, I may not see them alive again.

I'm sure that Jesus, in His humanity, felt sadness and grief, because as He delayed, He knew that Lazarus would die and the sisters would grieve. Jesus waited four days before going to see them. That must have been difficult. But Jesus, being God's Son, also knew that He would raise Lazarus from death in order to bring glory to His Father in Heaven. Consequently, the sisters, the disciples, and others would see the miracle and know Jesus was from God. God would get the glory—not man.

Father God, I have received sad messages in my life. But through everything, You have given me strength and peace. May You be glorified through it all. Amen.

JANUARY 13

"... I stand at the door and knock. If anyone hears my voice and opens the door, I will come in and eat with that person, and they with me" (Revelation 3:20).

It was grocery day, and after shopping, I came out of the supermarket with Laurieann in my arms. I unlocked the passenger door first. Laurieann was a year old and a very pleasant child. She laughed as I secured her in her car seat. Then I put my purse and keys on the driver's seat. I reached in, pushed the lock down on the passenger door, and closed the door.

As soon as I closed the door, I realized that I had locked Laurieann, my purse, and my keys in the car. What was I to do? I couldn't get into the car. My daughter was inside, and my groceries were in boxes outside the supermarket. I tried to get her to pull up on the lock, but she didn't understand and just laughed at the gestures I made.

I ran back into the store and approached a man working there. Almost crying, I said, "My keys are locked in the car, and my little girl is inside. Please help me."

Two men came out to the car with me, and one of them brought a wire coat hanger. Laurieann wasn't distressed and thought it was all in fun. One of the men opened up the coat hanger and made a sort of hook to go over the round knob on the top of the lock. He slid it over the top of the window, and within minutes, the lock was lifted and the door opened. I was so happy and relieved. I thanked them, picked up my groceries, and went home. When I remember this day, I immediately think of the verse above. Jesus waits at the door to our hearts, and we're the only ones who can open it.

Father God, I know that You don't force Yourself into our lives. Nothing resides in my heart unless I allow it. Thank You that when I opened my heart's door, You came in and sat down with me. From a thankful heart. Amen.

JANUARY 14

"But after Jehoiada's death, the leaders of Judah came and bowed before King Joash and persuaded him to listen to their advice"
(2 Chronicles 24:17, NLT).

There are all kinds of advice in this world. There's good advice and bad advice. Do you remember the Dear Abby advice columns in the newspapers? She gave advice on everything, from how to set a table to how to improve your marriage.

Today the Internet is littered with self-help sites and advice on any topic you can think of. Most of us know that you can't trust Internet advice. You must research the reliability of the advice you accept.

The passage above is part of the story of King Joash, who was raised by his uncle. Although the uncle was a good man who worshipped God, he didn't teach Joash what he needed to know to be a good king by putting God first.

After his uncle's death, the leaders persuaded the king to abandon the Temple of the Lord and worship man-made idols instead. This was his downfall. When a prophet of the Lord tried to intervene and give advice, they killed him. Joash was judged by God, and after being wounded in battle, he was killed on his own bed.

As a young king, Joash followed his uncle's guidance and beliefs. But Joash didn't have his own personal relationship with God. Consequently, He quickly fell away from God.

If you don't know God personally, who are you listening to? It's time to get the right advice. What advice are you hearing?

Father God, help me improve my relationship with You every day so that I will hear and follow Your advice in all that I do. Amen.

JANUARY 15

"Mightier than the thunder of the great waters, mightier than the breakers of the sea—the Lord on high is mighty" (Psalm 93:4).

Years ago in Newfoundland, every fisherman or fishing family had their own small wharf where they tied their boat. They unloaded their catch and prepared it for market right on their own stage. Most of the fish were salted and dried on drying flakes. As the bigger fish plants began to appear and more fresh fish was processed, the government funded the building of a bigger wharf that would be the central place for all the fishing boats to unload and dock. In Chance Cove, just as in most fishing communities in Newfoundland, there's a government wharf and a breakwater.

They built the breakwater outside the government wharf and towards the outer edge of the cove to protect the wharf from storms. This breakwater resembles a big wharf, filled with boulders and topped with concrete. It acts like a large, solid wall against the wave energy. When the sea is rough or a storm is coming, it protects the fishing boats and gear from the power of the ocean.

The breakwater acts as a buffer zone, reducing the waves' force so they cause less damage even when they reach the wharf. When there's a storm, the waves toss the boats around, but they still remain intact.

Did you know that if Jesus is in your heart, He protects you from the full force of harmful circumstances? Everything you go through is already buffered by Him.

Father God, thank You for the breakwaters that protect the fishing boats from storm damage, and thank You for protecting me during the storms in my life. You are mightier than the breakers of the sea. Amen.

JANUARY 16

"And there by the Ahava Canal ... We prayed that he would give us a safe journey and protect us, our children, and our goods as we traveled" (Ezra 8:21, NLT).

My good friend Lorraine taught me the importance of praying before setting out on a journey. Whether short or long, and no matter the type of transportation, she always prayed, "Lord, give us journeying mercies." Some people call it, "travelling mercies."

We took many trips together. We went camping, hunting, and visiting together. We went to church camps and to women's weekends. We always prayed before leaving. We were always safe.

I remember leaving St. John's to drive home and calling Lorraine to pray me home. Of course, she did just that. It didn't matter how early or how late it was when I called.

When it was time for our church women's group to go on our annual weekend event, all the ladies gathered together in the church parking lot where, before driving on the highway, we prayed for a safe journey. The practice of praying before travel increased my faith and personal walk with God.

My journeys were tiny compared to those of the people Ezra prayed for. They travelled approximately nine hundred miles on foot through some dangerous territory. But no matter how our journey compares with theirs, we can all pray and ask God for "journeying mercies." Ezra 8:23 says, *"So we fasted and earnestly prayed that our God would take care of us, and he heard our prayer"* (NLT).

Father God, how I thank You and praise You for keeping me safe on all my journeys. Thank You for my friend who taught me to ask You for "journeying mercies." Amen.

JANUARY 17

"Simon replied ... at Your word I will [do as you say and] lower the nets [again]'" (Luke 5:5, AMP).

I walked along a golden road.
There was no sun or moon.
All around me was sparkling light,
Tiny jewels in the air and on the road.
As I walked along, alone, but not alone,
I talked to the One who was with me.
I talked about my dear ones.
I remembered the times they were safe from danger,
The times they were healed of sickness,
And the times they were blessed with good things.
I thanked the One who was with me.
I talked about the concerns I have for my dear ones.
The One who was with me listened.
I thanked the One who was with me.
I talked about my day and recounted where I failed.
The one who was with me listened and said, *"Try again tomorrow."*
I walked along a golden road.
Home appeared so quickly.
I thanked the One who was with me.

Father God, thank You for Your encouragement to try again. Amen.

JANUARY 18

"The Lord says, 'Then I will heal you of your faithlessness; my love will know no bounds, for my anger will be gone forever'" (Hosea 14:4, NLT).

We were excited to be moving into our "new old" house. This was the very first house of our own. It was new to us, but it was actually almost one hundred years old. All we could see was potential. Other people saw something different. My mom and dad helped us move in and were very worried about the task ahead of us. I had a small baby and a three-year-old. How would we do it? In fact, my mom cried all the way home.

Yes, it had leaky windows, patchwork floor coverings, apple crates for kitchen cupboards, two fireplaces, three porches, and a very overgrown backyard. But it had potential to be something great.

We lived there for nine years and lovingly and carefully restored it from top to bottom. We restored the large backyard, and my husband made it better than before with beautiful flower gardens, fruit trees, and a vegetable patch.

Restoration is hard work. The book of Hosea is about restoration. You can read it for yourself and see how the restoration takes place. God uses Hosea's story to illustrate His love for us. The Lord pursues us with His love. God promises that when we repent, or turn away from our sins, He redeems, restores, and gives us a new beginning.

Father God, I'm grateful for this lesson about restoration. Just as we restored our old house, You restore us when we're truly sorry and turn from our sins. Thank You for new beginnings. Amen.

JANUARY 19

"And that you may love the Lord your God, listen to his voice, and hold fast to him" (Deuteronomy 30:20a).

Do you remember the old black and white television sets with the rabbit ear antenna on top? I remember them too. Some houses even had a large antenna attached to their roof. Of course, that was before cable, satellite TV, and fiberoptic. It seemed that whenever something came on that we wanted to watch (except the news), the TV would get all snowy and we'd have to turn the rabbit ears this way and that. Some people attached tin foil balls or wire coat hangers to the antenna, all in the hope of getting a better picture.

If Mom was baking and turned on the mixer to stir up the cake batter, the picture on the television would turn wavy with squiggly lines. We couldn't wait for Mom to turn off the electric mixer.

Do you remember the old transistor radios? My pop listened to the news, the messages, and the fishermen's broadcast on the radio. He'd turn the dial one way and then the other until he got the best sound, because sometimes there was a lot of static.

Just as we adjusted the TV antenna or turned the radio dial to get a clearer signal, we must tune in to hear God speaking to us. We must set aside time every day to talk to Him and then listen to what He says. God is always talking to us. Most of the time, though, we're not listening or tuned in. Are you blocking out the interference from the world and listening to what God has to say to you? Get tuned in and spend time with God today.

Father God, thank You for always talking to us; we just have to tune in to hear it. Your Word says to be still and know that You are God. Help me to remain alert to Your voice. From a thankful heart, in Jesus's name. Amen.

JANUARY 20

"God saved you by his grace when you believed"
(Ephesians 2:8a, NLT).

Have you arrived at the place in your life where you realized you need God's forgiveness? Maybe you read or heard somewhere that the Bible says you are saved by grace. So you asked God to forgive you and He did. He washed away your past mistakes and put you in right standing with Himself. He gave you a new perspective and a new purpose. The Holy Spirit was given to you, and you embarked on the Christian life.

What if God does nothing else for you for the rest of your days? Is grace enough? Of course, you're assured of salvation and a place in Heaven with Him. But what if while you're on this earth, God does nothing else? The rest of your life is marked by trials and troubles. Are you okay with that? Would the grace you received at salvation be enough to sustain you to the end?

Sometimes we look at God like a fairy godmother or a genie in a lamp. We want Him to give us things, to tell us what to do, to feed us, to keep us from illness and tragedies and anything else we can think about. Can we say like Job said, *"Though he slay me, yet will I trust in him"* (Job 13:15a, KJV)?

Yes, God wants to bless us, and He also wants us to trust in Him. But God's purposes for trials and troubles are beyond what we can understand. He sees into the future and knows how it will affect generations to come. Can we trust in Him through this life, even though it has many difficulties? Can we trust Him to know what's best for the future? Paul writes in Colossians 3:2, *"Set your minds on things above, not on earthly things."* When we focus on the right thing, grace is enough.

Father God, thank You for the grace You gave me and continue to give me every day. Help me to focus on heavenly things and not worry about the day-to-day troubles. Amen.

JANUARY 21

"Get wisdom, get understanding; do not forget my words or turn away from them" (Proverbs 4:5).

When I sat at the table to complete my homework, Mom asked, "What do you have for tonight?" I said, "I have to read a story in my literature book, answer the Chapter 3 questions in my geography book, and learn my spelling words."

Each night the homework was similar. Sometimes there were history questions, sometimes arithmetic, sometimes French, but there were always spelling words to learn. At the end of each week, we had a test on all the words we'd learned that week. I was a pretty good speller, and I only remember one time I spelled a word wrong on a test. The teacher wasn't too happy. After that experience, I don't think I had a spelling word wrong again.

Today, words are spell-checked on the computers as you type them. I think that's helpful, but we should learn how to spell them in our minds too. We learn the words by studying them and repeating the letters over and over.

You can apply the same principle of studying spelling words to studying what you read in the Bible. By reading and repeating, God's truths are embedded in our minds. We remember them and recall them when we need them. Psalm 119:11a says, *"I have hidden your word in my heart ... "* Recalling the scripture you've learned will bring you comfort; it will make you wise, and it will be your weapon against evil. Scripture will help you stay focused on God's strength through the difficulties of life.

Father God, thank You for Your written Word, the Holy Bible. Help me to apply my mind to studying and learning the words You have preserved for our good. Amen.

JANUARY 22

"Your love has given me great joy and encouragement, because you, brother, have refreshed the hearts of the Lord's people"
(Philemon 1:7).

One summer my grandson went with me on a little trip across the island. He had some spending money with him, so we did a little browsing and shopping at the local stores. He wanted to buy a certain item for his friend who needed it, and he also purchased another as a birthday gift for someone else. One time he gave some of his birthday money to a local charity. He did all this without prompting from his mom or dad.

Recently, my grandson video-called his great-grandmother, who was staying with us, to sing "Happy Birthday" to her. How many eleven-year-olds these days think of doing that? He has no idea how much joy this gave her. I could learn something from this child about giving joy. My grandson gives us so much happiness. His thoughtfulness and concern for others go beyond his years.

When I was a child, we sang a little song in Sunday school that went like this: "J. O. Y, J. O. Y, surely this must mean: Jesus first, yourself last, and others in between." This little verse had never meant so much until my grandson demonstrated its meaning through his actions. When you put Jesus first and yourself last, you give joy to others. The wonderful thing about it is that he's not even aware that he is giving others so much joy.

Teach your children and your grandchildren about putting others before themselves. Love them and teach them to love, and they'll live their lives giving joy.

Father God, what a precious gift You have given our family. What a joy-giver he is to others. Bless him all his days, and may he always put others before himself. Amen.

JANUARY 23

"Do not harden your hearts as you did in the rebellion, during the time of testing in the wilderness" (Hebrews 3:8).

I watched a TV program about crab fishing on the Bering Sea. When the ship started its journey, it was clean and fast.

The ship sailed along, fulfilling its purpose of carrying men and setting crab pots. The fishermen pulled the pots and stored the crab on board. Then the ship encountered colder weather and storms. A hard crust of ice formed all over the ship. Layer upon layer, the ice thickened and the storm continued with no let-up.

By the time the storm ended, a thick, heavy layer of ice covered the ship, slowing its progress and making it treacherous for the seamen. The ship was in danger of turning over from all the top-heavy weight. It was no longer able to complete its purpose. The ice had to come off, but it wouldn't be easy. The ice was as hard as concrete.

The seamen carefully and slowly chipped away at the crusted ice. Little by little, the ice was removed, and the ship was freed to continue on her journey.

It's easy to let your problems get you down. When we experience hurt, we put a layer of protection around our hearts. Each difficult circumstance adds another layer. Eventually, the crust gets thick and hard. It weighs us down so much, we almost topple over. But we have a choice of how we react to life's problems. We can form a protective layer, or we can trust God to soften the hurts and our heart.

God is looking for a devoted heart: *"I the Lord search the heart"* (Jeremiah 17:10a).

Dear God, I want to trust You to get me through all of life's problems. Soften my heart when things hurt, and help me to let them go. Amen.

JANUARY 24

"All Scripture is inspired by God and is useful to teach us what is true and to make us realize what is wrong in our lives. It corrects us when we are wrong and teaches us to do what is right" (2 Timothy 3:16, NLT).

Today, many people dismiss the Bible or claim that it contains errors and can't be trusted. People may reject God's Word, but they can't destroy it: *"Forever, O Lord, your word is settled in Heaven [standing firm and unchangeable]"* (Psalm 119:89, AMP).

Down through the centuries, kings, emperors, and Caesars have tried to destroy the Scriptures but weren't successful. The written Word survived in spite of intense efforts to destroy it. The discovery of the Dead Sea Scrolls confirmed that our Old Testament is the same one from the time of Jesus. It was already centuries old when Jesus was born. The Jews of that time studied the Old Testament scriptures, and many of them memorized it.

Much of the New Testament has been preserved in manuscripts dating back to around AD 300 (after the time of Jesus). When the New Testament refers to Scripture, it's pointing to the Old Testament, which was the Scripture available at that time. Paul writes, *"And the Scriptures were written to teach and encourage us by giving us hope"* (Romans 15:4, CEV).

The Bible was written and preserved because it contains God's instructions to us for this life. It's our weapon against our problems and against evil. In Matthew 4:4 Jesus says, *"The Scriptures say: 'No one can live only on food. People need every word that God has spoken'"* (CEV).

Father God, I am so grateful that Your Word was preserved for me to study and feed on every day. Help me to continue in my study and understanding so that I can help others know You. Amen.

JANUARY 25

"... the Lord knows how to rescue godly people from their trials"
(2 Peter 2:9a, NLT).

One morning we had breakfast with Wayne and Wanda in Kippens. Wayne wanted Terry to drive his truck to the garage in Corner Brook for some maintenance work, and I would drive our truck.

It was snowing when we left, and by the time we passed the turnoff to Stephenville, the weather was much worse. We still had quite a way to go before arriving at the Trans Canada Highway. The snow was now very thick, and the wind whipped it up to whiteout conditions. I couldn't see the road or where I was going, and I couldn't see Terry in the truck ahead of me.

I drove very slowly, occasionally stopping to see the road. I couldn't see Terry or turn around, and I was afraid to stop or pull off to the side—if I couldn't see other vehicles, they couldn't see me either. So I kept slowly moving along.

Suddenly, I was in a complete whiteout and couldn't even see the front of my truck. I stopped and waited. In a few minutes, the wind lessened and the whiteout cleared. When I looked ahead, I saw that I was on a sharp turn, facing the woods and almost off the road. For a few seconds, I panicked. Then I said a prayer for safety, popped in an upbeat worship CD, and sang at the top of my voice, "Our God is an awesome God. He reigns from Heaven above." I turned the wheel to straighten up the truck, turned on my hazard lights, and drove on. I still didn't know where Terry was. He could have been off the road, and I wouldn't even know. Finally, I reached the highway and saw Terry right ahead of me. Praise the Lord!

Father God, my experience with the snowstorm reminds me of the accounts in Your Word of how You rescued Noah and his family, and also how You rescued Lot. Thank You for hearing my prayer and rescuing us from this danger. Amen.

JANUARY 26

"Are you the Messiah we've been expecting, or should we keep looking for someone else?" (Matthew 11:3, NLT)

I remember when the television show *CSI* (Crime Scene Investigation) first came on. I found it fascinating to learn how they gathered the evidence from a crime scene and then interpreted it to solve the "whodunit" mystery. They followed the evidence to get to the truth.

People may doubt what you say, but the evidence tells the truth. In Matthew 11, John the Baptist was in prison. He must have been having doubts about Jesus being the Messiah and even his own purpose. If John was to prepare the way, why was he in prison? Sometimes what we think has happened might not be correct at all, but when we examine all the evidence, we learn the truth.

We may have doubts about our faith, but Jesus tells us in Matthew 11:5 to remember what we've heard and seen: *"the blind see, the lame walk, those with leprosy are cured, the deaf hear, the dead are raised to life, and the Good News is being preached to the poor."* (NLT). This is what He told John's disciples to tell John. In other words, the evidence confirms that Jesus is the Messiah who was prophesied about in the Old Testament.

When you have doubts about whether you're forgiven or saved, look at the evidence of God in your life. How has God changed your heart and attitude? Instead of turning away or staying away, be a student of the Scripture; examine your life and the evidence for yourself.

Father God, when I read Your Word, I learn more about You and the evidence throughout the Bible. However, I only need to look at myself to see the evidence I need. Thank You for changing me. Amen.

JANUARY 27

"Can anything ever separate us from Christ's love?"
(Romans 8:35a, NLT)

I read a book titled *In the Grip of Grace* by Max Lucado. A man in the Bible—Paul—often talked about God's grace. He described himself as a prisoner of grace (Ephesians 3:1, 4:1; Philemon 1:9; 2 Timothy 1:8). Paul was held securely to God by grace.

When I think of things held securely, I picture hugging my grandson tightly, making sure he always feels loved. I also imagine fishing boats tied securely to the wharf posts, their rigging and knotted ropes holding them in place. Although God uses love and grace to hold us secure, fishermen use knotted ropes to hold things in place.

All around me, I see examples of God's grace enabling people to hold it together and stay on course. There's a senior who should be struggling with aging and loneliness, but grace keeps her joyful. A wife's husband was in a terrible accident, and she holds it together because of grace. A young teenager goes to church alone while his parents stay home, and grace keeps him coming back. Grace loves and cares for the children of a mother with cancer. I see a husband whose wife struggles with thoughts of suicide, and grace gives him strength. I see a pastor who preaches Sunday after Sunday, visits the sick, and buries the dead, and grace keeps him steadfast.

God's grace gives us what we don't deserve—unmerited favour. Are you a prisoner of God's grace? Romans 8:38–39 (CEV) Paul says, *"I am sure that … Nothing in all creation can separate us from God's love for us in Christ Jesus our Lord!"*

Father God, thank You for the evidence of grace that is in others and thank You that as the struggles increase, Your grace increases. From a thankful heart. Amen.

JANUARY 28

"Yet we hear that some of you are living idle lives, refusing to work and meddling in other people's business" (2 Thessalonians 3:11, NLT).

I've heard people say "There's not a lazy bone in his body" when talking about someone in particular who is very industrious and likes to work. I never saw or heard of my grandfather or father being lazy. You could say there wasn't a lazy bone in their bodies. They didn't like laziness and felt that everyone should be working at something. There was always something to do.

Most people from that generation seemed to be hard workers. They had to work or they'd starve. I heard that during the Great Depression years, people lived on six cents a day. These days, we don't even have cents (pennies) anymore!

Men and women were up before daylight and worked until long after dark. Just thinking about all that physical work makes me tired. Everything was done by hand. There were no electrical appliances or gas-powered chainsaws. They walked just about everywhere, even over long distances at times.

The Bible uses some harsh words to describe laziness: *sluggards* (Proverbs 13:4), *slothful* (Matthew 25:26, KJV), and *worthless* (Matthew 25:30). Scripture tells us that the outcome of laziness is *debt, poverty* (Proverbs 13:4), and *hunger* (Proverbs 19:15). To combat laziness, Paul says, *"Whatever you do, work at it with all your heart, as working for the Lord, not for human masters"* (Colossians 3:23). In 2 Thessalonians, Paul tells his readers to settle down and get to work and never get tired of doing good.

Father God, I know You dislike laziness. Please help me to remember what Your Word says about it, and help me to apply it to my life and my spiritual walk with You. Amen.

JANUARY 29

"This is the day the Lord has made. We will rejoice and be glad in it" (Psalm 118:24, NLT).

I'll be glad when 4:30 comes.

I'll be glad when it's time to go to bed.

I'll be glad when the summer comes.

I'll be glad when … Haven't we said this a time or two?

The day started off wrong from the moment I woke up. I was so tired, I didn't want to get out of bed. What do I have to get up for, anyway? It's another day of work, meetings, customer complaints, and bad attitudes. I have bills to pay, meals to cook, laundry that needs washing, and the dust! Where does it all come from? One of my children is out of work, and the other one works two jobs. Mom called and filled me in on all the family sicknesses and problems.

These days couldn't be the days the Lord made, could they? Only the good days—like holidays, birthdays, Saturdays, wedding days, Christmas Day, and graduation days—are made by the Lord. Is every day *the day* made by the Lord?

As I pondered over the day to come while showering and eating breakfast, I sensed in my being these words, "Yes, God made this day too." I made a choice to be happy *in* today, not after it's over! Give it a try.

Are you a prisoner in your home or hospital? Try singing or listening to some praise music. Are you away from family? Try writing in a journal or sending some old-fashioned letters to the family. They'll love them. Are you in the middle of painful circumstances? Pray, pray, pray.

Father God, thank You for all the days You've given us. It's difficult sometimes to appreciate the hard days, but You're there to help us through if we focus on You. Amen.

JANUARY 30

"As it is, if we had not delayed, we could have gone and returned twice" (Genesis 43:10).

"We have also brought additional silver with us to buy food. We don't know who put our silver in our sacks" (Genesis 43:22).

As you can tell from the verses above, Judah was frustrated with his father's lack of decisiveness. This portion of Scripture is part of the story of Joseph. Most of us are familiar with the story of Joseph's coat of many colours. Because Joseph's brothers were jealous of him, they sold him to slave buyers from Egypt. Eventually, Joseph rose to a high position, taking care of food supplies during a severe drought. His brothers were sent to Egypt to buy grain, and this is when this part of the story occurs. They didn't recognize Joseph, and he kept them guessing. He wouldn't let them return without the promise to bring back their youngest brother. One of the older brothers had to stay behind as a guarantee. When they got home, their father was distraught and delayed their leaving. This was the reason for Judah's frustration.

In verse 22, we learn that the brothers paid silver for the grain they purchased on the first trip, but while returning home, they found the silver back in their packs. They were afraid they'd be accused of stealing and worried about what would happen to them. I'm sure their frustration and anxiety were high. They thought things were out of their control, but little did they know that God was working according to His plan.

We've all experienced frustration at some time in our lives. It could be with certain circumstances, or with people, or with the way things are done or not done. But like Judah, we must learn to put others first and then trust God to unfold His plan.

Father God, sometimes I get frustrated when things aren't going the way I want. Help me to put others first and to trust You for the outcome. Amen.

JANUARY 31

"And he arose, and rebuked the wind, and said unto the sea, Peace, be still. And the wind ceased, and there was a great calm" (Mark 4:39, KJV).

Listen!
I hear the waves singing,
Softly drumming out their song.
What is their song?
Why, every seaman knows the words.
Listen carefully!
In the early dawn
When the little boats are up.
Listen carefully!
In the cool of the evening
The waves speak of freedom.
They are free to protect or to destroy.

I love watching the sea on a day when the swells are high and the waves are competing to be first to the beach. The sea's energy has always fascinated me. I wrote this poem in high school. It speaks to me of the waves, sometimes calm and sometimes stormy. They have a voice, sometimes soothing and sometimes shouting. They're totally out of our control but not out of God's control. God lets the sea play and be lively for a while, and then He brings back the calm.

Father God in Heaven, I know that You are the Creator and that You alone control the power of the waves. You can bring calm and peace to any storm. Thank You for the lesson of the waves. Amen.

FEBRUARY 1

"... Be still, and know that I am God" (Psalm 46:10a).

"... when you are on your beds, search your hearts and be silent" (Psalm 4:4).

In the early morning when your body starts to stir and your mind starts to wake up,
Be still and listen.
Before you have a chance to fill your mind with thoughts of business, family responsibilities, and tasks,
Be still and listen.
Before the alarm clock rings, before your spouse is awake, before the dog wants to go out,
Be still and listen.
What is God saying to you today?
Be still and listen.
Praise Him, exalt Him, and thank Him.
Be still and listen.

Dear God, when I'm still and quiet, I think of You. I remember that You gave me life, You gave me family, and You gave me many other good things. I sense You are near. You give me a calm and a confidence to face the day. Amen.

FEBRUARY 2

"Above all else, guard your heart, for everything you do flows from it" (Proverbs 4:23).

Lately, there seems to be an epidemic of heart attacks amongst people that I know. Some of my cousins, some of my friends, and some people I know at church have had various degrees of heart attacks and surgeries. Some of them seemed to be perfectly healthy before the attack, which came as a surprise to them and everyone else.

Heart problems can have a number of causes. Poor eating, lack of exercise, harmful habits, and even genetics contribute to heart failure. Sometimes these problems build up silently until one day the heart fails. Fortunately, with advances in diagnostics, medicines, and surgeries, many people recover from heart disease.

It's important to take care of your heart and keep it strong and healthy. Just as the body can't function well without a healthy heart, neither can the Christian without a healthy spiritual heart. We'll be sluggish at our work, in prayer, and in worship.

The heart is the core of our being, and the Bible sets a high value on keeping our hearts pure. Everything flows out of our hearts, including our thoughts and decisions, which show up in our actions. What we let in has to come out. The heart must be kept healthy by what is said: *"Put away from you a deceitful (lying, misleading) mouth"* (Proverbs 4:24a, AMP); by what is seen, *"Let your eyes look straight ahead"* (Proverbs 4:25a, WEB); and by what is done, *"Don't turn to the right hand nor to the left"* (Proverbs 4:27a, WEB).

God is a heart specialist and will give you a new heart if you ask. What is the condition of your heart?

Father God in Heaven, thank You for Your Word, which tells me how to take care of my heart. Help me to live a healthy life not only physically but spiritually as well. Amen.

FEBRUARY 3

"On that day living water will flow out from Jerusalem ... in summer and in winter" (Zechariah 14:8).

One of my favourite memories is skating outdoors on the ponds and brooks. I remember skating along the frozen edges of the brook close to our house. My friends and I skated under the old bridge and along the shore. Sometimes ice candles hung from the bridge and from cliffs along the rocky shore. They were our outdoor popsicles—not much flavour, but cool and thirst quenching. They looked like upside-down candles. We'd break off an ice candle and suck on it. The ice melted to water in our mouths and was so refreshing.

On warm days when the sun came out, the water dripped from the tip of the candles. *Drip, drip, drip!* Every drop sparkled and shone in the sun. The sun melted the hard ice that formed on the cold winter days.

Is your heart like that hard ice candle that formed during the dark, cold days of your life? Sometimes life's circumstances cause us to be full of bitterness, anger, resentment, selfishness, and pride. Do you need forgiveness for something in your past, or do you need to forgive someone who hurt you? Why not ask God's Son, Jesus, into your life? His love melts hard hearts and changes attitudes and, sometimes, circumstances. You can have that inner joy that you want.

If you're expecting joyless days, ask God's Son to shine on your life. His love gives hope for the future.

Father God, thank You for Your Son, who shines on our lives in winter and in summer. Drop by drop, the hardness melts away. Just as the ice candles disappear under the power of the sun, so too our sins are forgiven under the power of Your Son, Jesus. From a thankful heart. Amen.

FEBRUARY 4

"Wisdom will multiply your days and add years to your life"
(Proverbs 9:11, NLT).

"You're daft in the head. You're some stun. He is stun as a lump. You haven't got a clue. Not the sharpest knife in the drawer." These are Newfoundland sayings that refer to someone's lack of common sense or good judgement, and they have nothing to do with the amount of education someone might have. Come on, I'm sure you know someone like that! True wisdom consists of common sense, good judgement and knowledge. Knowledge is knowing what fire is and how to start it. Wisdom knows that playing with fire carelessly can cause a bad burn.

The Bible talks a lot about wisdom. Someone once said that "The book of Proverbs alone is a book of such wisdom that if it was followed, the psychologists would run out of patients, the courts out of criminals, and the safe houses out of victims." Proverbs 8:11 says, *"For wisdom is far more valuable than rubies"* (NLT); *"A wise child brings joy to a father; a foolish child brings grief to a mother"* (Proverbs 10:1, NLT). Most people would rather be around a wise person than a foolish one: *"the babbling of a fool invites disaster"* (Proverbs 10:14b, NLT).

Wisdom means to apply knowledge in our daily living. It also applies to character and the ability to live a godly life: *"Respect and obey the Lord! This is the beginning of wisdom. To have understanding, you must know the Holy God"* (Proverbs 9:10, CEV).

How do you get wisdom? The Bible tells us to pray for wisdom: *"If any of you need wisdom, you should ask God, and it will be given to you. God is generous and won't correct you for asking"* (James 1:5, CEV). We are lost without Christ. When we begin our Christian journey, we're on the path to gaining true wisdom.

Father God, please give me wisdom along with knowledge, so that I can live a godly life. Amen.

FEBRUARY 5

"... they will walk and run without getting tired"
(Isaiah 40:31b, CEV).

A baby's first steps are magical. We excitedly encourage and applaud every effort they make to stand and then each step they manage to take. Even though they fall many times, they don't give up. They never seem to get tired of trying.

I remember when my oldest daughter, Laurieann, took her first steps. She started by first standing and then taking a few steps here and there on her own until falling again. One morning I was in the kitchen of our little two-bedroom apartment. I heard a laughing sound and then the sound of little feet running. It was Laurieann laughing as she ran back and forth in the hallway. She'd finally realized that she could run. After a time of learning to balance and then to just take a few steps at a time, she was now running! She was so excited that she laughed as she ran.

Whenever I read this verse in Isaiah, I think of Laurieann's first steps and when she discovered that she could run without falling. God has promised us that when we hope in Him, He will give us the strength we need each day of our journey. Just like my daughter, we can run and not get tired, walk and not faint. No matter how old we are or how far along on our journey, we can be assured that God is with us. We can fall and can get up again and run.

Father God in Heaven, thank You for our physical strength and abilities, but also for the strength You give our spirit so that we can joyfully live each day of our life in victory. From a thankful heart. Amen.

FEBRUARY 6

"Who can find a worthy woman? For her value is far above rubies"
(Proverbs 31:10, WEB).

Today I woke up, got up, and dressed up. I prayed for strength to do the next thing. I felt overwhelmed, and I felt I was missing the mark. I thought about the women I read about in the Bible. They seemed to me to be so much more than I could ever be. How can I live up to their example when I struggle sometimes to get through the day?

How do I be a good sister, daughter, wife, or friend, such as the unnamed friends that went through the roof of a house to bring their sick friend to Jesus for healing? Then there's Mary, the mother of John Mark, who was known for her hospitality and courage. What about Lois, the dedicated grandmother of Timothy, who taught him about God? There are the women who were disciples of Jesus, such as Dorcas and Mary Magdalene. Lydia was a businesswoman with good judgement who showed hospitality. Priscilla was a teacher, student of the gospel, and missionary. We can't forget Ruth, the best daughter-in-law ever.

Finally, I thought about the Proverbs 31 woman, who had it all together. She was a superwoman, a heroine, and every man's dream wife. I am none of these. I am the woman at the well looking for forgiveness. I am the woman who touched the hem of Jesus's garment looking for healing. I am the mother whose child is sick. I am all of the unnamed women in the Bible with their needs and their worries.

But then, I remembered what Jesus said to an unnamed woman: *"Daughter ... Go in peace and be freed from your suffering"* (Mark 5:34). Jesus knows and sees me just where I am.

Father God, sometimes I struggle to be like others. Help me to be who You made me to be. I know that You have a purpose for my life, and I want to honour You by accepting who I am in Christ. Amen.

FEBRUARY 7

"Don't be selfish; don't try to impress others. Be humble, thinking of others as better than yourselves. Don't look out only for your own interests, but take an interest in others, too"
(Philippians 2:3–4, NLT).

Are you so focused on what you don't have that you're blind to what you do have? It's time to remove the blinders.

Do you know your parents, grandparents, siblings, and cousins? Have you received education, healthcare, drug coverage, and police protection?

Do you have freedom to vote, shop, and walk the trails? Do you have a paycheque for your labour, money to pay for rent, lights, and phone?

Have you received gifts from parents, friends, and relatives? Do you have medicines and access to counselling for emotional or financial difficulties?

Do you know the joy of the companionship of a pet? Have you had opportunities for travel? Are you the recipient of gratitude, thanks, and appreciation for helping others?

Have you been complimented on your appearance, your smile, and your personality?

Now what was it you were saying about what you don't have and how bad life has been to you? It's time to look beyond yourself and see how you can help others.

God does indeed give sight to the blind. Much to be thankful for, don't you think? We are so blessed.

Heavenly Father, sometimes we forget and take for granted all the good things You've given us. Please forgive and remind us again. Amen.

FEBRUARY 8

"Teach us to number our days carefully so that we may develop wisdom in our hearts" (Psalm 90:12, HCSB).

When I made the decision to set a retirement date, I put a countdown clock on my computer screen. Every day it told me how many days I had left to retire. As the time got closer, I was frantically trying to accomplish things before my time was up. I set priorities and thought about the most important things to do before I retired from the workforce.

I threw out all the accumulated stuff of thirty plus years. I talked to staff about their own personal concerns and goals. I realized I only had a little time left to make a difference for the people I worked with. I wanted to ensure that they were taken care of. I tried to do the important things and leave the rest, but my time at work was limited.

I imagined this was similar to someone who was told that they had a certain amount of time left to live. Some people would spend it wisely by setting priorities and getting the most out of each day. They would concentrate on people relationships and talking about their souls. Other people would ignore it and spend their time selfishly.

This is why we ask God to *"teach us to number our days,"* so that we can spend them wisely. Being aware of how little time we have left helps us to live more wisely. It helps us to focus on the important things, especially people relationships.

We can spend our time sensibly, or we can waste it foolishly.

Father God, all our days here on earth are shorter than we like to think. Help me to make the most and best of each day. Amen.

FEBRUARY 9

"For the Son of Man came to seek and to save the lost" (Luke 19:10).

There are many examples of good problem solvers in the Bible. During the rebuilding of the temple in Jerusalem, Nehemiah solved many problems. He always prayed first and then planned and prepared. His enemies tried to sidetrack him on numerous occasions, but he remained focused.

Moses solved problems as well—and there were many along his forty-year journey. One particular problem arose when Aaron let the people get out of control. Moses focused on what was driving the activity—the morality, or lack of. He knew that the most damaging problems are not solved by correcting actions or behaviour. Some can only be resolved by a change of character, morality, and heart. Moses went to God, confessed the sins of the people, and asked for forgiveness. He solved the right problem.

Sin is the greatest problem in the history of the world. But God is the greatest problem solver. He had a plan before the world was created to send His Son Jesus to take care of this problem. Jesus said that all sinful behaviours are connected to the heart (Matthew 15:19). We can clean up our act, but we need help to clean our heart. God took the initiative to solve the sin problem. He came looking for the problem. He came looking for the lost.

How we handle our problems is up to us. After praying, planning, and preparing, we need to take initiative, be creative, stay focused, and solve the right problem.

I ask myself: What will I be remembered for? Will I be remembered for the problems solved, or for the problems created?

Father God, help me to learn from Your graceful approach to problem solving in all areas of my life. Amen.

FEBRUARY 10

"We do not want you to become lazy, but to imitate those who through faith and patience inherit what has been promised" (Hebrews 6:12).

On cold winter days, I don't feel very energetic. This time of year, I spend more time indoors than outdoors, so I'm not as physically active. For me, winter promotes a sedentary lifestyle. In the past, I'd walk through the snow on the trails, or brave the icy winds walking our street. These days, I prefer the comfort of the warm house. I usually choose comfort over more challenging conditions. I may even border on the side of laziness.

Even though I'm confined to the house more in the winter, I need to find ways to keep active, like stair walking, making use of my exercise machines, and, of course, there's always housework.

I wonder if this could be true sometimes of my spiritual life. When you're sedentary, your body loses muscle tone, strength, and endurance. The same thing is true of our spiritual body. If you're inactive in prayer, not reading your Bible, and neglecting worship, your spiritual life will be dull, weak, and unproductive. Just as you need to be disciplined in your physical activity, your spiritual life requires activity to stay fit and to be an effective Christian.

I read one time that *discipline, not desire, determines destiny*. It's no good to sit around dreaming about being fit. You have to do something about it. I want to be physically and spiritually fit. Let's strive to be disciplined in our physical and spiritual day-to-day lives: *"Never be lacking in zeal, but keep your spiritual fervor, serving the Lord"* (Romans 12:11).

Father God, forgive us when we get lazy in our spiritual walk. Remind us of the importance of staying active and disciplined in our daily prayers and devotions. Amen.

FEBRUARY 11

"But Jesus told them: You are always making yourselves look good, but God sees what is in your heart. The things that most people think are important are worthless as far as God is concerned" (Luke 16:15, CEV).

Bad hair days—I've had them. You've had them. "My hair is so flat today. It must be the wet weather we're having. My hair is so frizzy today. Look at that grey hair; I need to have my roots redone. My bangs are too long, and I need to get them cut. That last colour was too light (or too dark). Look at all those dead ends. I need a makeover."

Bad heart days—I've had them. You've had them. Gossip—"Did you hear about so and so?" Temper—"That boss of mine makes me so mad, I could …" Greed—"I'll take the best piece for myself. I deserve it." Grumpiness—"Don't bother me with your problems; I have enough of my own." Jealousy—"All right for her, she's in with that uppity crowd."

We place a lot of importance on how our hair looks, but the Bible certainly does not. It seems that the condition of our heart is much more important than the condition of our hair: *"Let your beauty come not from the outward adorning … but from the hidden person of the heart, in the incorruptible adornment of a gentle and quiet spirit, which is very precious in God's sight"* (1 Peter 3:3–4, WEB).

What kind of beauty would you prefer? The beautiful reflection in the mirror that lasts for a short time, or the beautiful reflection from the heart that lasts forever?

Dear God, I've had bad hair days and bad heart days, too. Thank You that I have hair and can make it into whatever style I choose. I'm glad You work on my heart and can make me what You would have me to be. Amen.

FEBRUARY 12

"Create in me a clean heart, O God; and renew a right spirit within me" (Psalm 51:10, KJV).

"Terry, there's someone at the door," I shouted from the kitchen. "You let them in while I go change."

Did you ever get unexpected company when you felt you were looking your worst? I've received company when I wasn't at my best, and my reaction usually was, "Sorry for the way I look. I haven't washed my hair yet, or showered, or put makeup on, or I was in the middle of doing my housework." We tend to make excuses for our appearance if we feel embarrassed or unprepared. We don't want people to see us at our worst.

Sometimes I make excuses to God when He wants me to do something that I don't want to do. Do you make excuses to God? Jesus sees into your heart and searches your mind. He sees your desires and the motives behind your actions. He knows and understands everything that makes you who you are today. He doesn't look at your outward appearance. He sees who we really are on the inside. You can't hide anything from God.

What would it be like to see inside someone's heart and see what Jesus sees? What would it be like to see someone's soul and not their physical appearance? When I think of Jesus looking at my mind and heart, I wonder what He sees.

Just in case He sees something in me that isn't right, I ask Him to give me a clean mind, a pure heart, and a right spirit. Even though my hair may not be styled, or my makeup on, or I may be in my scrubbing clothes, God loves me with an everlasting love and accepts me as I am.

Father God, thank You for Your promise to never leave me as I was. You are always there to forgive me when I do wrong and to set me right again. Amen.

FEBRUARY 13

"I believed in you, so I said, 'I am deeply troubled, Lord'" (Psalm 116:10, NLT).

COVID, COVID—Here we go again, counting the numbers. How many positive cases today? How many deaths?

The pandemic season of COVID-19 and its variants seemed, at times, to be never-ending. I listened to the news, and my mind could hardly comprehend what my ears were hearing. The number of infections was on a rapid rise; we had many variant viruses and several lockdowns. I wondered what lesson God wanted to teach us. Obviously, we haven't learned it yet.

In the book of Exodus, God sent ten plagues to the people of Egypt. These plagues had the specific purpose of softening Pharaoh's hard heart so that he'd give the Jews freedom from slavery. I wonder if this was the reason for the COVID-19 pandemic. Did God want to soften our hearts to free us from captivity?

Is something in our lives holding us captive and away from God? Are we making materialism the new god? What about self-gratification, power, or greed? Is God trying to soften our hearts so that we'll turn to Him?

In this fast-paced, selfish world, we seem to put a lot of things ahead of God. These things hold us captive, like addictions do addicts and like Pharaoh did the Jews.

God doesn't want us to be held captive. He wants us to have an abundant life in Him. The Bible tells us that God loves us with an everlasting love. He'll go to extreme measures to set us free. Do you have a Pharaoh in your life holding you captive?

Father God, thank You for Your love that frees us to live a more abundant life. Help me to put You first in everything. Amen.

FEBRUARY 14

"This is how we know what love is: Jesus Christ laid down his life for us" (1 John 3:16a).

Unconditional love—that's what we all look for. Pets—especially puppies—are good examples of unconditional love. They're always excited to see you. They want to please you. They don't look at the richness or poorness of their surroundings. All they want is a friendly word, a bowl of food, fresh water, and a warm place to sleep.

Dusty was our first dog. She was a slender, tall-legged, black-and-tan-coloured beagle. When we lived in a two-bedroom apartment in Mount Pearl, Terry came home after work one day carrying this little puppy. We loved her immediately, and she loved us in return. She asked for very little—just a warm spot in the sun, food in her dish, a hug, and a kind word from us. We took her everywhere we went, and Terry even trained her to hunt. Almost every weekend he went rabbit hunting with Dusty. She was a natural hunter and very loyal. She liked to please us.

One time when they were hunting, she was so excited that she kept chasing something in the woods and didn't return when Terry called her in for the night. He had to go home and leave her there. He left his jacket on the ground in case she returned so that she'd smell his scent. Sure enough, the next morning he found her lying on that jacket. Needless to say, we were overjoyed to have her home.

She was our devoted pet for seventeen years. A love like that is hard to find. First Corinthians 13:4 says, "*Love is patient and kind. Love is not jealous or boastful or proud*" (NLT).

Father God, I receive a type of love from my pets. I receive love from family and from friends. But nothing compares to Your extravagant love for us. Thank You for allowing us to experience all these different types of love. Amen.

FEBRUARY 15

"... let me hear your voice; for your voice is sweet ..."
(Song of Songs 2:14)

People may not remember the words you say, but they remember how you say them and how you made them feel.

The tone of your voice can be comforting and soothing. One time I was taking my daughter Tiffany to the Janeway Children's Hospital. She was only a year old and was very ill and crying. My cousin went with me to hold Tiffany while I drove. Betty and I talked on the way, and I think I talked the most. After a while, Tiffany quieted down. Betty said, "It was the sound of your voice while we talked. It soothed and quieted her." I realized she was right.

One time my parents planned to be in Florida for a few months. Mom called often to chat, but I didn't talk to my dad for quite a while. I missed him very much and wanted to hear his distinctive voice and laugh.

One evening I had company over, and while preparing supper, the phone rang. It was my dad on the line. I couldn't even speak, as I filled up with emotion and wanted to cry. It was so good to hear his voice; I just wanted to listen and not say a word. He talked, laughed, and asked me questions. All I could do was give short answers. When the call ended, I was overwhelmed and gave in to my tears. I can't remember the words he spoke, but I remember the sound of his voice and laugh.

Father God, thank You for giving me my dad. Thank You that our voices can be comforting, soothing, and loving. Help us to use our voices in ways that glorify You and help others. Amen.

FEBRUARY 16

"You move as gracefully as the pony that leads the chariot of the king" (Song of Songs 1:9, CEV).

The truck backed into our long driveway. I waited with held breath until it stopped and I could go and look inside of it. Terry and his friend led a skinny brown horse down the ramp. Tears came to my eyes as I looked at what was left of this beautiful animal. She was encrusted with dirt and feces. Her halter was embedded in the skin around her head. Her head tilted to one side, and she couldn't straighten it. Her ribs were visible through a somewhat thick winter coat. She stumbled and almost fell, and I thought, *This horse is not going to make it.*

My husband and I were members of a horse protection group. We lived on a farm and had a barn and a couple of horses. When the call came about this horse, my husband rescued her. With his care and patience, he gave her water, fed her a warm mash, and wrapped her in warm blankets. Over the next weeks, he cleaned her with warm water one little bit at a time. Her skin was extremely sore, and with his care and the attention of a vet, she improved.

By summer, she had recovered and looked like a different animal. Her neck was straight; the wounds from the halter had healed; and her coat glistened. She was a registered quarter horse, and her training made her a joy to ride as she pranced around the field. She was a gentle soul, and I was happy that we could restore her health and give her a safe place to live.

Who knows what kind of good life she'd had before she ended up in a bad place. There are people like this. They start off on the right path but through no fault of their own, they end up living a very poor life. They're just waiting for someone to rescue them.

Father God, give me eyes to see people who need help and the courage to reach out a helping hand. Amen.

FEBRUARY 17

"This is the bread that came down from heaven. Your ancestors ate manna and died, but whoever feeds on this bread will live forever" (John 6:58).

Newfoundlanders sure like their homemade bread. No other food in Newfoundland sparks memories of home quite like homemade bread—you can almost smell it, see it, taste it, and feel its warmth. It's a simple food, very basic, but necessary for our well-being.

Luke 11:3 records Jesus teaching us to pray by asking: *"Give us each day our daily bread."* I think we Islanders take this literally. As much as we like our slice of homemade bread, Jesus was probably referring to not only our physical food, but our spiritual food as well. Set aside time every day to read a little or a lot from the Word of God. Prepare yourself for reading by becoming quiet before the Lord. Remember that the purpose is for the good of your soul. Read slowly and pay attention to the words. Pause at the periods and take a moment at the commas. Don't be in a hurry. Give God a chance to reveal His message to you. You know what happens when you rush your meal—you get indigestion!

Bread is mentioned many times in the Bible. It talks about the earning of bread (Genesis 3:19); it tells us about miracles involving bread (Mark 8); it compares having no bread to lack of faith (Matthew 16:8); it describes a variety of grains and flours used in the making of bread (Ezekiel 4:9); and Jesus was recognized as He broke bread (Luke 24:30–31). Jesus said *"I am the bread of life"* (John 6:48).

Let me ask you, "What's this bread of life mean to you?"

Father God, thank You for all good things. As the Bread of Life, You comfort and sustain us in our daily living. When I make my homemade bread, I think of You. Amen.

FEBRUARY 18

"If you enter a town and it welcomes you, eat whatever is set before you" (Luke 10:8, NLT).

My best friend and I were boarding at a house in Arnold's Cove where we attended high school. An older couple offered to take us in and give us a room and meals during the weekdays. On the weekends, we went home. Their home was a warm and inviting simple bungalow. We shared a room and basic facilities. Each morning, Mrs. Lockyer put a basin of warm water in our room for washing. After this, we ate breakfast and went to school.

They were a very kind and friendly couple, but sometimes it was hard to understand what they said. One day she asked us if we liked "erring." I asked her to repeat it, but I still didn't know what she was talking about, so we said yes. At suppertime, I found out that she was talking about a type of fish called herring. We had a great laugh over this as we ate our supper.

In the New Testament when Jesus sent out seventy-two followers to the places He would later visit, He gave them certain guidelines. One of these was to eat whatever was put before you, just as my friend and I ate the "erring." We wouldn't think of refusing, as that's not how we were raised.

Many of the younger generations today don't have the experience of boarding away from home with strangers in order to go to school. They don't know what it's like to sit at a table and graciously accept what's offered to them. Instead, they're accustomed to asking for something different, or even going to a fast-food restaurant or takeout place.

Are we like that in our daily walk with God? Are we more eager to eat fries and hamburgers at a fast-food place than to sit in His presence and enjoy the healthy meal He offers?

Father God, thank You for Mr. and Mrs. Lockyer, who opened their home to my friend and me. Help me to be as hospitable as they were. Amen.

FEBRUARY 19

"But now you must also rid yourselves of all such things as these: anger, rage, malice, slander, and filthy language from your lips"
(Colossians 3:8).

Out of the corner of my eye I caught a glimpse of a dark object running across the floor. Was that what I thought it was? Yes, there was a mouse in the house. He was fast, but not fast enough to go undetected. He scampered along the wall by the television and then disappeared under the couch. I jumped up, yelling as I went, *"Mouse!"* I ran through the kitchen to the porch and grabbed the broom. I said to myself, "I'll get that little freeloader."

I chased him around from room to room, swiping with the broom, but he disappeared down a tiny hole by the heating pipe to the basement. What to do now? I hoped there weren't any others with him. I said to myself, "Out he must go."

The next step was to set traps. I set them here; I set them there. I set them everywhere. When I finally settled down, I went to the kitchen to wash dishes. Suddenly, I heard a snap! It came from the cupboard under the sink, where I'd put one of the traps. I didn't want to look but knew that I had to check.

I opened the door. There was a mouse in my trap. I had him! That no good freeloader. Success was sweet. I got rid of him and continued on with my work.

If only getting rid of our bad behaviour and thoughts was as easy as getting rid of that mouse.

Father God, just as I set traps for the mouse, help me to get rid of my wrong thoughts and actions by following the example and truths You set for us in the Bible. Amen.

FEBRUARY 20

"You hem me in behind and before. You laid your hand on me"
(Psalm 139:5, WEB).

Years ago, I watched President Obama's inauguration on television, and I noticed that he walked openly and with confidence. It must have given him comfort and security knowing that wherever he went, he was surrounded by the best security in the nation.

He walked through the masses of people but was hemmed in on every side, back and front, with a wall of bodyguards. I looked at the guards and took note of where their focus was. They were looking at the crowds of people and the surrounding buildings. They weren't looking at the President. Their job was to spot trouble before it had an opportunity to get to the President. If they kept their eyes only on him, he could be assassinated right before their eyes. But before that could happen, it would have to pass through the guards first.

As born-again Christians, we are God's children, under the protection of the Almighty. Nothing comes to us that hasn't already passed through Him. We're surrounded by armies of angels. We have no idea the number of disasters that our guards have intercepted for us.

If we could see with our spiritual eyes, we might see the forces of evil like crowds of people pressing in along the streets. We'd also see the Lord's angels positioned around us like a shield. The Bible tells us that *"The angel of the Lord encamps around those who fear Him, and he delivers them"* (Psalm 34:7).

Father God, thank You for the assurance that because I'm Your child, I have Your protection. Help me to remember this and not to fear but walk with confidence. Amen.

FEBRUARY 21

"For everyone has sinned; we all fall short of God's glorious standard" (Romans 3:23, NLT).

Most of us like the idea of a hero to save us from bad things. I remember watching superhero television shows like *Superman* and *Wonder Woman*. I was amazed at their strength and ability to defeat evil. They fought crime and rescued people in distress. Did you have a favourite hero when you were a child? Maybe it was a TV hero like the Lone Ranger, a crime solver like Nancy Drew, or maybe some fairytale hero like Prince Charming. For some people, it could be a father, teacher, or friend. Maybe your hero is a doctor, policeman, or some other profession.

With all the evil in the world, it's natural to look for a saviour. We don't want to see people oppressed and suffering. We don't want evil and bad people to win. The world is full of people with evil thoughts and ways. Sin means doing what goes against God's standards. The Bible tells us that everyone has sinned. That's why God sent His Son. He knows we need a Saviour more than we need anyone else.

But no matter how much God does for us, we still reject God. This is true of people all through the ages. Jesus came to give us salvation and eternal life in Heaven. But we must believe in Him and accept Him in our hearts and lives.

Do you want a superhero or a Saviour?

Father God, even though we may still have heroes, help us to realize that we need a Saviour more than anything else. Thank You for forgiving us of our sins, and help us to forgive others who wrong us. Amen.

FEBRUARY 22

"It was late autumn, and the king was in a winterized part of the palace, sitting in front of a fire to keep warm"
(Jeremiah 36:22, NLT).

Extreme weather watch! This alert popped up on my phone. I opened up the weather app and saw: "Blizzard warning: Your area is under an extreme weather watch. Stormy conditions are predicted with high winds." Time to go to the store and stock up on bottled water, batteries, matches, candles, non-perishable food, toilet paper, and, of course, storm chips (ha ha).

What do you do in a storm warning? Do you make sure you have your emergency supply kit packed with the essential items? I like to have emergency phone numbers close by, flashlights and candles where I can easily find them, and warm blankets and clothing ready in case the power shuts off. If you have an emergency generator for power supply, make sure you buy extra gas and test its operation.

If you have a wood stove or fireplace, you need to get the splits ready to light the fire. You should also store an emergency supply of non-perishable food and water, secure items that might blow away, and ensure all your electronic devices are fully charged. These are just some things you can do to prepare.

How do you prepare for a spiritual storm? Get your emergency supply kit packed by learning what the Bible says about trials (Romans 12:12). Secure yourself with scripture verses that teach us about God's character (1 John 4:8). Memorize emergency verses that affirm God's promises to us (Jeremiah 29:11). Lastly, pray as though your life depends on it—because it does (Philippians 4:6).

Father God, I want to be prepared for all the storms and trials in life, but sometimes I fail in one or two areas. Thank You for being there to lift me up again. Amen.

FEBRUARY 23

"For wisdom will enter into your heart. Knowledge will be pleasant to your soul" (Proverbs 2:10, WEB).

My memory of the two-room school where I attended until grade seven reminds me of pictures in an old photo album of a time long ago. The colour is faded, the sharpness is blurred, and the edges are frayed. But in my memory, I see in the centre of the classroom a round, black wood-burning stove (called a pot-belly stove) with a door in the front and four legs to hold it off the wooden floor. There are rows of wooden desks—the kind with the seat attached to the top. The desks have unique stories of their own, with marks here and there from the numerous owners. Most of them had several globs of dried gum stuck underneath.

The sun shone through the windows, and the snow outside sparkled. I guess that's why there were so many mitts around and under the stove. During recess, we'd be outside making snowballs and throwing them at our friends. Sometimes, when the stove got too hot, we could smell the burnt odour of the woolen mitts.

I remember spelling tests, essays, and geography. We wrote everything by hand in scribblers and exercise books. Everything had to be neat without too many eraser marks. There were no computers, cell phones, libraries, or indoor toilets. These surroundings, combined with the innocence of childhood enhanced my ability to learn. I learned to play and socialize with friends and to respect my teacher. With no mechanical noise, I learned to appreciate quietness.

I personally didn't have the stress that students have in today's schools. Maybe we need to get back to a simpler way of life to appreciate what God has given us.

Father God, thank You for the school I attended in those early years. I look back with fondness at those memories and the time I had to be just a child and enjoy every day. Amen.

FEBRUARY 24

"If you remain in me, and my words remain in you, you will ask whatever you desire, and it will be done for you" (John 15:7, WEB).

Do you have difficulty praying? Maybe you can't find the words sometimes because you have trouble expressing your thoughts and feelings to God. Do you think you need just the right words for God to hear your prayer?

Do you have trouble talking to your friends or family? Do you talk to them naturally, or do you talk really grand? If they're like my family, they'll make fun of you if you try that. Whichever way you talk to them, you can do the same with God. Don't be afraid to express something the way you'd express it to others. God knows your heart, and you can't surprise Him. You may wonder why God doesn't always give you what you want. Ask yourself if it's in line with God's will or His Word. Is it a selfish request that may be harmful to you or someone else?

How do you know if you're praying and asking according to God's will? One way to know is to say Scripture verses back to God. The Word of God is the will of God. There are verses in the Bible to match anything you want to ask or say.

When you memorize or write down verses that stand out to you or reflect your heart's thoughts, say them back to God. The Bible tells us that when we pray according to God's will, we can be assured that God hears our prayer and will answer.

Father God, sometimes I like to imagine that You're sitting at my kitchen table with me, having a cup of tea or coffee. The Bible tells me that "The Lord directs the steps of the godly. He delights in every detail of their lives" (Psalm 37:23, NLT). Thank You from the depths of my heart for entering into conversation with me at my table. Thank You for directing my days. Amen.

FEBRUARY 25

"Five times I received forty stripes minus one from the Jews. Three times I was beaten with rods. Once I was stoned. Three times I suffered shipwreck. I have been a night and a day in the deep"
(2 Corinthians 11:24–25, WEB).

The old barn housed the horse, along with a few chickens and ducks. Pop cared for the horse and the birds, but the ducks were Pop's pride and joy. He had a small pond made for them in the little brook that went through the property.

One rainy morning, my nan went to the barn with the scraps of food for the birds. There was a narrow wooden walk to the entrance of the barn, where the ducks and chickens lived. This was where they were fed with grain, chicken feed, and table scraps. The boards were wet and slick, and my grandmother slipped and fell. She broke her hip. It took her quite a while to recover, as this was her second broken hip.

My grandmother lived next door to us, so I visited often. She was a resilient woman who'd had many mishaps and sicknesses throughout her life. She lived a life of service to her family, the church, and the community. She was a teacher, a midwife, and a shop owner. But throughout her life and no matter the circumstances, she was thankful for what she had.

In the verse above, the apostle Paul is relating the hardships he suffered because of his ministry as a missionary bringing the gospel of Jesus Christ to people. He rejoiced in his suffering because it helped to advance the gospel (Philippians 1:12, 18b).

It's hard for us to imagine suffering as a reason to rejoice. But we need to look beyond the suffering and ask God to use it to help others and to tell them about His Son, Jesus.

Father God, I want to have faith like my grandmother. I want to live above my circumstances, not beneath them. Remind me of this when I need it. Amen.

FEBRUARY 26

"One of the two which heard John speak, and followed him, was Andrew, Simon Peter's brother" (John 1:40, KJV).

Have you ever received good news that you just can't wait to tell someone? You just heard something that was too good to keep to yourself. I'm sure we've all experienced this at one time or another. That's what happened to the men in the verse above. They had such good news that they couldn't wait to tell others.

Among the first men Jesus called were two disciples who followed the teaching and preaching of John the Baptist. When they heard and met Jesus, they left John to follow Him. One of them was Andrew. He then went to his brother Simon and said, "We have found the Messiah."

Then Philip joined the followers of Jesus and recruited Nathanael. They knew what the Scriptures said about the arrival of the Messiah. Of the many prophecies about the birth of the Messiah, one of the most well-known is found in Isaiah 7:14: *"… the virgin will conceive, and bear a son, and shall call his name Immanuel"* (WEB). These followers were familiar with the prophecies, and they were waiting for the Messiah to come. They believed Jesus to be the Messiah, so they followed Him.

Like Andrew, we can tell others that we've found the Messiah, the One the Bible talks about and the Saviour we were waiting for.

If you've heard about Jesus and asked Him into your heart, it's important to be a personal witness. Our message should be the same as Andrew's: I have found the Messiah.

Father God, thank You for sending Your Son, Jesus, as the Messiah. Thank You for all the people who believed and witnessed to others. Help me to be quick and bold to witness for You. Amen.

FEBRUARY 27

"... taking up the shield of faith, with which you will be able to quench all the fiery darts of the evil one" (Ephesians 6:16, WEB).

What an odd thing to see in the storage room of an old general store from the 1950s. Maybe that's why I remember them. They stood out from the assortment of crates, barrels, and other things you'd expect to see there. I was curious about them. It was a pair of leather boxing gloves hanging from the rafters. The leather was stained and faded brown. Where had they come from? Who'd used them and why were they there? Someone told me they were worn by my Uncle Reg. Boxing was a favourite sport of the family, and Uncle Eric boxed as well.

Once part of a sporting ensemble, they served a definite purpose, proudly worn by the owner in battle and in victory. They protected the boxer's hands and lessened the impact to the opponent. They were the fighter's tool. When held in front of the face, they were used in defence by the wearer. They protected his face from his opponent's punches.

The gloves remind me of the verses in Ephesians 6 that tell us to take up the full armour of God: the belt, shoes, breastplate, helmet, shield and sword. The belt of truth against Satan's lies. The shoes of peace of the gospel, or Good News, to share with others. The breastplate of God's righteousness to protect the heart. The helmet of salvation to protect our mind from doubt. The shield of faith to stop the fiery arrows of insults and temptations. And the sword, the Word of God, our weapon against the enemy. Make sure you wear your armour every day.

Heavenly Father, may we never forget to use the weapons You gave us, and especially to pray in the Spirit at all times and on every occasion. May we stay alert and be persistent in our prayers for all believers everywhere (Ephesians 6:18). *Amen.*

FEBRUARY 28

"Faith in Christ Jesus is what makes each of you equal with each other, whether you are a Jew or a Greek, a slave or a free person, a man or a woman" (Galatians 3:28, CEV).

"Oh no, not another girl," I said as I answered the phone. Mom was calling from the Grace Hospital in St. John's to let me know that she'd delivered another baby to add to the present family of mom, dad, and four girls.

I'm the oldest sister in my family, and when my youngest sister, Monique, was born, I was home on break from university. While my mom was in the hospital in St. John's waiting for her baby to be born, I took care of my sisters. Of course, I didn't mean what I said on the phone. It's just that we had four girls already, and a boy would have been nice. At least that's what I thought at the time.

Today, I wouldn't change her for any boy. Monique is my baby sister and a rare gem. From an early age, she put her trust in God. Her faith has never wavered, and she sets a good example for all of us. There are many examples in the Bible of women in the ministry of the gospel. In Romans 16:1, Paul mentions Phoebe, who was a church deacon. This tells me that women are important to God and play a vital role in the fulfilling of His purpose and plan.

Boy or girl, it didn't matter to us, and it doesn't matter to God. We're all important to Him. He gave His life for us. He desires that in our hearts, we recognize Jesus as Lord of our lives. God is our heavenly Father, and He does not say, "Oh no, not another girl!"

Father God, thank You that whether male or female, we're all of value to You. Forgive us when we view some people as more important than others. Help us allow You to be Lord of our lives. Amen.

MARCH 1

"She went and did according to the saying of Elijah; and she, he, and her household ate many days" (1 Kings 17:15, WEB).

Aunt Effie—she wasn't really my aunt, but everyone called her that—lived in a saltbox-shaped, two-storey house by the brook. I remember visiting her with my friends when we were children, mainly because she gave us cookies. Her speciality was chocolate chip cookies—my favourite. She always had a supply of cookies in her cookie jar.

She was a kind woman and made the children feel welcome. Her house was on a little yard surrounded by a small fence with a gate in the middle. When we'd knock on her door, she'd invite us to come into her cozy, warm kitchen. We rarely saw her husband, Charlie—a tall man—who worked in the woods and was a fisherman.

How fortunate I am to have this warm, comforting memory of one of my neighbours. When I read the verse in the Bible about the widow who fed Elijah, I immediately thought of Aunt Effie. She was welcoming and caring to all the children. She was an example of an older woman giving hospitality, and I think that's a good thing to be remembered for. The Bible tells us to be hospitable. *"Be not forgetful to entertain strangers: for thereby some have entertained angels unawares!"* (Hebrews 13:2, KJV). Now, wouldn't that be something? I think in my case, it was Aunt Effie who was the angel.

Father God, thank You for people who show their hospitality to those in need and to strangers. Help me to always be willing to open my home to help others and be an example of a servant heart. Amen.

MARCH 2

"And they took up twelve baskets full of the fragments, and of the fishes" (Mark 6:43, KJV).

What's in your basket? When I think of a basket, the first thing that comes to my mind is my laundry basket. I suppose it's my first thought because I use it almost every day. If you're like me, it seems as though there's always some dirty laundry waiting for a turn in the washer. I drag that basket around from upstairs to downstairs, to the bathrooms to the laundry room, and to the clothesline. It's the most used basket in my house.

Many other baskets come to my mind besides laundry baskets. Picnic baskets carry food, Easter baskets contain Easter eggs, and gift baskets could have just about anything in them. There are many references to baskets and their use in the Bible. You might be wondering what I'm talking about and how it relates to you.

Let's go back to our most used basket—the laundry basket. What else do you carry around in it besides laundry? Likewise, what do you drag around from day to day that weighs you down, limits your joy, and prevents you from living a full life? Is it a dress of regret, a hat of shame, shoes of hurt, a scarf of worry, all wrapped up in a coat of guilt? It's a heavy load, isn't it? No one can blame you. You've had your share of troubles.

When you decide that you've had enough of the laundry basket, ask God to lighten the load of worry, anxiety, fear, shame, unforgiveness, and hurts. We choose what we carry—a basket of dirty laundry, or a basket of God's promises. God says, *"as I was with Moses, so I will be with thee: I will not fail thee, nor forsake thee"* (Joshua 1:5b, KJV).

Father God, help me to give You all the unnecessary burdens that I carry around. I want to carry Your promises instead. Amen.

MARCH 3

"… in quietness and in confidence shall be your strength … "
(Isaiah 30:15b, KJV)

Here we are in Florida for the winter. Every morning, I put on my swimsuit, coverup, and flip-flops and walk across the green lawn to the pool for the morning water aerobics session. There are some cold mornings, but we're fortunate in this park because the pool is heated.

On warm days after each session, I lie in the sun and chat with a few of the ladies who exercise with me. It's a peaceful time of day before lunch and before the regular pool-soakers arrive for the afternoon. It's relaxing, and I often find myself reflecting on God's surprises and blessings in my life. Not only am I soaking up the sun, but I'm soaking up the Son. I'm so thankful for this time, and I want to remember it for the days and winters when I'm not here.

It feels like a timeout from real life. I bask in the knowledge that Jesus is part of me. I'm grateful for the Christian friends we've met both in the park and at church. There is much time for reflection on my life and the goodness of God throughout. I pray for our family at home and know that God is with them too. I am rejuvenated in the silence, the sun, and the Son.

> When prayer is at its highest, we wait in silence for God's voice to us; we linger in His presence for His peace and His power to flow over us and around us; we lean back in His everlasting arms and feel the serenity of perfect security in Him. (William Barclay)[1]

Father God, thank You so much for this rest and timeout. Please help me to remember that in You I find rest. Amen.

---

[1] "William Barclay Quotes," AZ Quotes, accessed October 12, 2025, https://www.azquotes.com/author/912-William_Barclay/tag/prayer.

MARCH 4

"Inside the Ark were a gold jar containing manna, Aaron's staff that sprouted leaves, and the stone tablets of the covenant" (Hebrews 9:4b, NLT).

In Nan's bedroom in the old two-storey saltbox house there was a trunk. As a little girl, I dreamed about what treasures it contained. Nan's old trunk seemed like a treasure chest to me, but it was off limits to the children.

Today, I have a trunk in my bedroom, given to me by my husband, who got it second-hand from a friend. It was covered with splotches of paint and hadn't been taken care of. I restored the finish and the metal latches. The paper lining inside wasn't damaged, and it's a grand looking trunk now. I use it to store my treasures from my childhood and from my children, and souvenirs that I've kept from various interests. Nan's trunk gave me a love of old trunks and trinket boxes. I store the things that are important to me, and they remind me of the story of my life—of my journey.

The Ark of the Covenant is the name given to the chest that God directed Moses to have built. Exodus 25:10 says, *"Have the people make an Ark of acacia wood—a sacred chest 45 inches long, 27 inches wide, and 27 inches high"* (NLT). I imagine the Israelites must have wondered what the Ark actually contained. Maybe they wanted to look inside but were too afraid of the consequences.

God wanted the items in the Ark preserved as a reminder to the Israelites of their forty-year journey through the wilderness. They were to remember the commandments that God gave them through Moses. God wanted them to remember how He provided for their greatest needs.

Father God, thank You for these reminders of Your care and provision. Thank You for the lesson of the trunk and all the treasurers it contains. Everything I have is a gift from You. Amen.

MARCH 5

"He gives snow like wool, and scatters frost like ashes"
(Psalm 147:16, WEB).

Many, many winters I've heard this said: "Winters aren't as bad as they used to be when I was growing up." Back then, the snow seemed higher, the ice thicker, and the winters more fun. These last few winters have been kind of mild with a moderate amount of snow.

However, this winter seems like an exception, like an old-fashioned winter. Today is March 4, and we've had snow on the ground since November. We had heavy snowfalls during December. January was a mixed bag of snow, ice, and a little rain. February was very, very cold with high winds. This is the wintriest winter that I remember for a very long time.

Everyone is talking about global warming, and I guess it's happening, but it certainly doesn't seem like it this winter. At times like this, I remember that the earth has undergone many types of changes in weather patterns. I also remember that God created the earth. He knows the current weather patterns and the changes that will happen. Psalm 148:8 tells us that God commands the weather: "*lightning and hail, snow and clouds, stormy wind, fulfilling his word*" (WEB).

Sometimes we just want to remember the worst. On this cold winter day, the sun is shining and the snow sparkles like a sea of diamonds. The days are longer now, and the sun is still shining at suppertime. We can either focus on the negative around us or focus on the positive and all that God has created. No matter what the weather, God is with us. When you think about it, winter really isn't all that bad.

Father God, I'm so thankful for these longer days and the promise of springtime. Thank You for being with me through this cold, stormy winter. Amen.

MARCH 6

"I speak to him face to face, clearly, and not in riddles! He sees the Lord as he is. So why were you not afraid to criticize my servant, Moses?" (Numbers 12:8, NLT)

Miriam and Aaron criticized Moses because he married a Cushite woman. I wonder if they felt free to do this because they were siblings? Miriam was Moses's older sister and may have felt that she had the right to criticize him. The lesson in this portion of scripture, though, isn't whether Moses did wrong by marrying a non-Israelite woman but that Miriam and Aaron criticized the one God had chosen to lead them out of Egypt. By criticizing Moses, they were also criticizing God. They didn't respect Moses's leadership. God was very angry with them. Miriam was punished with leprosy, while Aaron immediately cried out for mercy.

I had an employer once who taught me that if you complain about a situation or a person, you better have all the facts and a possible solution to the problem before bringing it to him. In other words, complaining and grumbling solve nothing and change nothing; instead, they create negativity and a feeling of discontent.

The cost to Miriam was leprosy and banishment for seven days. Aaron had the sense to immediately repent and ask for mercy.

What is the cost of complaining? Do you want to find out?

Father God, You have blessed us with good things beyond measure. Have mercy and forgive us when we're quick to complain. Instead, help us to gather the facts and seek You for a resolution.

MARCH 7

"For he satisfieth the longing soul, and filleth the hungry soul with goodness" (Psalm 107:9, KJV).

When I was a young girl in Chance Cove, my friend Norma would sometimes invite me to her house for Sunday supper. Her mother, Doris Rowe, prepared the most delicious Sunday supper—a traditional Newfoundland cold plate. I remember the cold salads, the meats, and the homemade bread. The salads and meats were leftovers from Sunday's cooked dinner. If there wasn't enough leftover meat, a can of meat was opened to supplement the meal. The bread was always so fine-textured and soft; it tasted delicious. Often there was jelly and custard for dessert.

According to Exodus 16:12, in biblical times, there were usually just two meals a day—morning and evening. There are many references to food in the Bible, and a variety of food was eaten, including vegetables, grains, spices, and fish. Meat wasn't eaten every day but was saved for special times.

Just as there were traditions in the Bible about foods and when to eat, there are Newfoundland food traditions too. The younger generation might not be as traditional today, and many like to eat in restaurants on Sunday. But when I was young, we always had a cooked Sunday dinner and cold plate for supper. Today you can find recipes on the Internet for Newfoundland cold plate. It consists of several different kinds of salads and meats with pickles and bread. Newfoundlanders love their cold plate suppers. Our food traditions satisfy our physical hunger, but the verse above tells us that God satisfies the thirst and hunger of the soul.

Father God, thank You for our food and for all the times we get together with family and friends to share a meal. Help us to remember that only You satisfy our hungry soul. Amen.

MARCH 8

"You saw me before I was born. Every day of my life was recorded in your book. Every moment was laid out before a single day had passed" (Psalm 139:16, NLT).

We were excited to learn that we would be grandparents. I thought it would never happen. We kept in touch with our daughter for daily updates on her progress. Finally, enough time had passed for an ultrasound. We could get a picture of our grandchild before the birth. We may even know whether we'd be grandparents of a boy or a girl.

When I was carrying my daughter years earlier, this technology was new. It was only used to rule out medical problems or complications with the upcoming birth. Nowadays, it's normal for all pregnant women to have an ultrasound. I was eager to see the life growing in my daughter's womb. This child was becoming very real to us.

We received the ultrasound picture from our daughter, and I cried when I saw the tiny body of a baby being formed into the likeness of God: *"So God created man in his own image, in the image of God created he him; male and female created he them"* (Genesis 1:27, KJV).

Immediately, we thought of names. We wondered who the baby would resemble the most. We thought of things to teach him, his first words, and his first steps. We realized that there was so much more to consider in his development. In our minds, we saw plans for his future. But we're told that God saw him before we did and already had his days laid out and recorded. We realized that our grandson's life was planned by God, and He has a purpose for his life.

Father God, thank You for this new technology that allows us to see an unborn baby. Help me to be the grandparent You designed me to be. Amen.

MARCH 9

"For we are God's masterpiece. He has created us anew in Christ Jesus" (Ephesians 2:10, NLT).

In my grandmother's house there was a front bedroom where my nan and pop slept. It was upstairs and faced the road, overlooking the ocean.

Nan's doll hung on the bedroom wall by the foot of the bed. The sun would shine through the bay window as I'd stare at the beautiful doll. I'd touch her dress in awe, and I liked to look at her. She had long brown ringlets and a beautiful porcelain face with soft features. I think her dress was satin, and she wore shoes. She was about two feet long. Her legs and arms were made of soft material, but her hands were porcelain. I wondered where the doll had come from and who had made her. The maker put a lot of care into her design and crafting. She was beautiful to me, and I marvelled at her. She was a masterpiece for sure.

The verse above tells us that we are God's masterpiece. Now, some of us might not be beauty queens. Some are born without full mental or physical abilities. I was born with genetics that I wouldn't choose to have—those that cause disease. But the Bible tells me that I'm God's *masterpiece*. Who am I to question God's work? Doesn't the artist have the right to design in the way He chooses? We should be asking how we can honour the Creator with our lives. How can I use my weaknesses and strengths to fulfill my purpose?

Never forget, some of the most powerful testimonies and ministries are from those who don't fit the regular mold.

Father God, sometimes I struggle when I see how others seem to have no troubles working and witnessing for You. Forgive me when I may question Your design for my life. Keep me in Your will. Amen.

MARCH 10

"Return to your house, and declare what great things God has done for you" (Luke 8:39a, WEB).

Being a witness to your own family and hometown friends about your newfound faith in Jesus is not an easy thing. The people who've known you the longest and the best have a difficult time believing that you've changed. They know all about your past failures and weaknesses.

The man in the verse above had obviously changed so much that his family had to believe. In the previous verses, Jesus had delivered him from demonic possession. The people in the region who saw this became afraid and asked Jesus to leave. The man who'd been healed wanted to go with Him, but Jesus told him to stay and witness to others. Jesus returned to the boat and left the area. The Bible tells us that the man became a missionary to the area: *"He went his way, proclaiming throughout the whole city what great things Jesus had done for him"* (Luke 8:39b, WEB).

Had Jesus allowed the man to go with Him, who would have been left behind to tell others what had happened and serve as proof? Jesus knew what the people needed in that area, and this man would be the best witness. They were, to some extent, afraid of Jesus, but they would listen to the testimony of the healed man.

Jesus brings us many opportunities to tell others about Him and what He's done for us. We have to be aware of those times and not be afraid to take advantage of them. Never underestimate the importance of witnessing and telling others about Jesus.

Father God, thank You for everything You've done for me. Give me confidence and strength to be the witness I should be. Amen.

MARCH 11

"Call to me, and I will answer you, and will show you great and difficult things, which you don't know" (Jeremiah 33:3, WEB).

When I was growing up, my mom went to Home League (the Women's Ministry program at the church) on Wednesday nights. If Dad was in the sawmill that he owned with his father, we were left on our own that night.

In later years, Dad never answered the phone if Mom was home. When I'd call on Wednesday nights, Dad would say, "Your mother has gone to Home League." Often I'd purposely call on Wednesday nights so he'd have to answer and I could talk to him without him saying, "Well, here's your mother."

Memory is really important. This hit home to me the year I lost my dad. I found that I wanted to remember every word he ever said to me, every moment I spent with him, every laugh we shared, and all the lessons he taught me. *"Keep on being faithful to what you were taught and to what you believed. After all, you know who taught you these things"* (2 Timothy 3:14, CEV). I trusted my father to teach me from his knowledge and experiences.

My dad taught me that when something bad happens or life throws you a mess, don't stay down, don't dwell on it for long, and don't wallow in self-pity. Set a goal and make a plan to go forward one step at a time, and stick with it. Yes, I miss my dad and his voice. I am so thankful and filled with certainty, because I know I will see and talk to my dad again in Heaven, and I look forward to that day.

Dear God, You are my heavenly Father, and I'm grateful that You listen when I call, just like my dad did on Home League night. Amen.

MARCH 12

"You shall not be afraid of the terror by night, nor of the arrow that flies by day" (Psalm 91:5, WEB).

Are there days when you feel like you should have stayed in bed? From the time you put your feet to the floor until you put them back in bed at night, the day was nothing but trouble. Some days are not golden. My husband says these are the rusty years, not the golden years.

Daily living can bring many problems. One day while getting out of bed, I twisted my back the wrong way. I looked out the window and saw that we'd received thirty centimetres of snow overnight that had to be shovelled. Before I got my coffee and breakfast, one of the girls called with a problem. Everything thawed in the freezer, which was only six years old. The doctor called with the not-so-good results of my blood test. Finally, I turned on the radio to hear some music, but instead, I heard about another mass shooting and another virus similar to COVID that was making people sick. And you know what else? This was all before lunch time.

When I read Psalm 91, I realize that our lives are just like this. It talks about the terrors of the night, the dangers of the day, the plague in darkness, and the disaster at midday. But then, in verse 7, you get the promise: *"Though a thousand fall at your side … these evils will not touch you"* (NLT). Verses 9 and 10a add this condition. *"If you make the Lord your refuge, if you make the Most High your shelter, no evil will conquer you"* (NLT). Verses 11 and 12a give the reason: *"For he will order his angels to protect you wherever you go. They will hold you up with their hands"* (NLT).

Father God, I am so happy to know that no matter what troubles come to me, You promise to hear my cry for help and be with me through it all. Amen.

MARCH 13

"Jesus said to him, 'The foxes have holes and the birds of the sky have nests, but the Son of Man has nowhere to lay his head'"
(Matthew 8:20, WEB).

One day I visited my friend Edna, who lived directly across the road from our house. Her house was a two-storey, saltbox-shaped house similar to ours, and it was very close to the salt water. Her mom, Florence, told me to come on in, and we ran upstairs to play. It was my first time upstairs, and I was curious about the bedrooms. It seemed that there were several. At that time, our great-grandmother Sarah was still alive and lived with them. She was very old, and in my childlike thinking, I thought she might be one hundred, but she really wasn't that old.

Edna said, "Come into Grandma's bedroom and I'll show you the bed." Well, in we went and jumped on the bed. Down we went, almost disappearing in the feather mattress. I'd never seen one before, and I was amazed at its softness. It was great fun to sink down in the feathery sea. It was a great place to lie down and rest. It was soft and wrapped around your body like a comforting cocoon.

Matthew tells us that Christ said that He had no place to lay his head. Sometimes the cost of following Him is that we won't have the things or people we relied on before. Are you willing to count the cost? But then Jesus says in John 14:2a that, *"My Father's house has many rooms."* He's saying that God has room for all who believe in Him.

Father God, thank You for giving us what we need daily to live. Thank You for the worldly comforts You allow us to have. Help us to give up anything that hinders our relationship with You. I look forward to my room in Heaven with You.

MARCH 14

"So we are Christ's ambassadors; God is making his appeal through us. We speak for Christ when we plead, 'Come back to God!'"
(2 Corinthians 5:20, NLT)

Most of us know that ambassadors are diplomats (messengers) of the highest rank, with full authority, sent by one country to a foreign country to represent the governing body.

In the verse above, the apostle Paul tells us that Christians are called *ambassadors* for Christ. This is because we are the Lord's representatives in a secular world. Sometimes we forget that we're ambassadors and that we have authority to represent Christ.

Although our roles are similar to those of a government ambassador, we are not to conform to the pattern of this world. Yet we should build and maintain positive relationships; we should live in and promote peace as much as possible. We should help people meet their physical needs, and we should use knowledge and leadership skills to teach others about the gospel. In addition, we should encourage others to reconcile with God.

In Ephesians 6:20, Paul says, *"I am in chains now, still preaching this message as God's ambassador. So pray that I will keep on speaking boldly for him, as I should"* (NLT). Even though Paul was in prison, he still considered himself an ambassador for Christ. He didn't give up telling others about Christ's love, sacrifice, and resurrection. He continually encouraged them to reconcile with God. Are others seeing us as ambassadors for Christ? Our lives must show that we do everything God expects His ambassadors to do.

Father God, I am overwhelmed that You would appoint me to be an ambassador for Christ. Even though I often feel weak and underqualified, I know that Your Spirit is with me to encourage me and make me bold. Amen.

MARCH 15

"Mary stayed with Elizabeth for about three months and then returned home" (Luke 1:56).

I've learned that God is so gracious and kind that He brings people into our lives when we need them. They cross our path sometimes for a short time, sometimes longer, and then they're gone.

I think of a good friend I had for about fifteen years until she passed. From a call to a hug and a cup of tea, I could count on her help. Many women have touched my life in different ways. One was an encourager when I needed it. One could make me laugh. Another one trusted me to pray. And still another one always had a hug.

I thought about Mary (Jesus's mother) staying with Elizabeth (the mother of John the Baptist). Mary was a young, inexperienced girl, and Elizabeth was much older. Also, her baby was due to be born before Mary's.

The Bible doesn't say, but I can't help but think that the purpose of Mary's visit was to be there for the birth of Elizabeth's baby so that she would know what to do when her own baby would be born. Mary was quite young—some say around fourteen years of age. I'm sure that God took all of this into consideration when He made His plan for Jesus to be born. He knew that Mary needed a wise, strong woman to mentor and encourage her.

Elizabeth was six months pregnant when Mary went to visit her. Mary stayed with her for three months. Is the timing of this just a coincidence? Mary later gave birth to a son, and they called him Jesus. The Bible doesn't say, but I'm confident that Mary learned a lot from Elizabeth.

Father God, thank You for all the help You've given me through the friendship of other women. Each of the ones You sent my way have blessed me, encouraged me, and helped me to grow in my faith. May I be that kind of woman to someone else. Amen.

MARCH 16

"Rejoice in the Lord always. I will say it again: Rejoice!"
(Philippians 4:4)

"Finally, be strong in the Lord and in his mighty power"
(Ephesians 6:10).

Today is Dad's birthday. I rejoice and thank God for the dad He gave me. I rejoice for the seventy-seven years that my dad had. I rejoice for the days I was able to spend with him.

I want to tell you about a birthday card I gave my dad. The day before his birthday, I went to the drugstore with my sister. We were staying in St. John's with my parents at a relative's house while Dad was having radiation treatment. We went to the drugstore to get a few supplies. The next day was his birthday, so I walked down the aisle of birthday cards.

It felt so surreal, and I felt out of place. This would be Dad's last birthday. What kind of card do you buy? What words do I want on the card knowing that it's the last one I'll ever buy for him?

I picked up a few cards and read all the words that my dad couldn't read right now. The brain tumour had taken away his ability to read. Some had nice pictures and fancy paper. Finally, I saw a card that was very plain. It had a little red heart and the words "Dad" and "Happy Birthday" on the front cover. Written on the inside were these words: "This card contains all the love I sometimes don't express. Dad, I love you."

This was the perfect card. It said everything that needed to be said in a simple way that he could understand.

God blessed Dad on his last birthday. He was well enough to enjoy a birthday lunch and visits from family. God gave him and us strength for the day.

Father God, thank You for my dad. Thank You for blessing his life and giving him a good birthday. Thank You for giving me strength and peace through that time. Amen.

MARCH 17

"For forty years you sustained them in the wilderness, and they lacked nothing. Their clothes did not wear out, and their feet did not swell!" (Nehemiah 9:21, NLT)

Imagine wearing clothing that never wears out. I think I have some clothes like that. It seems that sometimes you buy a coat, a pair of boots, or a blouse that lasts forever. No matter how many times I wear them or wash them, they're still like new. That could be a problem these days, because the styles change so frequently that you need to buy new stuff to keep up with the times.

I remember the style of clothing my grandparents wore when I was a little girl. It's funny now when you look at old pictures and see the old styles. We can laugh and wonder how they ever wore that type of clothing. They usually only had a few changes of clothing, and their styles didn't change as often as ours do today.

Even when I was young and living at home, my clothes closet was very small, and it wasn't packed with clothing like it is today. Some old houses didn't even have closets. They just had a few hooks on the wall. We wore our clothes until they were worn out or handed down to the next child. Even so, I can't imagine keeping the same clothing for forty years, as the Israelites did. We're more of a wasteful society today.

It may not have seemed like a blessing to the Israelites that they wore the same clothing that didn't wear out, but it was miraculous. I think the lesson is that through our wilderness experiences, God is with us and can provide for us in unbelievable ways. We may not see it or appreciate it until years later. How has God provided for you in your life?

Father God, thank You for Your provision in ways that we don't always see. Open my eyes to see all the ways You bless me. Amen.

MARCH 18

"See! The winter is past; the rains are over and gone" (Song of Songs 2:11).

Even though we still have a good depth of snow in our yard, and even though it snowed last night, I am not perturbed. This morning as we went to the car to go to church, I heard the sound of hundreds of songbirds announcing that spring is coming. The trees around our property were filled with birds, and it was as if they were singing winter down. There's a saying we have in church: If you speak too long, you'll be sung down.

Well, I'm officially saying goodbye to winter today. Maybe the calendar says something different, but if the birds can give winter the boot, I can too. "Winter, you've been here long enough."

I must say, though, that I'm thankful for God's care this winter. I enjoyed my winter activities and I continued to write. Here I am in March thinking the winter wasn't too long after all. Who would have thought I'd be saying this today?

I'm thankful for the time at home and the time spent with family. I'm thankful for snowblowers and for neighbours who helped us sometimes with snow clearing. I'm thankful that what fell on us was snow and not bombs from war. We have much to be thankful for in this part of the world, and I ask for God's forgiveness for complaining. Genesis 8:22 tells us, *"As long as the earth remains, there will be planting and harvest, cold and heat, summer and winter, day and night"* (NLT). Let's be thankful for these things.

Father God, thank You for the songbirds that herald the approach of spring and a change of seasons. I'm thankful for all things but especially for spring and summer. Amen.

MARCH 19

"Though he brings grief, he will show compassion, so great is his unfailing love" (Lamentations 3:32).

Lately it seems like I've been crying, or on the verge of tears all the time. But that doesn't mean I don't trust God or that I'll stop praising and thanking Him. I must confess that sometimes I alternate between praising and pleading. Sometimes when we're going through a hard time, our pain is front and centre. We can't see or hear God clearly. I was focusing on the pain way too much.

It's not always easy to be praising, but that's what David did in the Psalms. They're full of his fear and tears but also his praising. In Psalm 138:1a, David says: *"I will praise you, Lord, with all my heart."*

God is always worthy to receive our praise. When I take the time, I remember that little extra help He gave. The time He kept our daughter safe during the accident, and when He stayed the hand of the drugged-up robber from our eldest daughter. The time He kept us safe during that bad snowstorm when we were driving. The time He sent someone to pray with me and make me laugh. The time He provided the job, the groceries, the car, and all the other necessities of life. How can I help but praise Him?

Whatever the experience, I know that God is still God. God is still good, and His mercy is new every day. Death and sickness can't take away from the grace that He showed me when He saved me. That's reason enough to praise our God. I will still have sadness. I will still cry, and my heart will still break, but I will praise Him because He is worthy to be praised.

Father God, I praise You because my circumstances don't change who You are. Thank You for allowing me to see You in every life event. Amen.

MARCH 20

"But Moses sought the favor of the LORD his God. 'Lord,' he said, 'Why should your anger burn against your people, whom you brought out of Egypt with great power and a mighty hand?'"
(Exodus 32:11)

The people had turned away from God and made a golden calf to worship. God was very angry and would have brought a disaster against them, except Moses prayed. Moses interceded and pleaded for God's mercy. God heard his prayer and withdrew the threat.

Scripture contains numerous examples of prayer changing circumstances. In the Old Testament, in 1 Kings 18, Elijah prays for rain. Seven times he falls to the ground in prayer, and on the seventh time, the rain comes. In the New Testament, in Acts 12, the apostle Peter is miraculously released from prison by an angel, because Christians gathered at a home for prayer.

Sometimes we only see the impossible, but with prayer, it becomes possible. When all you see is the impossible, continue to pray and believe. Prayer does make a difference. It's important to pray for others, because when you pray, Heaven is moved to act on your request. Why do we sometimes make it the last resort?

Prayer causes change—sometimes within you, and sometimes within others or in life circumstances. God is a merciful God and the Bible says, *"The insistent prayer of a righteous person is powerfully effective"* (James 5:16b, WEB).

Father God, forgive me when I momentarily forget the power of prayer. Change my heart and create a steadfast prayer discipline in me. I want my prayers to be powerful and effective so that I can intercede for the people in my family and for others. Amen.

MARCH 21

"Many in the crowd spread their garments on the road ahead of him, and others spread leafy branches they had cut in the fields" (Mark 11:8, NLT).

I remember seeing spruce boughs on the paths and wood roads around the area where I grew up. At that time, many people kept horses for pulling logs from the woods, and I'm sure the paths were often muddy. It was quick work to cover the mud with spruce branches.

Most wood roads today are maintained regularly with heavy equipment. As well, our modern-day ATV vehicles are faster than horse and sleigh, and they seem to speed over many spots without a problem.

During the Easter season, and specifically on Palm Sunday, I often wondered about the significance of putting branches on the road before Jesus. I'm sure it wasn't simply to cover mud or boggy ground. I learned that in the past, conquerors and princes were honoured by putting greenery and flowers on the road. This was a mark of respect. So when Jesus entered Jerusalem on a donkey, the people honoured Him as they would a king. John 12:13 tells us that the branches were from the palm tree. Furthermore, palm branches represented joy and victory.

It's ironic that the same people who celebrated Jesus's arrival in Jerusalem this way put Him to death just a few days later. They didn't realize that the King of kings was there to deliver them from their sins and eternal death, and not from the Roman rulers of the day.

Father God, forgive me when I mistake Your purpose in my life to be one of ease and smooth sailing. As much as I would like to always have sunny skies, I know that wouldn't be good for me. How would I know my need for You without some stormy seas? Amen.

MARCH 22

"I don't really understand myself, for I want to do what is right, but I don't do it. Instead, I do what I hate" (Romans 7:15, NLT).

Sometimes we discover things about ourselves that we don't like. I discovered that I can't be all things to all people. It's totally distressing to me to know that I fail miserably every day. God doesn't fail, but I do.

Parts of me are still led by my own selfish desires and motives. I'm not totally selfless. Pride still shows its ugly head. I look at women I admire and wonder why I can't be more like them.

Like Paul, I know the things I want to do, but I don't do them. Instead, I do the things I hate to do. No matter which way I turn, I can't make myself do right.

In my study today, I learned that I can't overcome these failings with my own willpower. As hard as I try to do it, I can't. Instead, I have to avail myself of the power available to me, and that is the power of Christ. Sometimes I forget that I have the Holy Spirit living in me. The Bible promises that when I fail, He reaches out to me and lifts me up again.

In the passage above, Paul talks about this very thing. Sometimes we're slaves to our sinful nature. Paul says, *"Thank God! The answer is in Jesus Christ our Lord"* (Romans 7:25a, NLT). It's a good thing God put a plan in place to save us. I definitely can't save myself. Even though I may still fail, Romans 8:1 tells me, *"If you belong to Christ Jesus, you won't be punished"* (CEV).

Father God, thank You for saving me. Thank You for forgiving my sins. Help me today to do the things I want to do that I know are right and please You. Amen.

MARCH 23

"Pray also for me, that whenever I speak, words may be given me so that I will fearlessly make known the mystery of the gospel" (Ephesians 6:19).

Do you know the mystery of the lodge? When I was growing up, a number of my family members were members of the Orange Lodge. We heard many stories surrounding the Lodge Order. There seemed to be a lot of mysteries that kept us wondering what it was all about.

To my friends and me, it seemed that they had secret meetings, and no one else was allowed to be there. We didn't know what they did there or what the purpose of the Lodge was. Of course, our imaginations ran wild as we envisioned tall tales of the goings-on.

Every year, there was an Orange Lodge parade. All the members dressed up in their regalia. They wore sashes and funny hats. The parade was led by someone on a big white horse.

I still don't know much about it, but an Internet search tells me it was originally formed in Ireland in 1795 and named after King William of Orange. The Loyal Orange Association in Canada is a Christian, Patriotic, Benevolent, and Protestant Society.

Now that some of the mystery of the Orange Lodge has been revealed, let me ask you, "Do you know the mystery of the gospel?" It was a mystery that was hidden for a long time. But when Jesus came, the mystery was revealed. As stated in the verse above, this was Paul's mission: *"to make known the mystery of the gospel."*

There is no longer any reason to wonder about the gospel. Everyone can learn about the gospel through the Word of God. It's the good news about Jesus. He came to save us and give us peace.

Father God, help me to be a student of Your Word, and help me to tell people the good news about Jesus so there is no more mystery. Amen.

MARCH 24

"And I will pour out ... a spirit of grace ... They will look on me, the one they have pierced, and they will mourn for him as one mourns for an only child, and grieve bitterly for him ... " (Zechariah 12:10)

One of the products of the Spirit of grace is a new awareness of sin. In the past, we might not have realized how sinful we are. But the Bible tells us in Romans 5:12 that we are all sinners because we inherited a sinful nature right from birth.

After receiving the Spirit of grace and salvation, we immediately become aware of our sins and our sinful nature. We mourn over our sins and regret the choices of our past. When we realize that Jesus took all our sins upon Himself on the cross, and that He suffered and died for us to be forgiven, we weep bitterly for what we've done. The Bible tells us in the verse above that we grieve as if He was our only child. The indifference to our own sin is gone.

Each of us has to stand alone before God and account for our sin. We grieve alone for the cost. We mourn for what was lost—our innocence and what it cost. When the Spirit of grace is poured out on someone, their eyes are opened to their own sins and to what that meant for Jesus.

God sent Jesus to be crucified because of His great love for us. Don't reject Christ's forgiveness. He died so that all might be forgiven and saved. In 1 Timothy 2:4, Paul writes that God *"desires all people to be saved and come to full knowledge of the truth"* (WEB).

Father God, thank You for Your grace that was poured out for me. Thank You for patching up the holes left by sin. Help me to continue in your grace by immediately confessing sin. Amen.

MARCH 25

"There will be plenty of goats' milk for your food, for your family's food, and for the nourishment of your servant girls" (Proverbs 27:27, WEB).

"… land flowing with milk and honey, the most beautiful of all lands" (Ezekiel 20:6b).

Do you remember drinking sweet tea mixed with Carnation milk and poured out in your saucer? When I was growing up, Carnation canned milk was used for all cooking and baking. I liked it warmed and poured over puffed rice (which is a type of dry cereal).

Newfoundlanders love their Tetley tea with canned milk. The brand of choice is Carnation. When I was a child, we didn't have access to fresh milk all the time. Most of the time, we drank Carnation milk mixed with water. We used it on our cold cereal, hot cereal, desserts, and fresh blueberries. In fact, many babies were raised on Carnation milk. My oldest daughter was content and healthy on a Carnation milk formula in her bottle.

In the time of the Old Testament, having plenty of goats' milk meant God's blessing upon the land and the people. Goats' milk, eggs, and bread were the staples of their diet. When the people worshipped and obeyed God, He blessed them. Their land was lush and fertile.

God wants us to enjoy the blessings of life as much as is good for us. When we're honest in our dealings with others and diligent in our work, we can expect God's blessing on our lives.

If you ask any Newfoundlander, they'll tell you that Carnation milk is a definite blessing and is still much-loved today.

Father God, thank you for all the blessings on my life. Thank you for the place we live and the freedoms we enjoy. Help me to never take these things for granted. Amen.

MARCH 26

"But when you pray, go away by yourself, shut the door behind you, and pray to your Father in private" (Matthew 6:6, NLT).

When I was a teenager, my bedroom was the first one on the left at the top of the stairs. It was the smallest bedroom of the four, but I didn't have to share it with one of my sisters.

I remember wearing flannel pajamas and keeping them folded under the pillow during the day. I remember the homemade quilts, the chenille bedspread, and the thick satin eiderdown comforter folded at the bottom of the bed. Under my feet was a canvas floor with a braided mat by the bed. There were lace curtains and jack frost on the inside of the glass window. There was a bureau for clothes and a small closet on one wall. On the wall over my bed was a picture of a little girl with hands folded in prayer (I still have this picture). I loved to read, so there were a few books besides schoolbooks. I loved the quietness of my little bedroom. It was a cozy, comfortable place to read and occasionally do homework.

The Bible tells us to find a quiet place to talk to God, because it's easier to talk to God and listen if there aren't any distractions. My little bedroom was the perfect spot. The décor was plain, and there was no phone, television or video games.

Today our lives are filled with distractions. Sometimes I have to remind myself to make a point of setting aside a quiet time for God every day. I try to get time early in the morning before too much activity begins. I encourage you to look at your day and decide where and when you can best meet with God, even if it means getting up earlier or turning off your phone.

Father God, help me to find and take advantage of quiet times throughout the day to meet with You. Amen.

MARCH 27

"Let them praise his name with dancing and make music to him with timbrel and harp" (Psalm 149:3).

*B*ang! Bang! Bang! Clang! Clang! Clang! These noises came from somewhere downstairs, and someone sang very loudly, "Up from the grave He arose, with a mighty triumph over his foes."

I awoke with a start. What in the world was that noise? Someone was downstairs in the kitchen making some very loud noises with pots and pans and singing at the top of their voice. It sounded like Uncle Eric. You never knew what he would do next. He loved to do the unexpected by surprising everyone—very loudly.

It was about 6:30 a.m. on Easter Sunday morning. It was time for everyone to be up if they wanted to be in the Easter march. We soon heard the drums and saw the march coming around Back Cove Hill. The Salvation Army flag was in front, flapping in the wind. Next came the big drum with its *boom, boom, boom*, and the little drum with its *rat-a-tat-tat*. The band members marched in time and made a joyful noise with their brass instruments. We heard the tambourines and saw the ribbons flying. Everyone was singing and marching along in step.

Uncle Eric made sure we didn't sleep in. He wanted us to see the Easter march. The Bible tells us to make a joyful noise by praising the Lord (Psalm 100:1). Uncle Eric believed in making lots of noise and being joyful. He always laughed a lot. I'm sure he's doing the same thing in Heaven! *"Awake, harp and lyre! I will awaken the dawn"* (Psalm 108:2).

Father God in Heaven, thank You for Easter Sunday and the reason we celebrate that day. Help us always to praise You joyfully and with music. Amen.

MARCH 28

"She gets up while it is still night; she provides food for her family and portions for her female servants" (Proverbs 31:15).

"My people will live in a peaceful habitation, in safe dwellings, and in quiet resting places" (Isaiah 32:18, WEB).

I don't know what time my mother got up in the mornings when I lived at home, but she was always up before me. I'd come downstairs, and the woodstove would already be warming up the kitchen. Our breakfast was ready, and the smell of toasting bread made my mouth water.

The kitchen woodstove was a thing of beauty. It was shining black from Mom's polishing technique and it had shiny chrome decorative framing. A warming compartment was attached on top, and a hot water box was on the side. It was the centre of the home, and on cold mornings, we warmed our clothes on the oven door before getting dressed for school.

My mom kept the fire going and cooked our meals on the stove. It was a comforting place to be, with the smell of baking bread and jam simmering on the back burner. I don't think there could be a more peaceful memory of home. I'm so thankful that God blessed me with my family, especially my mom.

Isaiah spoke of the day when Jesus (the righteous King) would come back: *"When the Spirit is given to us from Heaven … You, the Lord's people, will live in peace, calm and secure"* (32:15, 18 CEV). Just as I had a peaceful home to grow up in, the Lord's people, with the help of the Holy Spirit, can experience peace too, even though there may be troubles to contend with.

Father God, thank You for the peaceful home my parents provided. Thank You for the promise of peace to those who trust and believe in You. Help me to provide a peaceful home for my family and to point them to You. Amen.

MARCH 29

"So we rebuilt the wall till all of it reached half its height, for the people worked with all their heart" (Nehemiah 4:6).

Bough whiffin—a temporary tent, a lean-to of boughs. This type of shelter was a crude lean-to that you could put up in an emergency. It had a roof, but sometimes not all the sides were filled in. When I was growing up, my friends and I would build one for fun. In years past, it was an essential shelter for anyone who found themselves having to stay in the woods overnight.

I remember when the Salvation Army church in Chance Cove was being renovated—actually, it was completely transformed. The inside was turned around so that the main entrance was now at the opposite end. The whole building was made new. I remember my dad telling me about the dedication of the Salvation Army officer who made it all happen. My dad was very proud of it and talked about the work of the volunteers and the people who supported it.

It took a lot of work and many long hours. The people sacrificed their time and donated materials. It was a labour of love. When it was nearly finished, my dad gave Terry and me a tour. He talked about the care and craftmanship that had gone into the finishing touches. He told me about how some of the original woodwork was reused. He was so proud of it.

The renovation of the church reminds me of the story in Nehemiah and the rebuilding of the wall in Jerusalem. It was a monumental task, but with the right people working with all their hearts, anything was possible.

Father God in Heaven, thank You for people who inspire others to work and achieve much more than they otherwise would on their own. This is the lesson in the book of Nehemiah, and this is the lesson with the rebuild of my home church. Help me to both inspire and be inspired. Amen.

MARCH 30

"And the peace of God ... will guard your hearts and your thoughts in Christ Jesus" (Philippians 4:7, WEB).

For many people, winters are symbolic of cold, bleak, lonely, and difficult times. Just like the season of winter, our spiritual *winter* can leave us discouraged, lonely, and depressed. I've had some of those winters too.

One time, I was caring for a sick family member through a prolonged illness. During this spiritual winter, I was living in a basement apartment in a different town. My normal routine was gone. I slept, ate, and did mundane tasks. I had little contact with family or friends. Some days, I had to stand on a step stool to look out the window and see over the top of the snow outside. Being a caregiver can be lonely, but I've often felt the closest to God during difficult times.

How do we survive our spiritual winters? Ask God to show you where He's working even in the smallest details of your daily living. Listen for that small voice, as this can be a time when He whispers new things. Ask God for His peace. When I look back, I see that is what God gave me. When the bad news just kept on coming, peace kept me from despair.

Sometimes, circumstances don't change. So what do we do then? Ask God for peace. The Bible tells us that God's peace is more wonderful than we can understand. I think peace of mind and heart are what all of us want. No matter what's happening in our lives, we can have peace.

I read about a woman who stood up in church to give her testimony. She said, "I praise the Lord for a deep, settled peace. The world didn't give it to me, and the world can't take it away."

Father God, I know there will be spiritual winters in my life. I know that Your peace will make all the difference in the world. Amen.

MARCH 31

"A happy heart makes the face cheerful, but heartache crushes the spirit" (Proverbs 15:13).

I was hanging out in the shop with my nan when the wholesale truck stopped outside. I loved to be in the shop when the trucks came to our little community. They made their rounds to all the little stores in the area and sold all kinds of grocery items and miscellaneous other things. There were meats, dry goods, and hardware items as well.

This was a great service, because before the roads were built, goods were brought in by train and schooner. The man came in the store to get Nan's order for groceries. As she listed off the items to the driver, she suddenly thought of something and said, "Juice! I want some juice." At that, we all burst out laughing. She stated it as though it were the most important item in the whole shop. Nan had quite a sense of humour. God created joy and laughter. A person who is joyful and laughing is infectious and pleasant to be around.

The Bible tells us that laughter is good for us: *"A cheerful heart is good medicine"* (Proverbs 17:22a) and *"[there is] a time to weep and a time to laugh"* (Ecclesiastes 3:4). Even during difficult circumstances, as in Job's story, God can fill you with laughter: *"He will yet fill your mouth with laughter and your lips with shouts of joy"* (Job 8:21).

May we never forget to look for joy and to laugh every chance we get.

Father God, thank You for the gift of laughter. I know people who laugh no matter what their circumstances. They are an example to me to have joy in my heart and not be serious all the time. Help me to show others that I have the joy of the Lord. Amen.

APRIL 1

"The thief only comes to steal, kill, and destroy. I came that they may have life, and may have it abundantly" (John 10:10, WEB).

"April showers bring May flowers." We've all heard this rhyme before, especially around springtime. Did you know it can be traced back to the mid 1500s, and maybe even earlier. The rhyme was originally a short poem that went:

Sweet April Showers

Do bring May flowers

But this isn't just a rhyme. It's an example of the cycle of renewal: spring, summer, fall, winter. The April rain puts water in the soil to help plants grow, and the water also helps the nutrients reach the roots faster so the plants grow faster and healthier.

"April showers bring May flowers" reminds us that even the most unpleasant things in life can bring about very enjoyable things—the heavy rains bring an abundance of flowers. This rhyme is a lesson in patience for us during the rainy seasons of our lives, and it reminds us to wait on the goodness of God as we grow in character.

Many of life's greatest things come only to those who wait, patiently and happily enduring the clouds and damp of April so that you can take in the sights and smells of May. The May flowers will come.

The benefits of waiting for the April showers to bring May flowers are abundant. Just as May is usually the beginning of the warmer months and leads into summer, we too can trust in God's promise to bring life in all its fullness.

Creator God, thank You for giving us the beauty of flowers, especially when they come after the rain. Without the rain, we'd miss out on this special blessing. Amen.

APRIL 2

"I revealed myself to those who did not ask for me; I was found by those who did not seek me" (Isaiah 65:1).

Oh, what fun we had playing hide and seek! There were lots of places to hide around the shop, the mill, and the barn. When my friends and I played this game, we counted and then shouted, "Ready or not, here I come."

This is the way it was with me and God. I didn't seek God. I was the one hiding. But God sought me. He used events in my life to put me in the right place, and He used trials to soften my heart to hear Him. During those years, God never abandoned me. He was always seeking me out. I was just living the life I felt I had to live. But God loved me too much to forget about me. I wasn't close to God, and I think God misses us when we're distant, just like we miss our children and grandchildren when they're not around us.

One day, I realized that there must be more to life. I asked God into my heart. I asked Him to show me how He wanted me to live. From then on, a new life was set in motion. I had no idea it would unfold as it did. It's still unfolding and I'm still learning about grace, mercy, love, and forgiveness. Because of Jesus and His death on the cross, I have a new heart and a new life.

I know that I could never be deserving or righteous enough on my own to be in God's presence. I couldn't go before God without Jesus vouching for me. But because of the cross, I don't have to. I was made right in God's eyes when Jesus died for me.

Father God in Heaven, thank You for not forgetting about me. Thank You for Your Son, Jesus, who made it possible for me to go where You are. Help me always to be close to You. Amen.

APRIL 3

"'Come now, let us settle the matter,' says the Lord. 'Though your sins are like scarlet, they shall be as white as snow'" (Isaiah 1:18).

We all know that stubborn stains are hard to remove and need special treatment. Over the years, I've had to wash out some pretty bad stains on my laundry. I've used all kinds of stain-remover products and some home remedies as well. On grease stains, I like to use some good old Lestoil cleaner.

I've read that you can remove yellow stains from white clothes by soaking them in a mixture of cold milk, ice cubes, and water. Another mixture I heard about is hydrogen peroxide, dish soap, and vinegar, which is supposed to remove tomato-based stains. Chocolate stains may be removed by rinsing in cold water and washing with dish soap. Coffee stains are a little harder to remove, but you can use white vinegar, cold water, and then colour-safe bleach.

I'm sure you've tried many techniques. But there are always stains that are hard to remove. Psalm 51:1–2 says, *"blot out the stain of my sins. Wash me clean from my guilt. Purify me from my sin"* (NLT). The Bible gives us the three steps to stain removal: 1. Blot the stain to soak up the excess. 2. Wash it to remove the loose dirt. 3. Purify it to eradicate any trace or unseen particle left behind. When Jesus died on the cross, His blood not only cleaned us of sin but purified us so that no trace is left behind.

First John 1:9 says, *"But if we confess our sins to God, he can always be trusted to forgive us and take our sins away"* (CEV). Be assured that when God says you are forgiven, you are forgiven indeed.

Father God, thank You for your Son, Jesus, who takes away our sin and purifies us from every trace. Amen.

APRIL 4

"His accusers didn't go inside because it would defile them, and they wouldn't be allowed to celebrate the Passover" (John 18:28b, NLT).

These accusers were the Jewish leaders. They couldn't go inside the Praetorium because the Passover Feast was coming. If they went inside, according to Jewish law, they would be defiled and couldn't attend the Passover. So they turned Jesus over to the Roman authorities to be condemned to death. They were more interested in the feast than the real reason for it.

In Exodus 12, we're given the origins of the Passover. The Israelites were slaves in Egypt, and God sent Moses to free them and bring them out. Of course, there was opposition from their enslavers. Finally, God said he would kill all the first-born males in that place. The Israelites were instructed to kill a lamb and put its blood on the doorposts of their homes. When the destroying angel saw the blood, he would pass by their house. This first Passover pointed the Israelites (Jews) to the time when Jesus would come and be sacrificed for the sins of the world.

Now fast forward to the New Testament and the books of Matthew, Mark, Luke, and John. These books state that Jesus came as the Messiah foretold in the Old Testament. He preached, healed, and forgave sins. The Jewish leaders didn't like it and they didn't recognize Jesus as the Messiah—the Passover Lamb for the whole world was right in front of them. The accusers didn't realize that it would soon be Jesus's blood they would be spilling: *"For you know that it was not with perishable things ... that you were redeemed ... but with the precious blood of Christ, a lamb without blemish or defect"* (1 Peter 1:18–19).

Father God, just like some people celebrate Christmas without a thought of Jesus, these Jewish leaders would celebrate Passover without a thought of the real Passover Lamb. Help us to focus on You, the real reason for these celebrations. Amen.

APRIL 5

"For what I received I passed on to you as of first importance: that Christ died for our sins according to the Scriptures, that he was buried, that he was raised on the third day according to the Scriptures" (1 Corinthians 15:3–4).

In my family, we had a tradition at Easter time of placing our shoes by our bed or outside our bedroom door the night before Easter Sunday for the Easter eggs. We always used Dad's shoes, because they were the biggest in the house. When we'd get up in the morning, the shoes would be filled with Easter eggs and other goodies. Occasionally, we'd get a new skipping rope, a new ball, or a game of jacks. It was the one time of the year when we could fill up on chocolate before breakfast. I don't know where this tradition started, but we certainly enjoyed it.

As I got older and learned about why Christians celebrate Easter, I wondered what Easter eggs and an Easter bunny had to do with Easter anyway. According to tradition, eggs signify new life. In some cultures, Easter is a celebration of new life at springtime. Later, bunnies were associated with Easter because they are very prolific and also symbolize new life.

For Christians, the meaning of Easter is much deeper. It's when we remember that Jesus came to die for us. The cross is central to our faith: *"without the shedding of blood there is no forgiveness"* (Hebrews 9:22). But we know that He rose on the third day. Jesus didn't stay dead. There are many recorded witnesses to this both in the Bible and in the secular work of Josephus (AD 37–100).[2] God raised Him to life again, and we have this assurance of new life too.

Father God, help us to celebrate Easter for the right reason and to always remember that the cross allows for eternal life. We will tell others that we celebrate our new life in Christ. Amen.

---

[2] Josephus' Account of Jesus: The Testimonium Flavianum, Josephus.org, accessed October 12, 2025, https://josephus.org/testimonium.htm.

APRIL 6

"She got a papyrus basket ... Then she placed the child in it"
(Exodus 2:3).

After I was born and brought home from the cottage hospital, I didn't sleep in a cradle. I slept in a cardboard box.

Every year on my birthday, my dad would say, "I can remember when we brought you home from the hospital—we put you in a box." Most birthdays he said it was a butter box. On one birthday, he said it was a prune box. It seemed like every birthday was a different box! I'm not certain what kind of box it was, but I do know one thing for sure, as verified by other family members—I did sleep in a box. There was no shortage of boxes, because my grandmother had a shop, and boxes were plentiful.

I'm not sure why they put me in a box. Knowing the way my mom thinks, it was probably because the small butter box was warm and cozy. Whatever the reason, it doesn't matter. I was well cared for and loved. One time, someone told me that their mother put them in a bureau drawer. I'm sure this too was a warm and sturdy place for a baby.

In Bible times, there were no cardboard boxes, but there were handmade woven baskets. People used the baskets in the same way we use boxes today. They stored food and carried goods from one place to another in them. As we read the story of Moses, we discover that they used a special type of basket to hold babies. They even made them waterproof.

So why shouldn't I have slept in a cardboard box? What I want to know is, "Was it an Eversweet butter box, or a Good Luck butter box?"

Father God, thank You for giving me two parents who loved me. I know that loving and caring for others is important to You. Help me to follow Your example and that of my parents too. Amen.

APRIL 7

"Jesus said to her, 'I am the resurrection and the life. The one who believes in me will live, even though they die'" (John 11:25).

How good is good enough? Remember back to your school days, when all you needed to pass to the next grade was 50 per cent. When I finished high school, grade eleven was good enough to get a teaching job. These days, you need at least one or two university degrees to teach.

Do you ever wonder if you're good enough to get a place in Heaven? Now, I've met some good people in my life. But I wonder who decides who's good enough, and what standard they use. Is 50 per cent enough? How good do you have to be?

You might say, "I've lived well. I'm kind and generous. I love my family, and I help my neighbours. I'm probably good enough to go to Heaven." You get a place in Heaven not because of your goodness but because of the goodness of Jesus.

Luke 23 contains the account of Jesus's crucifixion. Two thieves were on crosses next to Jesus. One thief realized who Jesus was and asked Him to remember him when He went to Heaven. This thief probably never did one good deed in his whole life. But Jesus told him that he would be with Him in Paradise that day. The thief was saved not because he was good enough but because he believed that Jesus was who He said He was, and because Jesus gave him salvation. Jesus said, *"The one who believes in me will live, even though they die."* That's good enough for me, and I hope that today it's good enough for you.

Father God in Heaven, I'm so glad that I don't have to rely on my own goodness. I know that if I did, I'd never get to Heaven. Thank You for Your goodness and Your promise that if I believe in You, I will be with You in Paradise. Amen.

APRIL 8

"Jesus answered, 'The work of God is this: to believe in the one he has sent'" (John 6:29).

"God sent his Son into the world not to judge the world, but to save the world through him" (John 3:17, NLT).

Many people wear a necklace with a cross on it. When I wear mine, I remember the Easter story and all the things I've learned about the cross. It reminds me that I belong to God. But what else can the cross mean to us?

From a Christian perspective, it's where Jesus gave up His life for us. He was crucified on a cross. Personally, I think of it as a crossroads—a place where you have to make a choice.

The two thieves who were crucified with Jesus were given a choice. When they were confronted with Jesus, one thief believed, and one didn't believe. They both had a choice. One thief accepted Jesus, and one turned away. The Bible tells us that everyone has sinned: *"For everyone has sinned; we all fall short of God's glorious standard"* (Romans 3:23, NLT). Because we're all sinners, every one of us needs to accept Jesus if we want to go to Heaven.

That is why I'm glad for the cross. It's where sin is forgiven and where we're confronted with Jesus, the man of the cross, God's Son. We have an opportunity to believe or not, to choose life in Heaven or not.

God sent His Son into the world to save it. That's the message of the cross. You can't be confronted with the cross and miss the man of the cross. But you can be confronted with the cross and miss its message. Believe in the Son of God, and the message will be clear to you.

Father God in Heaven, thank You for sending Your Son into the world. Without the cross, we wouldn't be forgiven or have life in Heaven. I thank You for confronting me with the cross. Amen.

APRIL 9

"Grace and peace to you . . . and from Jesus Christ ... who loves us and has freed us from our sins by his blood"
(Revelation 1:4-5).

My arms are tired,
My legs are weak.
I cannot stand
Upon my feet.
Your arms are strong,
Your hands enfold
My flesh and bones
That have gone cold.
I was in darkness,
But then Your light
Shone all around
And dispelled the night.
There was warmth,
And it was red,
Flowing from You,
Covering my body and head.
You held me up
Through all the pain.
My soul was cleansed,
Never to be the same.

Father God, thank You for Your Son, who gave His life so that we could be forgiven. Amen.

APRIL 10

"Before she goes into labor, she gives birth; before the pains come upon her, she delivers a son" (Isaiah 66:7).

The arrival of a new baby is an exciting occasion. Today, the actual birthing process is often a family affair. Husband, grandparents, and siblings all cram into the hospital to witness the great event and see the new baby immediately after birth. This is different from the old days, when only nurses and doctors were allowed there.

When my oldest daughter, Laurieann, was born, Terry dropped me off at the hospital on his way to work. The staff put me in a wheelchair and wheeled me to the registration desk. After the registration, they moved me upstairs to the birthing area, where the real work began.

Everyone around me were strangers until later in the day, when my Aunt Alicia arrived. She was a retired nurse who had worked in the delivery room and was there to assist me. My daughter was born at 4:20 p.m., just as Terry returned to the hospital after work. (Pretty good timing, don't you think?) I'm sure that some of you have funny birth stories to tell as well.

Many years later, I had the privilege of being in the room with my oldest daughter when my precious grandson Ethan was born. He was born by C-section, and when my daughter looked at him, she said, "He's perfect, Mom, isn't he?" I said, "Yes, he is perfect." Pictures were captured and footprints stamped in ink—everything to document that momentous occasion. I will never forget the joy of that moment.

The birthing ordeal is most times painful, stressful, and hard work. It is an experience like no other. Every birth is a miracle, but especially the birth of God's Son, Jesus.

Father God, thank You for the people who assisted me when I was giving birth. And thank You for the privilege of being in the room when my precious grandson was born. Amen.

APRIL 11

"'I'm going out to fish,' Simon Peter told them, and they said, 'We'll go with you.' So they went out and got into the boat ..." (John 21:3)

There's not much I like to do more than cod fishing. I like trout fishing too, but fishing for cod is my favourite. I love the scenery of the ocean, the sharp outlines of the cliffs, the sculptured rocky beaches, and the noisy seabirds. I love the blue of the sea and to smell the salt in the wind.

On the ocean, you don't have to swipe at the mosquitoes. Your view isn't obstructed by buildings, trees, and hills. You can see for miles. It's usually not hot and sticky on the ocean (at least not in Newfoundland waters). Sitting in a boat, feeling the wind, and seeing the open water gives me a sense of peace. It's a place to get away from all the cares and worries of life.

I can understand why Peter went fishing, especially after the traumatic events of the past few days that we call Easter. A lot happened to Peter leading up to and after the Easter period: Jesus was arrested, and then Peter failed Jesus by deserting Him and then denying Him three times. To top it all off, Jesus was killed, and all Peter's hopes were dashed. Peter was distraught. He went to the sea, where it was peaceful and quiet and he was in a familiar, comforting place.

Much to Peter's surprise, Jesus was waiting for him on the shore. Peter was overjoyed to see Him, and it was there that Jesus restored Peter's faith and position as a disciple.

Jesus forgave Peter for his denials and failures. He will forgive us as well. Put your trust and faith in God, and you will be amazed where He takes you.

Father God, thank You for giving us a second chance. You have a purpose for each of our lives. Please help us to trust You in all things. Amen.

APRIL 12

"And he carried his cross to a place known as 'The Skull.' In Aramaic this place is called 'Golgotha'" (John 19:17, CEV).

Once upon a time, in a faraway forest, there was a tree. The tree thought, *When I'm fully grown, I will be exquisitely decorated and placed in someone's home, or maybe crafted into a beautiful furniture piece.* But year after year, the tree was overlooked, and all around him other trees were selected.

Years went by, and the tree waited to be chosen. One day, some people came to the forest and pointed to him. He was so excited. *Finally,* he thought, *someone wants me in their home.* They cut him down and carried him away. But much to his dismay, they took him to a place where they cut off his beautiful branches, stripped off the bark, and shaped his trunk into a plank.

Next, he was carried to a courtyard, where soldiers placed him on the shoulders of a man who'd been badly beaten. He was forced to carry the plank all the way to the top of a hill. The soldiers nailed the man's hands to the plank, then both of His feet to a long beam. Then they stood him up. The man suffered a lot, and the plank was sorry for him. His blood stained the plank and ran to the ground. Eventually, two men came and took down the man's body.

The young tree had wanted to be placed in someone's home as a beautiful ornament. But this tree was chosen for a much greater purpose. We may be a lot like this tree who wanted a glamorous life of ease but instead found a life of adversity and trouble. You see, God's plans for us aren't always our plans. God sees the whole picture. His purposes are for the good of all humanity.

Heavenly Father, I have many plans in my heart, but I want Yours to prevail. Help me to realize when my plans need to be set aside for Your purpose. Amen.

APRIL 13

"Now that same day two of them were going to a village called Emmaus, about seven miles from Jerusalem" (Luke 24:13).

We were out for a drive and almost to Gull Pond by the highway when all of a sudden, everything went black in the car. The engine sputtered, and Terry managed to turn the wheel so that we were off the road and over to the side.

It was in the spring of 1973. I was dating Terry Wheeler—a tall, dark, handsome young fellow I'd met in trade school. He was from Port aux Basques and came home with me on the weekends. It was a Sunday night, and we went for a drive. The next thing we knew, we were stranded on a dark road, miles from home. We broke down right next to a bog, and it was very foggy. Not one car came along, so we decided to walk. As we walked, we talked. Before long, we could see the lights in Chance Cove. Finally, we got to a house and called my father.

The road we walked on was quiet and lonely—much like the Emmaus Road that the two disciples walked. It was about the same distance as the Emmaus Road, so I imagine how they felt. How long and dreary the road must have seemed. Then Jesus joined them and talked with them. The time passed more quickly, and before they knew it, they'd walked the seven miles and arrived at Emmaus.

It must have been wonderful to have Jesus there, talking with them, looking at their faces, and stirring up dust clouds. They walked with Jesus and didn't know who He was. He'd seen that their faith had been tested, so he came to encourage them. He'll do the same for us on our journey. How many miles have we walked and not known that Jesus was walking with us?

Jesus, I love to walk with You today and every day. Thank You for being with me no matter where I am or where I go. Amen.

APRIL 14

"Going over to him, the Samaritan soothed his wounds with olive oil and wine and bandaged them" (Luke 10:34a, NLT).

The wound was open and oozing. There were bits of sand and rock embedded in the torn skin of my knees. I was crying, and my mother was consoling me. Many times, I went to my mother with skinned knees, scraped elbows, and cuts on my hands.

My mother gently cleaned the wounds with water and a cloth. She put antiseptic cream or liquid on the wounds and then applied the band-aid. Every day she cleaned the wounds and put on a fresh bandage until it was completely healed.

Receiving the hurtful words of other people, living with the consequences of our own sinful actions, being in the fallout of someone else's mistakes, and dealing with the tragedies of life can leave us with deep wounds. God is the ultimate in wound care. Can you picture it? He cleans, He applies pain control, He stitches it together, He pours on soothing oil, and He applies the bandages.

The Bible tells us in Psalm 147:3 that *"He heals the brokenhearted and bandages their wounds"* (NLT). Often when we give our burdens to the Lord, we don't leave them with Him but take them back and look at them again. We're like a child who constantly lifts up the bandage to look at the wound. When it starts to heal, we pick at the scab. We just can't leave it alone.

How do we leave our wounds with the Lord? Don't lift up the bandage. Don't pick at them. Don't continue to give them life by talking about them over and over. Instead, ask God to give you a different focus to take your thoughts and attention away from the wound.

Father God, thank You for Your promise to heal hearts and wounds. Help me to leave my burdens with You instead of removing the bandage to look at them again and again. Amen.

APRIL 15

"… I live by faith in the Son of God, who loved me and gave himself up for me" (Galatians 2:20, WEB).

As I looked through the glass, I saw rain falling on the patio outside. The heavy drops bounced off the boards, and the sheets of rain were so thick, it was hard to clearly see the details of the garden. The grey clouds darkened the sky, and to top it off, I hadn't cleaned my patio window of all the winter grime. Still, I knew the sun was out there.

I listened to the radio, and the host was talking about trusting God through the dark days and cloudy skies. I thought, *This message is so appropriate.* That day, my vision was blurred by the dirty window, the dark, cloudy sky, and heavy sheets of rain. I had to concentrate to imagine a sunny day and picture the garden with its beautiful blooms. Still, I knew the sun was out there.

Sometimes we have dark days, even when the sky is sunny, and it's hard to see the Son. Still, the Son is there.

I sat down at the kitchen table and read a prayer by Thomas Merton:

My Lord God, I have no idea where I am going. I do not see the road ahead of me. I cannot know for certain where it will end. But I believe that the desire to please You does in fact please You. And I hope I have that desire in all that I am doing. I hope that I will never do anything apart from that desire. And I know that if I do this You will lead me by the right road though I may know nothing about it. Therefore, I will trust You always though I may seem to be lost and in the shadow of death. I will not fear, for You are ever with me, and You will never leave me to face my perils alone. Amen. [3]

---

[3] Henri J. M. Nouwen, *Encounters with Merton: Spiritual Reflections* (New York: The Crossroad Publishing Company, 1981), 133.

APRIL 16

"Jesus looked at them intently and said, 'Humanly speaking, it is impossible. But with God everything is possible'" (Matthew 19:26, NLT).

I learned something about myself the other day: I will play the hand of cards I'm dealt to the best of my ability. I'll play them wisely and strategically. I'll use them to gain points to win the game.

However, if I'm dealt a poor hand, I'll play the cards, but I won't take a gamble on them and bid higher to win, as I'm afraid that I'd lose. I'm not willing to take chances on poor cards. Some people will put everything on nothing and still win. Sometimes I wish I could be more like that.

I'm an adventurous person, but I still like to play it safe. The Bible tells me that with God, all things are possible and that God can take nothing and turn it into something. I need to believe that God can take my nothing and turn it into something worthwhile. I'm not talking about playing cards but about my faith to endeavour to do more for God. An excerpt from a prayer by Sir Francis Drake says,

> *"Disturb us, Lord, when we are too well pleased with ourselves, when our dreams have come true because we have dreamed too little, when we arrive safely because we have sailed too close to the shore. Disturb us, Lord, to dare more boldly, to venture on wider seas where storms will show Your mastery: where losing sight of land, we shall find the stars. We ask You to push back the horizons of our hopes: and to push into the future in strength, courage, hope and love. Amen."*[4]

---

[4] Sir Francis Drake, "Disturb Us, Lord," Renovare, accessed October 6, 2025, https://renovare.org/articles/disturb-us-lord.

APRIL 17

"They have pierced my hands and feet" (Psalm 22:16b, WEB).

I have several memories of playing with my nan's hands. One time, we were sitting on the daybed in her kitchen. I held her hands, felt her long fingers, and stroked the thin skin. The veins that popped out on the back of her hands fascinated me. They were dark and big like rope. Underneath the skin on one hand was a small black object, which was the lead of a pencil. She'd had an accident in school and never had it removed. I used to touch it through the pale skin. She told me that although the lead was still there, it didn't hurt anymore. The lead in Nan's hand reminds me of the hurts we keep inside that are hard to get out. David Roper says:

> Not all our hurts can be healed in this life. Some … we will bear all our lives. But, if you hold your wounds up to the sunlight of God's love, they will never fester and in Heaven they will be healed.[5]

Sometimes it's hard to let the hurt go. We need help from someone else—someone who can extract the pain and heal the wounds. Even though some hurts remain (like the lead in Nan's hand), they don't have to fester. The marks might still be there, but they won't hurt anymore. *But he was pierced for our rebellion, crushed for our sins. He was beaten so we could be whole. He was whipped so we could be healed"* (Isaiah 53:5, NLT).

Father God, thank You for the memory of my Nan's hands. Thank You for Your Son, Jesus, who came to heal us. Help me, Lord, to trust You and to give my hurts to You. Amen.

---

[5] David Roper, *The Song of a Passionate Heart* (Grand Rapids, MI: Discovery House, 1994), 170.

APRIL 18

"He breathed the breath of life into the man's nostrils, and the man became a living person" (Genesis 2:7, NLT).

"He himself gives life and breath to everything..."
(Acts 17:25b, NLT)

Are you aware of the breaths you take? Can you even remember your first breath? Most of us are not aware of our breath until it's limited in some way.

My daughter has asthma and for most of her life has been aware of every breath. My ancestors and many of the family on my dad's side have an inherited gene that causes a lung disease called pulmonary fibrosis. We are well aware how this disease affects our breathing.

Thankfully, my daughter has medications that help alleviate the symptoms of asthma and help her to breathe more freely. In addition to lung transplants, there have been advancements in medications for pulmonary fibrosis that prolong the life expectancy of my affected relatives. With funding and ongoing research in medical interventions, many lung problems are being treated more effectively than in the past.

Without our breath, we can't live. The fact that God breathed life into man makes us different from all other life on earth. They received their breath from nature and the earth. We received the breath of God and became living souls. We should never take our breath for granted.

Father God, thank You for the breath of life and the breath in my lungs. Sometimes I'm not aware of this silent miracle, but I know people who struggle to breathe. Help them to breathe more easily. Amen.

APRIL 19

"'Can anyone hide from me in a secret place? Am I not everywhere in all the heavens and earth?' says the Lord" (Jeremiah 23:24, NLT).

The area around my dad's sawmill and under the floorboards of the mill were packed tight with mountains of sawdust. It was the perfect place to dig tunnels. So naturally, my friends, sisters, and I did just that. We dug tunnels under the floor and out into the yard. We crawled through the tunnels, hid in them, and had fun. Our imaginations fueled our playtime as we play-acted all kinds of adventures. It didn't matter that we were covered in sawdust—we had fun.

The Bible contains many examples of people trying to hide or run away from God. Adam and Eve hid in the garden after they disobeyed God. Jonah ran away from his responsibilities when God told him to go to Nineveh. David hid in a cave because he was afraid of his enemies. Of course, even though we hide from others, it's impossible to hide from God. We're really only hiding from ourselves. We don't want to confront the thing that causes us fear and pain. We don't want to be reminded of our mistakes and failures. Sometimes we're fearful of reproach, reproof, or reprimand. Nobody wants to be reminded of their failures. Instead, they want to be loved and accepted.

Fortunately, the Bible tells us that God's love drives out the fear of these things (1 John 4:18). When we put our trust in God, He replaces the fear in our lives with His love. His love for us enables us to face the challenges ahead.

Father God, thank You for Your perfect love. With Your love in our hearts, we need not fear anything. Help us to come out of hiding and show that love to others. Amen.

APRIL 20

"If we are not faithful, he will still be faithful. Christ cannot deny who he is" (2 Timothy 2:13, CEV).

I remember when my girls became teenagers. One morning I woke up, and strangers were in their place. What had happened to my beautiful, loving, talkative little girls?

Who were these girls that had taken their place? They spent hours in the bathroom, hours in their room, and hours on the phone. Their clothes were everywhere, but the closets were empty. No more conversations or after-school talks. Mood swings and arguing with each other were the order of the day. They seemed to care more for friends than family. It was so frustrating to see them that way. How long would it last? But then I remembered what I was like as a teen. How did my mom and dad put up with me?

My Christian life is similar to this. Once I was a little girl and walked in the Christian faith. I went to church and Sunday school. I played in the band and was in the Bible study group. I enjoyed all these things, but later on, I became selfish and cared more for friends and the world. For a long time, I was a stranger to God. But God didn't forget about me. Even though I was like a rebellious teenager, God kept His eye on me and brought me back to the right path again.

As I developed in my Christian faith, I realized how much God loves me and always has my best interests in mind, even when I may not understand it.

Father God, thank You for not forgetting about me but continuing to love me. Thank You for forgiving me when I was doing my own thing. Amen.

APRIL 21

"Keep your Creator in mind while you are young! In years to come, you will be burdened down with troubles and say, 'I don't enjoy life anymore'" (Ecclesiastes 12:1, CEV).

One day, Judy, Joan, and I visited their mom, who was my Aunt Stella, while she was teaching school in Chance Cove. She taught in the old Salvation Army two-room school at the top of the hill. One room held grades primer to five, and the other held grades six to eleven. She taught the higher grades.

We weren't old enough to go to school yet, but we had decided to walk up the road until we got there. She invited us into the classroom, which I thought was very exciting. It was my unofficial first day at school and was a very positive experience. I never forgot it.

Most youth are known for living in the present and being spontaneous. They celebrate life and find joy in ordinary things. They don't carry the burdens and worries that age sometimes brings. When you're older, you reflect back on your life and wish you'd been wiser in your youth. When you're young, you delight in each new day and experience. How exciting it would be to worship and trust God as a young person again without the troubles that life experiences bring!

Teach your children and your grandchildren about the Creator. Teach them to worship with joyful hearts. When they're older, they'll remember to trust God to give them what they need—salvation and a home in Heaven.

Father God, thank You for the positive influences in my youth and what they taught me. I remember the things I learned about You and how it helps me even to this day. I'm so glad I had godly influences in my youth. Amen.

APRIL 22

"Then if my people who are called by my name will humble themselves and pray and seek my face and turn from their wicked ways, I will hear from heaven and will forgive their sins and restore their land" (2 Chronicles 7:14, NLT).

During the COVID pandemic, I heard this verse quoted many times. This verse contains the definition of "repentance." It differs from other verses on repentance because most of them deal with personal repentance, whereas this verse talks about national repentance. In order to heal the nation, all people must turn away from sin and turn instead to God.

The first part of the verse says *"if my people,"* and I think this refers to all people who believe in the one true God. The CEV version translates it this way: *"If my own people will humbly pray and turn back to me and stop sinning, then I will answer them from heaven. I will forgive them and make their land fertile once again."*

We often talk about revival, and I think this verse is telling us that if all believers earnestly seek God, then revival and restoration are possible. We can't expect people or circumstances to change unless Christians wholeheartedly follow God's ways. First, we have to examine ourselves, turn from wrongdoing, ask for forgiveness, and then pray.

Revival and healing are possible, but only if your heart belongs to God. When all believers everywhere give themselves wholeheartedly to God, then anything is possible. Revival and healing start with you and me.

Father God, please forgive me when I do wrong. Help me to do right and to place You first in everything. I pray for revival in me. Amen.

APRIL 23

"Keep your lives free from the love of money and be content with what you have, because God has said, 'Never will I leave you; never will I forsake you'" (Hebrews 13:5).

We moved into our very first apartment today. We're newlyweds and very excited to have our own place. We have a new baby too and are looking forward to setting up the baby room.

We didn't have much in the way of furniture and household items. Nonetheless, when you're young, you have many plans, hopes, and dreams for the future. Terry's mom and dad sent us some used furniture by train, and that was the day it arrived. The truck backed into the driveway, and the men unloaded our things. The couch was brought in, and I was a little embarrassed to see that it was well worn. Still, we had something to sit on, and I easily put a nice cover over it. I was thankful.

We'd bought a little chrome table and chair set for the kitchen, along with a small fridge and an apartment-sized stove. I unpacked our wedding presents and realized I didn't have to buy too much to complete the kitchen.

We'd bought a new bedroom set for our room, and in the baby's room we had a single bed and a crib given to us by Aunt Alicia. Most everything else was second-hand from our parents. It was fun to set up house and be on our own. Terry worked and I stayed home with the baby for a year. We paid our rent and bought groceries. We were as content as anyone could be. On the weekends, we spent time with friends or visited my parents in Chance Cove.

As I look back, I see that these were simple days full of hopes and dreams. We were content with what we had, and God blessed us.

Father God, thank You for those times. We had little, yet we had a lot. We were rich in youth, health, energy, and life. Amen.

APRIL 24

*"Who dares accuse us whom God has chosen for his own?
No one—for God himself has given us right standing with himself"*
(Romans 8:33, NLT).

If you cut your finger, you'll see droplets of red blood coming out of the cut. However, when you look at the droplet under the microscope, you'll see that your blood is made up of a liquid containing red cells, white cells, and platelets.

The red blood cells carry oxygen. They pick up oxygen in the lungs and deliver it to every part of your body. You can't live without oxygen. White blood cells fight off infections from viruses and harmful bacteria. They're your built-in physician. Platelets rush to the site of wounds and form blood clots. They produce a sticky, fibrous substance that plugs the hole and heals it. The liquid part of your blood is the plasma and is made up of 90 per cent water. The plasma transports nutrients and maintains stability in the body.

Blood makes life possible. It picks up oxygen from our lungs when we breathe; it protects the body; and it heals the body. Blood saves lives. If someone loses too much blood, they can receive a blood transfusion.

If our blood can do this much, how much more can Jesus's blood do? His blood gives us new life, fights off the infection of sin, protects us from further infection, and heals our wounds. Isaiah 53:5b says, *"and by His wounds we are healed."*

When Jesus gave up His life in the flesh, He gave up His blood—His life for ours. Hebrews 9:22b says, *"without the shedding of blood there is no forgiveness."*

Father God, thank You for Your grace, the sacrifice of Your Son, and the forgiveness of my sins. Help me not to forget the importance and power of the blood of Jesus. Amen.

APRIL 25

"That night the king could not sleep, and he had a servant read him the records of what had happened since he had been king"
(Esther 6:1, CEV).

Have you ever made a plan only to have it change? It's disappointing at the very least. That's what happened to Haman in the story of Esther. He planned to get rid of Mordecai, and he thought that the queen and king favoured him and would give him a place of honour in the kingdom. Not only that, but he also plotted to exterminate the Jews.

While Haman plotted for evil purposes, he didn't know that God had a greater plan for good. God placed Esther in the right place for the right time. She was brought into the king's palace and then chosen as queen. Through her courage, God used her to save the Jews.

> Then Zeresh his wife and all his friends said to him, "Let gallows be made fifty cubits high, and in the morning speak to the king about hanging Mordecai on it. Then go in merrily with the king to the banquet." This pleased Haman, so he had the gallows made. (Esther 5:14, WEB)

The gallows Haman had built became his sentence instead. Imagine his surprise when he realized that his evil plans had been destroyed. Remember, when others have evil plans against us, God has a plan for our good. He's always a step ahead. His timing is perfect, and He weaves our lives together into His plan.

Father God, thank You for Your plans that we don't even realize are there for our good. When others mean harm, You can turn it around for good. Help us to trust You in everything. Amen.

APRIL 26

"So God's message continued to spread. The number of believers greatly increased in Jerusalem" (Acts 6:7a, NLT).

When I think about world events such as wars, storms, drought, disease, and suffering, it gives me a helpless feeling. The magnitude of pain and hurt in the world seems overwhelming to me.

My neighbour had a yard sale today to raise money for an orphanage in Ukraine. That's a specific action for a specific need. This has an impact. I asked myself what I could do, as I'm only one small person in one small area of the world. I thought about my life and influence as being in a circle. I remembered when I first started attending Women's Ministries at our church. After each program and before eating, the women formed a circle around the room, held hands, and prayed our closing prayer and the blessing on the food. That circle left a deep impact on me. Each week I held hands with someone new, and soon bonds began to form with the women as we connected through prayer.

We need to widen our circle beyond family and close friends to include neighbours and community. Find ways to connect with them and discover their needs. These are the people your life touches. Maybe you can meet their need, even in a small way. Pay it forward. If someone does something for you, you do something for someone else.

I don't have to save the whole world by myself. I just need to help the people around me, who in turn help people around them. We can share our faith and belief in Jesus in the same way. Who knows what far-reaching impact it will have?

Heavenly Father, help me find ways to help others around me and to share my faith. Amen.

APRIL 27

"You keep track of all my sorrows. You have collected all my tears in your bottle. You have recorded each one in your book"
(Psalm 56:8, NLT).

Even though I don't cry often, I do a good job of it when I do. I'm thinking that God must have a really big bottle for my tears. The verse above reminds me of the bottles people find in the oceans with messages in them. I saw a movie once titled *Message in a Bottle*. It was a love story that made me cry.

I remember throwing bottles into the sea. I'd get empty bottles from my grandmother's store, write something on scribbler paper, and put the top on the bottle as securely as I could. My friends and I would stand on the bank overlooking the ocean and throw the bottles as far as we could into the sea below. I don't know if they went very far, and I've wondered if anyone ever found our bottles. I haven't found a bottle myself, but I think it would be exciting to find one along the beach sometime.

I think my tears must be like messages to God. Each set of tears represents a unique life experience that has caused me to feel deeply. God cherishes these messages and keeps them in His care. I wonder if He has shelves full of bottled tears. When I look at my bottles of preserves in the cellar, I can picture Him looking at the bottles of tears on His shelves.

Don't ever think that God doesn't see your tears or that He doesn't care. The Bible tells us He records them in a book. Imagine that! So they must be very special to Him.

Dear God, I know You must love me very much—You even keep my tears. Thank You for caring for me and listening to my cries. Amen.

APRIL 28

"Then he said to Thomas, 'Put your finger here; see my hands. Reach out your hand and put it into my side. Stop doubting and believe'" (John 20:27).

Are you a doubting Thomas? I've been called a doubting Thomas a few times. Have you?

Some people believe everything they hear or read, even on the Internet, where some of the writers are questionable. Anyone can post on the Internet. Don't believe everything you read there without knowing if the source is legitimate. Even news media aren't totally truthful these days. Sometimes they embellish stories to get higher television ratings. Gone are the days when they actually reported news and not just stories of the social life of movie stars or celebrities.

I can understand Thomas's doubts. Some people like to have concrete evidence. In this day of information overload, we need proof to verify that what we're being told is true.

But Thomas had been a witness to Jesus's ministry and miracles. You would think he wouldn't need any proof. Maybe some of the other disciples had doubts too but didn't voice them. Thomas was honest with Jesus, and Jesus graciously provided what Thomas needed—proof. Jesus wants you to believe in Him. If you have doubts, be as honest as Thomas was and ask Jesus to help you believe.

Father God, You are so patient and gracious with us. Help us to believe in Your Son, whom You sent to us. Thank You for Your Word that points us to You. Amen.

APRIL 29

"Or hasn't the potter a right over the clay, from the same lump to make one part a vessel for honor, and another for dishonor?" (Romans 9:21, WEB).

I remember as a child getting the new Eaton's and Sears Catalogues in the mail. This was like a treasure book where we'd dream of the things we'd like to have. People often ordered from the catalogue because there were no department stores nearby. When the catalogue became outdated, it was placed in the outhouse (I don't have to explain why they were there) or used for lighting the fire. This may have been the beginning of recycling paper products.

In this day and age, we're all about recycling. I have blue bags to put recyclable items in for pick-up by the town. They go to a recycling plant that processes them for a different function. We can now take those items and give them a new use and purpose.

Sometimes less glamorous items are recycled for a more important use, or a more important item for a lesser use. Whether glamorous or plain, God has a unique purpose for each of us. What we think is a less important service, God uses to advance His work and plan.

We're wrong to think that some service is less important. In this world, we value high profile careers and high salaries. These things have no value in light of eternity. Our value is in who we are in God's eyes, not the world's. God's purpose for each one of us may have nothing to do with talent, wealth, or fame. God looks at our heart and our commitment to Him.

Father God, help me not to judge others by their outward looks or achievements. Help me to see them as You see them. Amen.

APRIL 30

"But everything exposed by the light becomes visible—and everything that is illuminated becomes a light" (Ephesians 5:13).

Spring is here. The days are longer. The sun is brighter, and its rays shine through my windows to warm our home. The dark winter days are over. Every day that the sun shines, the snow melts to reveal more of the sand and garbage that accumulated beneath it. Patches of dry, yellow grass are showing, and soon the robins will be here digging for worms. I love this time when winter loses its hold on us.

Everything that was hidden by the dull days is revealed: dust, cobwebs, and fingerprints. I see things now that I didn't see all winter. When the sun's light comes through, the dust is revealed. The light reveals everything that was previously hidden: dust on the furniture and in the air, cobwebs from the ceiling, and fingerprints on the windows.

Another Bible translation of the above verse says *"Light exposes the true character of everything"* (GW). When you live in the darkness of the world by following its ways and standards, you don't see the sin in your life. Without the light, you can't see the dust. As you learn about God and His ways, His light shines through your darkness and reveals the sin you didn't see before. Don't live in the darkness. Psalm 27:1a says, *"The Lord is my light and my salvation."*

Father God, thank You for Your Son, Jesus. When we become aware of His presence, we see our sinful selves more clearly. Thank You for Your sacrifice and grace that forgives our sins. Amen.

MAY 1

*"Then they returned to Jerusalem from the mountain called
Olivet, which is near Jerusalem, a Sabbath day's journey away"*
(Acts 1:12, WEB).

Why is a Sabbath Day's walk different from any other day? I did some research, and this is what I discovered: Before the time of Christ on earth, the Jews created many rules that they thought would ensure God's favour. Because the fourth commandment forbade work on the Sabbath (Exodus 20:8), they also made a rule about how far you could travel on that day. The distance was a short walk—some say about three-quarters of a mile. Consequently, the term "a Sabbath Day's walk," described a short walk.

When I think of my walk with Christ, I hope that it's not different on a weekday than it would be on a Sabbath Day (Sunday). I'm not talking about a distance walk but my Christian Walk. I'm talking about being a Christian every day of the week. People should be able to see Christ in me wherever I am. I should be just as close to God on Wednesday as I am on Sunday. Being a Christian is for every day of the week.

On Sunday, we attend worship services and maybe have a closer walk on that day. However, we need to walk with Him every day of the week: *"… walk worthily of the calling with which you were called"* (Ephesians 4:1b, WEB); *"… whatever you do, do all to the glory of God"* (1 Corinthians 10:31b, WEB).

Father God, thank You for Your commandments, because they help us live a moral and righteous life. Help me, Lord, to walk with You and worship You every day of the week. Amen.

MAY 2

"He alone shapes their hearts; He considers all their works" (Psalm 33:15, HCSB).

Terry designs and makes each of his woodworking projects uniquely. Although he uses a similar plan or drawing, the grain of the wood is different in each one, which gives each one a unique character. No two pieces are exactly alike.

One time he made a beautiful aspen wood table with benches to match. It shone from the many coats of lacquer put on it, and you could see the colourful lines in the wood. It was a work of art. Another time he made a lamp from a piece of a tree that had a big burr of knotted wood attached to it. You would never see another one like it. He made storage chests, deacon benches, and bookshelves. We have a beautiful rustic coffee table that he made to use in our cabin. He fit pieces of sawed logs together so that the outside edge of the table kept the shape of the log. I love this little table and there is not another one like it. Each piece made by his hands is unique.

I never know how his projects will look, but Terry has a picture of it in his mind. Even though he knows what it will look like, each piece has a character all its own. That's the way it is with us. God made each of us different and unique. We each have our own beauty, shaped by God. He knows our hearts, our minds, our desires, and our characters. When you give your heart to God and believe in His Son, Jesus, you become a child of God Most High. He made you for service in His workplace.

Dear God, thank You for the talent You gave Terry to make beautiful things out of wood. I know that You are my Creator and that I'm still a work in progress. You know exactly how I'll turn out. Amen.

MAY 3

"For God has said, 'I will never fail you. I will never abandon you'"
(Hebrews 13:5b, NLT).

A memory from my school days: It's almost past lunch hour, and I'm on my way back to school. As I pass my friend's house, I see her in the garden hanging the Monday morning washing on the clothesline before she goes back to school. There sure is a lot of washing, but it's a sunny, windy day, so as Newfoundlanders say, "Some day on clothes."

When you have a family to wash for, you have to hang out the laundry whether it's winter or summer, rain or shine, or cold. The little wooden pegs hold the washing in place. Sometimes it's so windy, the clothes blow off the line and across the garden. Sometimes it's so cold, the clothes freeze stiff on the line and you can stand up the pants. You have to wait for things to thaw before you can fold them.

There's an odd expression we use sometimes when referring to someone left to fend for themselves. We say that they were "hung out to dry." As I questioned what that meant, I thought about the washing being hung out to dry against all the elements of weather. Do you sometimes feel like you've been left to face everything alone? At times in our lives it feels like we're being hung out to dry against whatever life throws at us.

Fortunately, we are not the Monday morning washing. We have a Saviour who has not left us to face the weather of life alone. No matter what storms may come, He is always with us.

God loves you, and if you ask Him, He won't leave you to face life all on your own. He gives us wisdom, comfort, and peace.

Father God, thank You for loving me with an everlasting love. Thank You for not leaving me to face every day alone. Amen.

MAY 4

"Every word of every command that Moses had ever given was read to the entire assembly of Israel" (Joshua 8:35a, NLT).

During my beginning years in the workforce, I was a stenographer. That is, I was a secretary who could write down in shorthand my boss's correspondence and reports as he verbally dictated them to me. Then I used a typewriter to transcribe them back onto paper for my boss to sign.

After my second child, I was away from my career for almost two years. Before I returned to the workforce, I decided to enroll in a refresher course at the local college to bring my shorthand and typing speed back up to where it was. I was glad I did this, as I didn't have any trouble getting work when I finished. When I read the above passage, I thought about my refresher course at college. I needed to review and practise everything I'd learned in my earlier courses.

Joshua wanted to ensure that all of the people were familiar with everything that was written in the Book of the Law. Because they—like us—easily forget, he read the whole book to them again. Even though I read my Bible daily, I often forget some of the truths or insights I learned from previous readings. When I reread a passage or verse, I recall the lessons from the past. That's why it's so important to read and reread the Scriptures. From time to time, I discover something new that I didn't notice before. Make time for reading the Word that God gave us. It corrects and encourages us in our day-to-day living.

Father God, thank You for being so understanding and patient. You know that we easily forget what You did for us in the past. Thank You for providing the refresher courses of life. Amen.

MAY 5

"God's word is alive and powerful! It is sharper than any double-edged sword. His word can cut through our spirits and souls and through our joints and marrow, until it discovers the desires and thoughts of our hearts" (Hebrews 4:12, CEV).

Growing up, I sometimes slept at my nan and pop's house. When it was time to go to bed, Pop fixed the fire in the woodstove by adding a coal knob or two and closing the drafter in the chimney on the back of the stove. Then he'd take the alarm clock off the shelf and wind it as he headed for the stairs. He'd place the clock on the bureau in the bedroom he shared with Nan. The next morning, he'd bring the clock downstairs again and light the fire in the kitchen stove. These were simple tasks and habits of everyday life.

We all have activities we do daily without even thinking about them. Maybe it's locking the door or turning off the TV at night. Then in the morning, we unlock the door and turn on the television again. Some may read the newspaper, listen to the news, or catch the latest weather forecast. Checking email and Facebook messages are modern-day habits. How many of us are faithful to these?

I've read that when you repeat something seven times, you start to form a habit. It becomes automatic, and you don't have to think about doing it. If this is true, in one week we can form the habit of reading our Bible every day. That would be awesome!

Psalm 119 says that God's Word will light our way, help us make right choices, heal our wounds, settle our hearts, warn us of danger, lead us, and make us wise: *"my heart stands in awe of your word"* (Psalm 119:161b, WEB).

Father God, thank You for the Bible. It's my counsellor; it's water and life to my soul. Remind me to spend time each day reading Your Living Word. From a thankful heart. Amen.

MAY 6

"When he saw Queen Esther standing there in the inner court, he welcomed her and held out the gold scepter to her" (Esther 5:2, NLT).

"What is your request? I will give it to you, even if it is half the kingdom!" (Esther 5:3, NLT)

Today was the coronation of King Charles III. As I watched the solemn and majestic ceremony, I was awed by the opulent dress and the carefully orchestrated proceedings. During the ceremony, King Charles was presented with several key items. Among these were the golden orb with a cross on top, the jewelled crown, and the golden sceptre. As soon as I saw the sceptre, I thought about the story of Esther in the Bible.

Even though Esther was the queen, she couldn't approach the king without being asked. Doing so could have led to her death. The only way she could approach him was if the king held out the golden sceptre.

Because Esther had a burden on her heart to save her people from destruction, she showed great courage when she took a chance with her life and went to the king. The king was pleased to see her and held out the golden sceptre. He said he would grant whatever she requested, even half the kingdom!

I'm reminded that when I go to the King of kings, I don't need to be afraid to approach Him. He holds out the golden sceptre to even me. We sing a chorus that goes, "Whosoever will may come to Jesus." Jesus tells us in Luke 12:32, *"Do not be afraid, little flock, for your Father has been pleased to give you the kingdom."*

Father God, thank You for Your Son, the King of kings. Thank You for being approachable. I know I can go to You at any time with any request. Amen.

MAY 7

"Let everything that breathes sing praises to the Lord! Praise the Lord!" (Psalm 150:6, NLT)

One spring morning, I got ready for work as usual. I walked downstairs and looked out the window at the drab, frosty day. It was the end of a long winter, and I couldn't wait until the arrival of warm, sunny days. *There's not much good about the weather these days*, I thought. It was a cold morning and a work day on top of that. I put on my boots and warm coat and went outside with my dog, Olivia, for her morning walk and nature call. We only walked to the end of our back fence, but it seemed that she was really taking her time.

I walked along with my head somewhat down and looked at the snow. As we neared the back fence and the tall trees, my ears were suddenly attuned to a magnificent orchestra of singing birds. The sound filled the air with all kinds of beats, notes, tones, and individual songs. It blended together in a symphony of praise to the morning and the coming spring. I looked up at the surrounding birch and aspen trees, which were filled with several varieties of songbirds. The birds seemed to be praising God for the day. God's little creatures are quick to sing His praises. Then I thought, *Am I a thankful person? First thing in the morning when my eyes are barely open, is there praise on my lips?* Many of us spend our days complaining instead of thanking.

As the little birds sang their morning songs, I realized it was a lesson to me from God's little creatures. It was classical music at its finest! Instead of complaining, I would do well to praise God first thing in the morning, as the little birds do.

Father and Creator, thank You for this world and for the little birds that sing so beautifully. Thank You for each new day, whether sunny or cloudy, I know that each day is a gift from you. Please help me to remember the lesson from that morning and to praise You in all circumstances. From a thankful heart. Amen.

MAY 8

"We have decided that the families of priests, Levites, and ordinary people will supply firewood for the temple each year" (Nehemiah 10:34a, CEV).

It was my turn to bring a few wood splits to school so that the fire could be lit in the potbelly stove. I remember that I had a little bundle in my arms as I walked up the hill to the small Salvation Army two-room school I attended.

Some schoolchildren brought a few coal knobs or bigger chunks of wood to burn. All of the students took turns bringing wood or coal to school. When the fire got going well, the stove turned red and you felt like you were melting.

The school was on top of a hill that overlooked the cove. In the winter when the snow came and the wind blew from the ocean, we were thankful for the heat from the wood stove.

In the verse above, the families of the Israelites were required to bring wood to the Temple to be burned on the altar. The bringing of the wood was just as important as bringing their other offerings and setting apart their firstborn for service to the Lord. This is covered in the subsequent verses. This tells me that no gift or service to the Lord is too small. Do you think that what you do or give isn't important or needed? Every effort is important. Every little bit counts in God's Kingdom. Don't forget to do your part no matter how trivial it may seem to you. Rest assured—it is not trivial to God.

Father God, thank You for the little two-room school I attended as a child. I've learned many important lessons and look back at that time fondly. Help me to give and do what I can and not think that it isn't needed. Amen.

MAY 9

"Instead, Jonah ran from the Lord" (Jonah 1:3a, CEV).

"But Moses said to God, 'Who am I that I should go …?'" (Exodus 3:11a)

When I was little, my dad made a swing for me in our front yard. It had a thick rope attached to a wooden crossbeam, and a wooden seat at the end of the rope to sit on. I sat on the wooden board and moved back and forth to get it going. I couldn't go very high by myself, but when I got a push, I could almost reach the sky. Back and forth the swing went, higher and higher!

Through the years, there have been many times when I needed a push—not on a swing but with some goal I needed to reach. My parents pushed me to reach higher. My husband pushed me to reach higher, and God pushed me to reach higher. It's good to get a push now and then. It makes you reach higher and achieve more than you would on your own.

In the Bible, God told Jonah to go to Nineveh, but Jonah didn't want to go. Before he would listen to God, the sailors threw him off the ship, and a whale swallowed him. He'd been reluctant to go, so God pushed him.

In the book of Exodus, we read the story about Moses. God chose Moses to lead the nation of Israel out of Egypt, but Moses was reluctant to go. He questioned God and didn't want to go back to Egypt. So God pushed him to go.

When you feel the push from God to do something, don't hesitate but go forward, knowing that God is with you.

Father, thank You for being so patient and for giving me the right pushes when I needed them. Thank You for all the people You placed along my way who helped me to reach higher and not give up. Amen.

MAY 10

"Then the Lord said to Joshua, 'Do not be afraid or discouraged'"
(Joshua 8:1a, NLT).

"Don't be afraid." Throughout the Bible, God continually reminds people to not be afraid. How many times did God tell Joshua to not be afraid? He also said it to Abram after he rescued Lot. He said it to Jairus when someone told him his daughter had died. He said it to Mary when she was told she would be the mother of Jesus. He said it to Zechariah, the disciples, Paul, and John. How many times has He said it to me?

Fear of the future and the unknown is an epidemic—not just in the Bible but even in this present day. I often feel afraid of something that may or may not happen. When I feel like this, I remember God's words to not be afraid or discouraged. I remember that God loves me. I remember that He's already in the future, like a time traveller, working things out for my good.

To believers, the Bible says, *"And we know that God causes everything to work together for the good of those who love God and are called according to his purpose for them"* (Romans 8:28, NLT). All I have to do is trust, and God does the rest. All I have to do is the next thing and let God take care of the future.

Lord, I don't have control over all my living. I sleep, get up, breathe, eat, work, and go to bed. Everything else seems out of control sometimes. I don't know where I'm going. I don't know how or why. I only know I want to please You. Guide me through the uncertain days. Amen.

MAY 11

"He replied, 'The Lord, before whom I have walked faithfully, will send his angel with you and make your journey a success'"
(Genesis 24:40a).

The time has come for another road trip! It seems like I've been on the road all spring. I've been in the car or plane more than I've been in my own home. My suitcase is getting good use and my personal kit bag is always packed. I do enjoy some parts of the travel, though, because I have time to reflect, pray and think.

Each trip is similar, but there are differences, and that's what makes them unique and memorable. I've travelled through sunshine, heavy rain, and snow. I've stayed with my daughters and in hotels. I've eaten good food and bad. I've arrived at my destination with no luggage and, at times, with too much luggage. I've met grumpy people and happy ones. I've had restful stays and ones that weren't so restful. As I set out on each journey, I wonder what the trip will be like. Will the ride be smooth? Will the weather be fine? Will I encounter any equipment problems? Will my baggage arrive intact? What manner of people will I meet?

When I started my Christian journey, I asked some of the same questions. This is what I discovered: The ride is both smooth and bumpy. There may be all kinds of problems along the way. The weather changes often; sometimes it's clear and sometimes stormy. I can have as much to eat as I want, but I have to ask for it. Baggage gets dropped along the way. And although sometimes it seems that things may be running late, everything happens right on time. You will meet many people—some on the same journey and others not. However, I have the promise that God will make my journey to Heaven a success.

Father God, thank You for being with me on all my travels. Thank You for all the different experiences along the way. I know You will be with me on any future journeys. Amen.

MAY 12

"After I have uprooted them, I will once again have compassion on them and return each one to his inheritance and to his land"
(Jeremiah 12:15, HCSB).

Most Newfoundlanders my age know what the word "resettlement" means. For some it brings back memories of uprooting and turmoil. For others, it's a positive memory of starting over in a new place.

The resettlement program moved people from isolated fishing communities to larger towns and centres. People were moved from small islands that were only accessible by boat and from communities that didn't have roads. There were three such undertakings by the provincial government, running from the 1950s until 1975.

I was in grades nine and ten at the high school in Arnold's Cove when the government's second resettlement program was underway. I remember that there wasn't room at the high school to accommodate all the new students, so it was decided to set up temporary classrooms.

I'm sure this resettlement was stressful for the families involved. Many had to float their houses to the new location. The students, however, seemed to fit in just fine. They were excited to be in a newer school, meet new friends and have more opportunities for education.

Throughout the Old Testament, people were settled and resettled, especially the Israelites. But God gave them a promise in Amos 9:15: *"I'll plant your roots deep in the land I have given you, and you won't ever be uprooted again. I, the Lord God, have spoken!"* (CEV).

Father God, I want to be rooted deep in You no matter where I live. I know I can't go where You are not. Help me to be content wherever I am. In Jesus's name. Amen.

MAY 13

"You light a lamp for me. The Lord, my God, lights up my darkness"
(Psalm 18:28, NLT).

I long for the warm days and nights of summer. It's so nice to sit outside in the evening and enjoy a campfire and the night sky. It's perfect—except, of course, for the mosquitoes, hornets, and nippers. Those annoying pests buzz around you looking for any exposed skin. Before you know what's happening, your ankles, hands, neck, and face start to itch, and you're scratching like crazy. The insect bites turn red and swell, and the only relief is to call it a night and go inside.

But don't count me out of it yet. I want to tell you how I fight back. We have a bug zapper light in our backyard. We use it in the summer when all the annoying flying insects are out. At the first appearance of the mosquitoes, we plug it in. It uses electricity to zap the bugs. They're lured in by the light and then burned up by the electric energy. All night long you hear the buzzing and zapping of the insects hitting the zapper. It's music to my ears.

Occasionally, we're much like the bugs drawn to the zapper light. We are drawn to the wrong kind of people, actions, and things. We are drawn in like bugs to a zapper and get burned up. That's what sin does. It draws you in and destroys your life, just like our zapper. We have to stay alert to who or what is trying to gain our attention: *"Do not be misled: 'Bad company corrupts good character'"* (1 Corinthians 15:33). Make sure you are following the right light.

Father God, I am thankful for the Bible, which is Your Spirit-inspired book for us. I love to read it and discover the map of life You gave us. You are the Light in my life. Amen.

MAY 14

"She put him in the basket and placed it in the tall grass along the edge of the Nile River" (Exodus 2:3b, CEV).

No other mother's story from the Bible touches my heart as much as the story of Jochebed, the mother of Moses. She was a slave in Egypt. Pharaoh was afraid that the Jews would become too numerous and threaten his rule, so he ordered the midwives to kill all the newborn male Jewish babies.

When Jochebed's son Moses was born, she managed to hide him for three months. When she couldn't hide him any longer and was faced with the threat of his murder, she took a leap of faith and devised a unique plan to save his life. Most mothers would do anything to save the life of their child. Her anguish over the baby must have been tremendous.

I confess that it's not a plan I would have thought of. She had great faith in her God to protect her baby's life. She took a basket and coated it with tar to make it waterproof. Then she put Moses in the basket and set it afloat among the reeds in the Nile River. Imagine someone today having to do what Jochebed did. The Pharaoh's daughter saw the basket and rescued the baby, whom she raised as her own.

I don't know all the sacrifices my mom made for me, but I'm aware of some. I was the firstborn, and my mother was young. She left her home to go live in a different town with my dad. She worked very hard keeping a home and taking care of family. Never forget to honour your mother. You may not know the struggles and sacrifices she made to give you life.

Father God, I am so thankful for my mother. May she live a long, healthy life and pass peacefully into eternity with You. Amen.

MAY 15

"The Lord himself goes before you and will be with you; he will never leave you nor forsake you. Do not be afraid; do not be discouraged" (Deuteronomy 31:8).

When I was preparing to retire, I felt as though I was venturing into unknown waters. I was a little fearful, mainly because I didn't want to face a dull routine, day in and day out. I wanted to have a purpose each day, and I was used to a work schedule. Although I looked forward to retirement freedom, I didn't want to become useless. How would my husband and I spend our days? I was going into unknown territory.

It was a similar feeling when we were transferred to another town. What would it be like there? Where would we live? Would we miss our old friends? I imagine it's the unknown factor that distressed me. We often fear when we can't see what's ahead for us.

Many words besides "retiring" affect people in a similar way, such as "enlisted," "commissioned," "reassigned," "moved," and "hospitalized." We don't know what this change will be like for us. How will we manage?

I was encouraged by the verse above and also by Joshua 1:9: *"Be strong and courageous. Do not be afraid; do not be discouraged, for the Lord your God will be with you wherever you go."* I realized that I could never be where God is not. I knew that He would be with me, even in retirement and whatever changes come with that.

Dear God, thank You for Your reassurance to be with me. Maybe the upcoming change won't be so bad after all. Help me to make the most of each day knowing that You are with me and guiding me. Amen.

MAY 16

"He makes me as surefooted as a deer, enabling me to stand on mountain heights" (Psalm 18:33, NLT).

It was a bright, cloudless summer day in the Codroy Valley. My in-laws' cabin was nestled at the foot of the Long-Range Mountains.

Terry took me on an adventure to catch a few trout and see the waterfalls on the side of the mountain. We drove to the spot where the trail started alongside the stream. As the car stopped, I saw the glint of a sparkling stream weaving its way through the rocks and trees towards the great Codroy River.

Terry and I were quite young at the time, and he had no trouble navigating the stream. He jumped from rock to rock without slipping, and I don't think he even had to look where he was going. He seemed to be part of the surroundings. He was so surefooted that he quickly disappeared from my sight. I had to call out for him to slow down and wait for me. These days we're not physically surefooted as before. We can't navigate the rocky stream jumping from rock to rock; in fact, we're thankful to even navigate our daily lives.

Going through life is sometimes like a rocky mountain stream. There are obstacles, deep waters, and a steep climb. Terry has learned to rely on God to help him navigate his days. In this respect and with God's help, he's just as surefooted now as he was in his youth on the mountain stream.

Father God, I'm so thankful for Your guidance and leadership in our lives. You make us surefooted over the obstacles, and we're able to rise above the circumstances and stand on the mountaintop. Amen.

MAY 17

"The Lord is my shepherd; I have all that I need"
(Psalm 23:1, NLT).

One morning on the way to work, I fell into a hole—not a pothole in the road, but a trap from a bad attitude. I said, "I'll be glad when all this rain is over." I was grumbling to myself and looking at another day of dark clouds. I fell into the complaining pothole.

On the surface, that's not a bad statement. Sometimes, we do get tired of the wet weather. But I said it with real intention and the belief that my circumstances would be better after the rain stopped. The devil loves to see us in this hole.

Circumstances and rain aren't the problem. The problem is my attitude. So … What if the rain doesn't stop? What if the bills aren't paid? What if I get sick? What if the price of gas keeps going up? What if I have an accident? What if I lose my job? What if my friends leave me? What if there's a hurricane? What if? What if? What if?

Then I thought, *What am I doing?* I have God on my side, and He's with me everywhere I go and through every circumstance. He hears my cries and sees my tears. He'll provide everything I need. My heavenly home is safe from the storms of this life.

God's character never changes. The goodness of God is not affected by our storms. Don't fall into the trap. Wait out the dark clouds with joy while singing praises to God. Remember, God is good all the time.

Father in Heaven, thank You that You are unchanging. Help me to choose joy during my seasons of thunderstorms and rain. Thank You for hearing my prayers. Amen.

MAY 18

"We make our own plans, but the Lord decides where we will go"
(Proverbs 16:9, CEV).

Travelling! Isn't it exciting to plan a trip? This is the time of year for travel. Most everyone is talking about going somewhere. They've made their plans—when, where, and how. Flights and ferry boats are booked up. What trip are you planning?

Last weekend, Terry was on a trip to Prince Edward Island. On the way back, he picked up a Newfoundland and Labrador travel book. As I was thumbing through it, I was thinking about all the things we needed to do to prepare for a trip.

How do you decide where to go? You might get advice from a friend. You might go to a travel company and talk to the agent, who'll give you information on exotic destinations. You might search the Internet and travel books. You can even book your flights and hotels online.

Of course, you can't get anywhere without packing your suitcase. What will you take with you? You may need traveler's cheques and a passport, and it's always good to have a map.

You also need to tell your family and friends where you're going. You wouldn't plan to go on a trip to Europe, or on a cruise, or even to a cabin without telling someone where you were going, would you? Just the same, you need to tell everyone about your journey with God. People need to hear about God, and they need to hear it from you: *"You know where I go, and you know the way"* (John 14:4, WEB); *"Your word is a lamp for my feet, a light on my path"* (Psalm 119:105).

Father God, thank You for this journey of life. Help me to be prepared and arrive safely at my final destination. Amen.

MAY 19

"But Martha was distracted by all the preparations that had to be made" (Luke 10:40a).

Martha was well known for her hospitality, and in the verse above, she's very busy preparing for her guest. Meanwhile, her sister Mary isn't helping her but instead is chatting with the guest. Martha becomes frustrated with her sister, but Jesus reminds her that the most important thing is to realize who He is and to take time to worship.

My Aunt Fronie was a Martha because she was always doing for others: baking, cooking, and volunteering her time. She was a Mary too, because she took time to worship God, and she put her trust in Him. She was a take-charge kind of woman. My earliest memory of her is at Chance Cove. I can see her in my mind's eye standing over the little kitchen counter in Nan's house, with her hands in the bread dough and a funny hat on her head. It wasn't really a hat. Its purpose was to cover the hair when preparing food. But usually this item was worn underneath clothing, not on top of the head (nudge, nudge, wink, wink).

She was a master at organizing the kitchen, family crowds, and meals. When the relatives were together at Chance Cove, Aunt Fronie was usually the one giving orders. She could play a game with the children, tell a story, and sing like a bird. Her sense of humour brought a smile to our faces and joy to all who knew her.

She was a homemaker, a volunteer, and an instrument for God. Even though she was often a Martha, she was a Mary at heart. I remember her faith and the song she often sang: "It is no secret what God can do. What He's done for others, He'll do for you. With arms wide open, He'll pardon you. It is no secret what God can do."

Father in Heaven, thank You for my Aunt Fronie and the influence she had on the people she helped, but especially on me. Amen.

MAY 20

"A wife of noble character, who can find? She is worth far more than rubies" (Proverbs 31:10).

This woman, known as the Proverbs 31 Woman, can be overwhelming to think about. Every time I read this passage, I think there is no woman like this. It's generally thought that this passage was written as a guide for a son when looking for a godly wife.

The only way I can make sense of it is that it represents many women and tells me that a woman can have numerous roles and job descriptions. These are the words I came up with to describe the woman in Proverbs 31: She was a morning person, a merchant, teacher, farmer, manufacturer, manager, seamstress, realtor; she was an investor, importer, and upholsterer. She was generous, honourable, godly, and she had a sense of humour. She was physically fit, thrifty, and industrious.

Do you have any of these jobs or qualities? The list is a bit daunting, and I think I might only have a couple of these aptitudes. Seriously, who can possibly meet this standard? In addition to the list above, she was a wife and a mother.

The passage doesn't mean that every woman should have all of these attributes, but she should be a godly woman. Proverbs 31:30 says, *"Charm can be deceiving, and beauty fades away, but a woman who honors the Lord deserves to be praised"* (CEV).

Her assets, talents, and accomplishments were the result of a godly heart. In all her busyness, she didn't forget what mattered most—to honour God in all she did.

Father God, thank You that I don't have to try to do all the things that this ideal woman can do. But help me to honour You in everything that I can do. Amen.

MAY 21

"Care for the flock that God has entrusted to you. Watch over it willingly, not grudgingly—not for what you will get out of it, but because you are eager to serve God" (1 Peter 5:2, NLT).

Sometimes caring for the flock isn't a very glamorous job. I remember the sheep my Uncle Sam raised in the garden across the road from our house. They were often out of the pen and wandering along the road. They had to be chased back inside the fence. They didn't care about cleanliness either, and they often looked very dirty. They only looked clean after shearing time in the spring. Of course, the newborn lambs were cute, but not so much the older sheep.

Maybe you could say the same about God's flock or the people under your care. Some are stubborn and wander away, or they're not as clean as you'd like them to be. Some are like newborn lambs, while others are like the older sheep.

God wants us to care for the people in our lives, whether they're family members, co-workers, neighbours, friends, members of our church, or even strangers. We're to do this willingly and not for what we may get out of it. Sometimes it isn't easy or pleasant, because we're like those stubborn sheep. But this is where God has placed us, and when we care for others, it's our service to Him.

Remember that Jesus is your Shepherd. He's your Caregiver and will take care of you as you take care of the people around you.

Father God, thank You for taking care of me even while I take care of others. Forgive me when I lose my patience with them, and show me the right way. Amen.

MAY 22

"That is what the Scriptures mean when they say, 'No eye has seen, no ear has heard, and no mind has imagined what God has prepared for those who love him'" (1 Corinthians 2:9, NLT).

What is your style? What are your passions? I've learned that in relationships, there are different styles and passions. One person might have an earthy style, with a passion for the land, the forest, the mountains, and the soil and for growing things. The other person may be a sea lover. They hug the shoreline and gravitate to the beaches. They hear the wind as music and see the waves as refreshing.

I thought about this today as we worked in the garden. Terry spread mulch around our front flower garden, and I wondered what beach rocks would look like there instead. I love the feel of the sand on my bare feet. I love to collect beach rocks that have been smoothed by the constant rolling of the waves. Terry is an earth lover and farmer at heart. He loves working the land, being in the woods, and growing things. He loves to grow plants and raise animals.

Terry has taught me the ways of farming, but it isn't in my heart. I like the ocean with the salty air and the crashing waves. I like to look at it, smell the air, and feel the wind. We're two different people, but we've come together and shared our lives. I've learned to garden, and Terry walks on the beach with me.

To have a garden by the sea—now that would be something. Just the same, God has prepared an even greater place for me in Heaven. I can only imagine!

Father God, I can only imagine what it will be like when I get to Heaven. Your Word says that it shines with the brilliance of God—like a precious jewel. Keep me in Your love until then. Amen.

MAY 23

"Be alert and of sober mind. Your enemy the devil prowls around like a roaring lion looking for someone to devour" (1 Peter 5:8).

We had several different feathered species in our barnyard, including turkeys, chickens, and a few geese. The turkeys were friendly and followed us around like trained pets.

One day as our daughters walked to the school bus stop at the end of the driveway, they turned around and saw, much to their embarrassment, that the turkeys were trotting along behind them. The girls were mortified and didn't want their friends on the bus to see the turkeys. Terry had to go to the bus stop to get the turkeys turned back. We laugh about it now, but at the time, the girls didn't think it was funny at all.

Along with the turkeys, we had chickens. Usually they weren't much trouble—except for the rooster. He always showed up when you least expected him, and he'd chase and attack us whenever we were nearby. Because of his aggressiveness, the girls and I were terrified of him. He was very territorial. He patrolled the fence and the barnyard like a policeman on duty. Whenever he saw someone enter his domain, he came after them with wings and spurs. Each of our daughters has a story to tell about being chased by that darn rooster.

The Bible tells us to watch out and be alert, because the devil is like that rooster. He's always looking for someone to attack. He's a schemer, a liar, and a strife maker. Peter tells us to take a firm stand against him and be strong in our faith.

Father God, thank You for warning us about the devil. Help us to realize when he's close, and help us to not fall for his schemes. Amen.

MAY 24

"God decided in advance to adopt us into his own family by bringing us to himself through Jesus Christ" (Ephesians 1:5a, NLT).

In the past, I lived what most people would consider an average life. I worked and raised children and coped with the ups and downs of doing all that. I had the usual worries of bills, sick children, and other family concerns. I enjoyed many hobbies and interests that kept me very busy. I was part of the world and all it had to offer. My focus was on myself and what I wanted. I considered myself just an ordinary married woman living an ordinary life.

But God had other plans for me. I found out that God wanted me as part of His family. He took an ordinary wife and mother and turned her life around. When I gave my heart and life to Him, He adopted me into His royal family and made me a child of the King.

This date marks the celebrated birthday of the late Queen Victoria. She was born into royalty. Even so, the royalty I've been adopted into is more significant because it will last for eternity. The Bible says that my citizenship is in Heaven (Philippians 3:20). I will be with God in His Kingdom.

Don't be concerned about being ordinary. Nobody is ordinary when they're a member of God's family. Everyone has a purpose and is equally important. God says, *"I will bless you with a future filled with hope—a future of success, not of suffering"* (Jeremiah 29:11, CEV).

When you ask God to forgive your sins and come into your heart, you are adopted into His royal family. You become a child of the King.

Father God, thank You for showing me that I'm more than an ordinary woman. I have a place in Your Kingdom and am royalty. Help me to accept the privileges but also live up to the responsibilities of who I am in Christ. Amen.

MAY 25

"Are not two sparrows sold for a penny? Yet not one of them will fall to the ground outside your Father's care" (Matthew 10:29).

As I played in the yard, I heard a faint sound and wondered where it came from. I thought it had come from the barn, so I went there to investigate. The barn was a little dark, but some light was shining through the cracks in the boards and through the half open door. The smell of hay and dried horse dung hit my nose. I listened, and again I heard the soft mewing.

I followed the sound, searching the stalls and then climbing to the loft. I found the source of the sound hidden in a corner, covered with a mound of hay. The barn cat had given birth to three little kittens, who were just a week or so old. They looked helpless and were crying for their mother. In my child's mind, I thought, *I hope she comes back soon. I'll watch from the yard to make sure she comes back.* Thankfully, the tabby cat returned to be with her babies.

The Bible says that God watches over the sparrows and other little creatures. I know He was watching that little family in the barn. If He values something so small, He certainly sees you. No matter what you're going through, He's with you, aware of your circumstances.

Hannah Whitall Smith says, "He who counts the very hairs of our heads and suffers not a sparrow to fall without him, takes note of the minutest matters that can affect the lives of his children and regulates them all according to his perfect will, let their origin be what they may."[6]

Father God, whenever I'm fearful and need reassurance, I remember this verse. If You care for the little birds, then I know You'll take care of me. Thank You for Your amazing love. Amen.

---

[6] "Quote by Hannah Whitall Smith," Bible Portal, accessed October 12, 2025, https://www.bibleportal.com/bible-quote/god-he-who-counts-the-very-hairs-of-our-heads-and-suffers-not-a-sparrow-to-fall-without-him-takes-note.

MAY 26

"For as the soil makes the sprout come up and a garden causes seeds to grow, so the Sovereign Lord will make righteousness and praise spring up before all nations" (Isaiah 61:11).

Our house is a nursery for new plant life. Every downstairs window provides sunlight to a tray of baby plants for the garden. Outside, robins pull worms from the tilled soil and then fly to their nests to feed the newly hatched babies. Trees are turning green with their summer garb. Everything around us is portraying new life.

The garden is alive with life: birds, insects, and plants. Everything is waking up from a long winter's slumber. I love the spring when everything becomes like new again. The grey and white of winter turns to a colourful world of living things.

Isaiah 61 describes a time when righteousness will come to the society of the day. It will be like the new growth in spring. But it also foretells the time when Jesus will come. In Luke 4, Jesus quotes from Isaiah 61, saying that He came specifically to preach the gospel to the poor (the spiritually poor who have no hope), to heal the broken-hearted (broken by sin), to proclaim liberty to the captives (release people from guilt and the bondage of sin), to give sight to the blind (to open their eyes to the truth of the gospel), to set at liberty those who are oppressed (mentally and spiritually by sin and addictions), and to proclaim the acceptable year of the Lord (to give us a time of liberation and fresh starts). This is the gospel of grace, healing, and deliverance. This is why Jesus came. He came for you and me.

Father God, thank You for Your Son, Jesus, who came to bring me His righteousness. Help me to teach others about the gospel of grace. Amen.

MAY 27

"Again, the kingdom of Heaven is like a merchant looking for fine pearls" (Matthew 13:45).

"When he found one of great value, he went away and sold everything he had and bought it" (Matthew 13:46).

The duck pond by the barn was a man-made swimming hole for the ducks. The mud around it was dark and sticky. But the ducks—Pop's pride and joy—loved it. Feathers would float in the water, and some stuck out of the mud. I loved to watch the ducks in the water.

Sometimes I'd walk around the pond looking for duck eggs. As I'd gaze into the water, I could just make out the shape of a duck egg. Sometimes they laid their eggs in the water by the edge of the pond. I'd gather them up and deliver them to my nan. It was like finding something of great value. When I read the verses above, I thought about Pop's duck pond and collecting the eggs from the muddy bottom.

I think everyone is looking for something—usually a better life. People want a life with no worries, no financial problems, no sickness, no wars, and no relationship problems. Some people think that if they could win the lottery, all their problems would be over.

In Matthew 13, Jesus says that the kingdom of Heaven is a greater prize, and it's worth trading all that we have to get it and become all that He created us to be. The only way to accomplish this is to give your life over to Jesus and follow Him with all your heart.

Jesus, thank You for giving me the greatest treasure of all—grace and forgiveness. I now have a place in the Kingdom of Heaven. Help me to follow You with all my heart. Amen.

MAY 28

"One day as Jesus was walking along the shore of the Sea of Galilee, he saw two brothers—Simon, also called Peter, and Andrew—throwing a net into the water, for they fished for a living" (Matthew 4:18, NLT).

I grew up in a small community where the main occupation was fishing for cod in the Atlantic Ocean. I observed that fishermen are resourceful people. They respect the weather and the sea. They fish to feed their families and to make a living. They go out in all kinds of weather to look for the fish. Even though they may enjoy fishing, it isn't done for fun. They are serious fishermen.

There are fishermen in a spiritual sense too. These fishermen are working for God and fishing for souls. They fish for many different reasons. Some people fish because their parents did it. Some people dress like fishermen but don't believe in it. Some fishermen just like to hang around with other fishermen. Some fishermen want to catch the most and the biggest.

In the Bible, two brothers—Simon (called Peter) and his brother Andrew—were fishermen. Then there was James and his brother John, who were fishing with their father, Zebedee. Jesus called them as his first disciples: *"Come, follow me ... and I will send you out to fish for people"* (Matthew 4:19). Jesus saw something worthwhile in these fishermen. Do you think He called them because of the way they dressed, or because of their parents, or because they caught many fish? I think Jesus called them because He knew the kinds of fishermen they would be for Him. He saw what they could become. They would give their hearts and lives to be "fishers of men."

Father God, thank You for this lesson from the fishermen. Help me to be serious and professional in living my life for You. Amen.

MAY 29

"Why, you do not even know what will happen tomorrow. What is your life? You are a mist that appears for a little while and then vanishes" (James 4:14).

There's no need to verify the time by checking the Internet. You can set your watch by the 4:00 p.m. fog in Chance Cove. Just about every afternoon when it's almost time to go in for supper, you can feel a shift in the temperature. From behind my mom's house, you can look up to the hills and see the first wisps of fog coming from across the Isthmus.

When I was growing up, I would enjoy a sunny day outside with my friends, swimming or beachcombing or bike riding. Then the temperature would suddenly feel cooler, and if we looked to the hills, we'd see the blanket of fog descending on the cove.

I was used to the fog. I grew up with it. In a way, it's kind of comforting. It wraps you in its misty cover. Things seem to be a little quieter and subdued when it's foggy. It limits your ability to see very far, so you focus more on the things nearby. We need that sometimes—to focus inward and reflect on our day and life.

A wise old man in Chance Cove once said, "Even a long life is short." Compared to eternity, our lives are like a mist or fog that appears for a short time each day and then is gone.

At the end of our life, may we be able to say, *"O Lord my God, you have performed many wonders for us … If I tried to recite all your wonderful deeds, I would never come to the end of them."* (Psalm 40:5, NLT).

Father God, thank You for the times of reflection. Help me to live in the present and make the most of each day before my life fades like the mist. Amen.

MAY 30

"You did not choose me, but I chose you ..." (John 15:16a)

I'll never forget one time when I went to the Salvation Army's Women's Camp at Twin Ponds. When Sunday morning came, I got out of bed, showered, and then dressed. In past camps, we'd worn our uniforms for service on Sunday morning, so I dressed with this in mind.

In the meantime, the other women got ready and went to breakfast at the dining hall. I was a few minutes behind, so I walked up the hill by myself. When I walked into the dining hall—where there was a few hundred women—I discovered to my dismay and embarrassment that I was the only one there (including clergy) wearing a uniform. To say I wanted to melt through the cracks in the floor and disappear is an understatement.

Apparently, I'd missed the memo explaining the relaxed dress code. How I even got that far without noticing that others weren't wearing their uniforms—or how someone didn't see me getting ready and mention it to me—I don't know. When I think about it now, I realize that it must have been a God-ordained experience to teach me a lesson.

God is so considerate of our feelings that during breakfast, He brought a Scripture verse to my mind: *"... God ... set me apart from my mother's womb and called me by his grace ... "* (Galatians 1:15). At that moment, I felt that verse in my whole being. So I went to the service wearing my uniform. Afterwards, I wrote in my journal that "even though I felt like a black seabird amongst colourful parrots," I knew I was set apart for God. I learned that sometimes being set apart is embarrassing; sometimes it's a struggle; and sometimes it's a sacrifice.

Father God, You taught me a valuable lesson that day. Being set apart isn't easy sometimes. Help me to remember that You chose me, and You will be with me whatever the situation. Amen.

MAY 31

"See, I am doing a new thing!" (Isaiah 43:19a)

Do you remember when you got your first bicycle? I was very young, but I remember it well. One day when my dad came home from work, he brought home my first bike—a two-wheel black beauty. As he unloaded it from the back of the truck, I got my first look at it, and I was very excited. It wasn't new, but it was new to me. I loved it! It had coaster brakes, which you applied by pedalling backwards. I think most bikes back then had only one speed.

After a few skinned knees, I quickly learned how to ride and took every opportunity to do so. I was so proud of my bike that every spring I painted it a new colour. My dad patched the tires and put new tubes in them. I was ready for another summer of bike riding. Up hills and down hills I went.

One day while riding my bike with my sister Arlette as a passenger on the crossbar, the bike's brake suddenly stuck. The bike stopped abruptly, and we flew over the handlebars, landing on the gravel road. We had cuts and scrapes. Arlette's front teeth went through her lip, and there was a lot of blood. But thankfully, she survived. I didn't take on a passenger again, but I didn't give up riding.

Learning to ride a bike is different for everyone. Some hardly have any mishaps, and some have many falls. I learned that even though I may occasionally fall, it's important to get back on and not give up. Life is like that, and the Christian walk is like that. Don't give up. Pick yourself up and keep going. God will do a new thing in you.

Father God, just like when I was growing up and learning to ride my bike, I'm learning to stay on this journey with You. Thank You for helping me each day to keep going. Thank You for helping me back on when I fall off. Amen.

JUNE 1

"So neither the one who plants nor the one who waters is anything, but only God, who makes things grow" (1 Corinthians 3:7).

Chance Cove is a small fishing community with lots of hills and rocks. I can't remember much farming or gardening being done when I was growing up. I do remember that some people grew potatoes and maybe turnip and cabbage. Once, I saw my dad and grandfather planting potatoes.

In the spring, everyone who planned to grow vegetables spread horse manure, seaweed, and capelin on the garden for fertilizer. A man who lived up the road grew potatoes in the garden by the beach. He had a big white horse that he hitched to a plough and led back and forth over the garden until all the fertilizer was tilled into the ground. When he finished, there were long rows of ditches and hilled-up dirt from one end of the garden to the other.

He placed the potato seeds in the trenches that he'd made. The eyes on the potatoes are the spots where the new shoots start, and they had to point up. Then he shovelled the hilled-up dirt on top. When they grew a little, he placed more dirt on top of the rows. They called this process "hilling-up" the potatoes. Then he added more of the stinky, yucky, messy fertilizer. The fertilizer was necessary for the best potato growth.

Potato growing reminds me of my life. Sometimes God uses stinky, yucky messes to help me grow and produce the fruit of righteousness in my life, which is right behaviour and relationships with others and God. Hang in there! One day you'll be like those beautiful potatoes fresh from the garden of life.

Father in Heaven, thank You for helping me grow into the person You would have me to be. Help me to remember that the messes in my life have a purpose, even though sometimes I would rather do without them. Amen.

JUNE 2

"Then they sat on the ground with him for seven days and nights. No one said a word to Job, for they saw that his suffering was too great for words" (Job 2:13, NLT).

Sometimes we know people who are suffering from disease or loss. We know their names. We know their particular hardship, and we pray for them and their need. We have long prayer lists at our churches for these people.

But many more people suffer silently. I heard a saying that went like this: "In every church pew there is a broken heart." We don't know their struggle or the turmoil in their lives. They need prayer but can't give anyone the details or put a name to it. As the verse above says, sometimes suffering is too great for words. Their prayer requests remain unspoken. God sees the anguish of these unspoken requests. He hears the smallest whispers of our hearts and understands the pain of these requests. Jesus knows what it is to live in human flesh. The Bible says, *"Trust in the Lord with all your heart; do not depend on your own understanding"* (Proverbs 3:5, NLT).

Unspoken requests are personal and often private. Sometimes they're too painful to talk about. Unspoken needs can be persistent. We need to be intercessors and prayer warriors, especially for the unspoken and unnamed prayer requests.

How do we pray for people with unnamed requests? Ask God to surround them with His love so that they feel God's presence and know He is with them. In James 5:16, we're instructed to *"pray for each other so that you may be healed."* Be assured that when no one else understands, God does.

Father God, even when our suffering is too great to put into words, let us know that You hear. We know that You care, and we expect You to answer. We come boldly to Your throne of grace, even when only our hearts are crying out. Amen.

JUNE 3

"But our citizenship is in heaven" (Philippians 3:20a).

What comes to your mind when you think of home? Is it a town? A house? If you close your eyes, what do you hear? Do you live by the ocean, a river, in the country, or in a town?

Is it a one-storey or a two-storey house? Is it white, blue, yellow, or red? Can you recall smells from the kitchen, the sound of creaking stairs, and the feel of the furnishings? I have a multitude of fond memories of my childhood home and the homes I've shared with my husband.

I believe all of us have a longing for home—not just a home or a house on earth but a home in Heaven. We try to fill that yearning by settling into our houses on earth. We want to be comfortable, secure, and happy. We want a piece of Heaven here on earth. Sometimes we even return to our childhood home to try and recapture the carefree days of youth. Because we're not home yet, the desire for home never goes away. No matter where we are, part of us longs for home.

The promise of Heaven is a gift from God when you believe in Jesus. The thought of going to Heaven gives me hope that I will be home at last, because there's no place like home.

Father God, thank You for the wonderful homes You provided for me on earth. I have such fond memories of each one. But I know that my heavenly home will be spectacular beyond my imagination. Help me to live my life with Heaven in my mind. Amen.

JUNE 4

"The Lord showed me all around, and everywhere I looked I saw bones that were dried out. He said, 'Ezekiel, son of man, can these bones come back to life?'" (Ezekiel 37:2-3, CEV)

Recently, I watched a documentary on a nature channel about elephants. They were filmed interacting with dried elephant bones. It seemed that they were paying homage to the bones of their dead. They gently touched the bones with their feet and sniffed the bones with their trunks, as if they were saying goodbye. The elephants have also been filmed gently touching the dying and then kicking the dead carcass of a calf elephant, as if to bring life back into it.

In the verse above, God took Ezekiel to a valley filled with dried bones. He asked Ezekiel if the bones could live again. Ezekiel could touch the bones and breathe on them, but he couldn't bring them back to life—just as the elephants couldn't bring life back into the bones of their kind.

God's people had become like those dried dead bones scattered around the valley floor. And then, God gave the promise that He would bring them back to their land and bring restoration to them both physically and spiritually. In Ezekiel 37:13–14a, God says, *"Then you, my people, will know that I am the Lord, when I open your graves and bring you up from them. I will put my Spirit in you and you will live ..."*

Just as only God can bring life to the dry bones, only God can bring life to someone who is spiritually dead. Won't you ask God to give you life?

Father God, only You have the power to give life. Thank You for giving me life and salvation. May I never be dead spiritually, like those dry bones. Amen.

JUNE 5

"Do two walk together unless they have agreed to do so?"
(Amos 3:3)

Can you remember the games you played with your friends at school outings and Sunday school picnics? I can! I especially remember the contests at school sport days and the picnics at Bellevue Beach Park.

We had tug of war contests; we played softball; we bobbed for apples; and we ran in all kinds of races. One race that comes to my mind was the three-legged race. There were a number of teams of two people each. One of each teammate's legs would be tied to the other, so that it looked like there were three legs and not four. When the whistle blew to start, all the teams had to walk or run to the finish line. The first team to get there won.

The three-legged race wasn't as easy as it appeared. Each two-person team had to run with the three legs and not trip up. This required working together and moving in rhythm. It required agreement on what leg moved and when. This was the only way you could get anywhere. Otherwise, you'd be flat on the ground. Of course, many of us did fall on the ground, but we quickly got back up and continued the race. It got a lot of laughs, and we had tremendous fun. We certainly learned a valuable lesson of cooperation. As the verse above says, two cannot walk together unless they've agreed to do so. Stay in a continual, uninterrupted walk with God.

Father in Heaven, thank You for fun times and lessons learned through the games I played as a child. Help me to remember and use them in my daily living and walk with You. From a thankful heart, in Jesus's name. Amen.

JUNE 6

"Even though I walk through the valley of the shadow of death, I will fear no evil, for you are with me. Your rod and your staff, they comfort me" (Psalm 23:4, WEB).

Some Bible translations of this passage leave out the reference to the shadow of death and instead call it a deep, dark valley or something like that. But for me, those translations don't fully capture the same picture as walking in the shadow of death. It's more than a shadow—it's a death shadow.

When my dad died, I felt as though I was walking in a shadow that wouldn't go away. It followed me everywhere. My heart ached, because that death left an empty space. Where once there was colour and light, now there was a grey shadow of emptiness. Through the valley, my life went on, and there were countless decisions to make and details to take care of.

Psalm 23:4 tells us that when we're faced with the time of death shadows, we don't need to be afraid, because during this time, God is especially attentive to us and employs His *rod* and *staff*. His rod gives us extra protection from harm, and His staff guides us in our daily decisions. Knowing that He was doing this gave me comfort. I was relieved that I wasn't in the shadow alone. His presence soothed my hurting heart, and I wasn't so anxious anymore.

"In 'pastures green'? Not always, sometimes He who knoweth best, in kindness leadeth me in weary ways where heavy shadows be" (Anonymous). Sometimes we might walk in the shadow of death, but the light will come and the shadow will disappear.

Father God, I will trust You always, even though I can't see You when I'm walking in the shadow of death. I will not fear, for I trust Your heart and Your promises to never leave me to face the shadows alone. From a thankful heart, in Jesus's name. Amen.

JUNE 7

"And he saith unto them, Follow me, and I will make you fishers of men" (Matthew 4:19, KJV).

In my career working for the government, I often had to advertise for and hire new employees to fill vacant positions. All the job ads followed a particular outline to make them concise, complete, and easy to read.

I thought about the accounts in the Bible of Jesus calling the fishermen to follow Him and be His disciples. I wondered what the job advertisement for the position of disciple would look like, and this is what I imagined it to be.

The position is titled *Fisher of Men*, and the successful applicant is required to travel. It's a permanent position with heavenly benefits. The main duty is to proclaim the good news of Jesus Christ to the world. The qualifications are as follows: "Must be early risers, hard workers, and dedicated. Must not be afraid to get their hands dirty or work in stormy seas. They will be close to nature, appreciating God's bounty and provision. They must be willing and able to work in teams with unity in all tasks. They must exhibit faith, especially when the way is unclear.

"The salary is not paid in earthly dollars but is the reward of eternal life in Heaven. Please send your résumé to Son of God, Foot of the Cross, Calvary, with the competition number as Disciple.4. Christ. Remember, this is a position of trust. Please note the closing date as the End of Time."

The Lord doesn't ask you to produce a college or university degree. He's looking for someone with a willing spirit and a repentant heart. Do you have what it takes to be a fisher of men? Won't you apply today?

Father God, I pray that as a result of this job advertisement, there will be many more disciples recruited for Your work here on earth. Amen.

JUNE 8

"And God said, Let us make man in our image, after our likeness ... " (Genesis 1:26, KJV)

Who is she? What does she look like? Where did she come from? What's her purpose here?

The Bible tells me I am made in the image of God. Only human beings are made this way. We have a special relationship with God, the Creator. He made us with a moral and spiritual awareness.

There are also many references in the Bible to heavenly beings, including seraphim, cherubim, and angels. The main role of both the cherubim and seraphim is to sit at the throne and worship God. Both are described as having four to six wings and four faces. However, angels who appear on earth aren't described as having wings but instead the appearance of a man.

Angels are God's military force; they are His messengers sent to minister to the saved (those who put their faith in God's Son). They guard, protect, and rescue us. They lead, guide, and strengthen us.

The Bible doesn't specifically say that humans become angels, but it does say that angels look like men. In Genesis 18, three angels looking like men visited Abraham. The writer to the Hebrews says, *"Do not forget to show hospitality to strangers, for by so doing some people have shown hospitality to angels without knowing it"* (Hebrews 13:2).

What will we look like in Heaven? The Bible says that in Heaven, Christ will transform our lowly bodies so that they'll be like His glorious body (Philippians 3:21), and we'll be recognizable just like Moses and Elijah were in Luke 9.

Father God, as I read Your Word, help me to focus not on how we look but on what is most important for me—my walk with You. Amen.

JUNE 9

"Still other seed fell on good soil, where it produced a crop—a hundred, sixty or thirty times what was sown" (Matthew 13:8).

Although I'm not a gardener, there are many of them in my family. Yes, I work in the garden, but gardening doesn't come naturally to me. Through the years, I learned some gardening skills from my husband, Terry, who is the gardener in our family. My nan was a gardener, and Aunt Carrie loved to garden too. They loved to work in the soil, plant the seeds and cuttings, and watch them grow. Gardeners are different from other people. They can spend hours poring over seed catalogues and gardening supplies—things that other people find boring.

A good gardener knows not to plant seeds where the birds can eat them or on rocky places where there's not enough soil. They don't plant the seeds among the thorns and weeds that choke them of nutrients and sunlight. A good gardener prepares the soil by tilling the ground and applying fertilizer.

God loves to garden, and He was the first gardener: *"Then God said, 'Let the land produce vegetation: seed-bearing plants and trees' ... And it was so"* (Genesis 1:11). Our lives are similar to the garden. God grows us into the person He wants us to be by preparing our lives like the soil in the garden. He provides sunlight and also rain—things like painful relationships, diseases, and all kinds of troubles that help us grow. It feels awful at the time, but that's how you get the best growth and the highest yield of fruit.

Father in Heaven, You know what's needed in our lives to make us receptive to Your influence. Besides the sun, sometimes we need a lot of fertilizer. Thank You for tilling up the soil of my life. Amen.

JUNE 10

"Yet I still dare to hope when I remember this: The faithful love of the Lord never ends!" (Lamentations 3:21–22a, NLT)

I hope it doesn't rain tomorrow, because I want to hang clothes on the line. I hope my knee doesn't hurt so that I can go for a nice, long walk. I hope the coffee is hot and the toast not burnt. I hope, I hope, I hope. Little hopes that we whisper all day long. What hopes did you have for today? Then there are the big hopes. I hope this disease ends soon. I hope my medical tests are normal. I hope my house doesn't need major repairs this year. I hope to see my family soon.

There are little hopes and there are big hopes. Job 17:15 says, *"where then is my hope—who can see any hope for me?"* Do you feel like Job sometimes? You just can't see any hope? The poet Emily Dickinson wrote, "Hope is the thing with feathers that perches in the soul, and sings the tune—without the words, and never stops at all."[7] Never stop hoping.

How much hope do you have? Sometimes, hope might be in short supply, and it's easy to lose hope due to the struggles of living, especially these past few years with the pandemic, mass shootings, the poor economy, and on and on. But we live every day with hope.

When I hope for something, I like to picture it in my mind. I remind myself that anything is possible with God. I think everyone needs to be reminded at times of the hope God offers to us. Be assured that Christ came for those who have no hope. I once read: "To pass words of hope to an emotionally drowning soul is to drag them into the life raft by hand."

Father God, thank You for Your promise of hope. Without hope, I can't live my life as You intended me to live it. Amen.

---

[7] Emily Dickinson, "'Hope' Is the Thing with Feathers," Poetry Foundation, accessed October 12, 2025, https://www.poetryfoundation.org/poems/42889/hope-is-the-thing-with-feathers-314.

JUNE 11

"Give us this day our daily bread" (Matthew 6:11, KJV).

My friends and I—and maybe a sister or two—found a corner of the barn to set up our playhouse. We used wooden crates of different sizes for a table, chairs, and cupboards. Of course, all these came from my nan's shop. We had play dishes and improvised with empty cans for other things.

We learned from our mothers by watching them, so we pretended to prepare meals for our children. We used sand, mud, grass, and whatever else we gathered from the yard. We mixed and we stirred. Someone was picked to be the mother, and the rest of us were the children.

These were carefree, innocent days as we play-acted what we observed from adults. We had everything we needed. God made sure our daily bread was supplied. But I wonder what that means to me today as an adult.

Nowadays, I can make bread—usually around four loaves or so. That's enough to last us a week or two, if we don't have company. Do you think that's the bread that Jesus was talking about? Could it be that God was talking about bread from Heaven? Give us this day our daily nourishment from God. Give us this day what we need in grace, strength, joy, faith, hope, and love. You see, the nourishment we received yesterday was for yesterday's living. God's mercies (favour and blessings) are new every day.

The next time you pray *"Give us this day our daily bread,"* remember exactly what you're asking and be thankful for all that God gives.

Father God, sometimes I repeat this prayer without thinking about the words. I want to remember what it means and be thankful for all that You give. Amen.

JUNE 12

"Though he brings grief, he also shows compassion because of the greatness of his unfailing love" (Lamentations 3:32, NLT).

They call it grief—this pain I have in my heart, soul, and entire being. Sometimes it's so tangible, I think it has form and substance. If you came near me, you could even touch it.

Grief is such a short word. It only has five letters. But it carries so great a pain. We try to describe it, but we can't. How can such a small word convey the depth and pain of someone's loss? It should be a long word, like "supercalifragilisticexpialidocious," which is a nonsensical word meaning something very great.

Let me tell you about another short word: "grace." It too has only five letters. But it covers a boundless amount of pain. Whether short or long, there is no limit to God's grace.

I heard a song that went, "No sorrow is greater than the grace of God." I thought about that word "grace," as it has come to mean a great deal to me. I discovered that although grief is great, grace is greater. *"Now the God of all grace, who called you to His eternal glory in Christ Jesus, will personally restore, establish, strengthen, and support you after you have suffered a little"* (1 Peter 5:10, HCSB).

Father God, You alone know the extent of someone's grief. When their heart is broken, Your heart is broken too. When they have no words except "help," You understand. When they need something to cover the grief, You provide the grace. Amen.

JUNE 13

"I press on toward the goal to win the prize for which God has called me heavenward in Christ Jesus" (Philippians 3:14).

I put one foot on the home base and held on to the bat with two hands. I watched the pitcher wind up and then throw the ball. I swung the bat, hitting the ball straight up the middle of the road. "Run," someone shouted. "Run!"

We called it baseball, but it was more like softball. We used a soft type of rubber ball instead of a hard baseball, and we used a piece of wood from Dad's sawmill instead of a normal bat. We put flat rocks on the ground to mark the bases. The children—young ones and older ones—would gather around. Before the game would start, we'd form two teams by choosing the captains and then the rest of the players.

The aim was very basic: hit the ball past home base and run as fast as you can and as far around as you can. If you made it to home base before one of your team struck out, then you scored a point. There was a lot of shouting, a lot of running, and a lot of cheering. Sometimes there were even disagreements. Most important, though, we played together on a team and had a lot of fun. We played until it was too dark to see the ball or until our parents called us home.

Choices are a part of life. There will be a time when you have to choose to be on God's team or the world's team. Whose team are you on? Joshua 24:15 says, *"… choose for yourselves this day whom you will serve … "*

Father God, thank You for giving me the freedom of choice. I'm so grateful to be on Your team. Help me to run towards the prize that You promised—a home in Heaven with You. Amen.

JUNE 14

"While he was at Bethany, in the house of Simon the leper, as he sat at the table, a woman came having an alabaster jar of ointment of pure nard—very costly. She broke the jar and poured it over his head" (Mark 14:3, WEB).

I have a collection of perfume bottles of all shapes and sizes. I don't use the perfume anymore, but I like the unique shapes and colours of the bottles. I often wondered what the alabaster jar of perfume mentioned in the verse above looked like.

I did some research and discovered that alabaster was a rich, marble-like type of stone often found in Israel. It was used in the decorations of Solomon's Temple. As well, it was used to make jars and boxes to hold expensive perfume, because it kept the perfume pure and unspoiled. Once the jar was sealed with wax, the perfume scent would be preserved. Sometimes, the neck of the jar would be broken to pour out the oil.

The perfume in the alabaster jar was spikenard or pure nard. According to online resources, it's a flowering plant of the honeysuckle family that grows in the Himalayas of Nepal, China, and India. The plant is now on the endangered species list. Even back in Jesus's time, the perfume was very expensive and would have cost the woman a year's wages. This was a costly gift coming from a heart of love. This was her way of worshipping her Lord.

I asked myself, "What is my alabaster jar, and would I offer it to the Lord? Is it a possession or is it my heart?"

Father God, when I read about this woman's sacrifice, I think that I often fall short of giving so extravagantly. I want to worship You like that. Help me to have a heart of love. Amen.

JUNE 15

"Don't lay up treasures for yourselves on the earth, where moth and rust consume, and where thieves break through and steal" (Matthew 6:19, WEB).

They built the old Orange Lodge on the ocean side of the road with the back of the building on a rock cliff facing the ocean. The rock cliff was almost straight down to the beach and looked like one piece of smooth rock all the way down. We called this rock "The Scrape." As children, we often navigated our way down the rock to the beach. It was fun exploring, and you never knew what you'd find on the beach. Because it's a small beach, we had to go at low tide.

We imagined it to be a place where pirates landed to bury their treasure, but we never found any gold, coins, or jewellery. What we found was a treasure only valuable to us—sea urchins, mussel shells, and driftwood. Pieces of old fishing nets and an assortment of sea life often washed up on the beach. This was our treasure.

Children's treasures are often a collection of things that have very little or no value to adults—worthless things to the world. But are they really worthless? Just look around you. What treasures have you missed? Have you seen the sunsets lately? Have you played a game with a friend? Have you laughed until you cried? Have you noticed the bright yellow of a dandelion? Treasures are all around us.

The dearest treasures come not in costly items of gold and silver but in what the Lord gives us: *"a rich store of salvation, wisdom and knowledge; the fear of the Lord is the key to this treasure"* (Isaiah 33:6b).

Father in Heaven, thank You for the fun I had exploring for childhood treasures. Most of all, thank You for all the priceless treasures You give us. Help me, Lord, to value what is important and to store up that kind of treasure. Amen.

JUNE 16

"Is it a time for you yourselves to be living in your paneled houses, while this house remains a ruin?" (Haggai 1:4)

What are my priorities today? I asked this of myself as I ate breakfast and enjoyed a cup of coffee. The list of things to do was long.

We were sorting and bagging all of the household and personal items in my mother-in-law's house. It comes to seventy years' worth of stuff, and it's a challenge to know what to do with everything. I still get meals, do laundry, walk the dog, talk to my family, video chat, visit my mother-in-law at the home every day, and shop for groceries. I'm sure there are things I'm leaving out, but you get the picture. It's a very busy time.

But I asked myself what was the most important thing to do today. My top priority is always to spend time with God before the day goes crazy. God must be first. My prayer each morning is for energy and strength for the day. I ask God to order my day, to help me set priorities, to help me to do the things I need to do and leave the rest. That's my prayer these days.

In Haggai, we learn that the Jews had returned from captivity but had forgotten about God. They were busy with their own lives and building their own houses. God sent the prophet to remind them to put God first. They were supposed to be rebuilding the Temple, but they didn't make it a priority. God demands that we put Him first in everything. In our busy world, it's easy to be too busy for God. Make a commitment to put God first and then ask Him to help you do just that.

Father God, I need You to be first and to bring joy and fulfillment to my life. Help me to live the life You want me to live. Amen.

JUNE 17

"... they came to a certain village where a woman named Martha welcomed him into her home" (Luke 10:38, NLT).

"There they made him a supper" (John 12:2a, KJV).

I completed grade ten at Arnold's Cove, but I wouldn't be returning the next year. My parents thought it best for me to attend another high school farther away, so I moved to Musgravetown and lived with my Aunt Stella, Uncle Al, and cousins Judy, Joan, and Renee. I shared a room with my cousin Renee, and the twins shared another room. We had so much fun and laughter that year. I enjoyed living there, and I loved their friendship.

Aunt Stella always made me feel welcome. She cooked delicious meals, gave me a comfortable place to sleep, and shared a laugh now and then. There was always room for one more at the supper table and for one more to sleep over. Aunt Stella turned no one away. She welcomed visiting family, the less fortunate, and the stranger.

The Bible tells us that from time to time, Jesus stayed at Mary and Martha's home in Bethany. This must have been a special place for Jesus. Just as Aunt Stella's was a special place for me, these friends were like family to Jesus. They welcomed Him and loved Him. He ate meals with them and rested there. Their home was a refuge for Him. Is your home like that?

Father God, thank You for our home and plenty of food to eat. Help me be a person who wholeheartedly shares my home and food with visitors. I want my home to be a place of welcome and rest for You and others. Amen.

JUNE 18

*"The people who walk in darkness will see a great light.
For those who live in a land of deep darkness, a light will shine"*
(Isaiah 9:2, NLT).

In the 1980s in Newfoundland, our government funded the building of several large hydroponic greenhouses in the city of Mount Pearl. It was thought that they could grow food all year around with artificial lighting. Residents living around that area complained that the grow lights were too bright in the night hours. The massive greenhouses shone through the dark winter night like giant spotlights on the city.

Light is powerful. It breaks through to the darkest corners. The Bible tells us in Luke 2:32a that several days after Jesus was born, Simeon prophesied that *"He is a light to reveal God to the nations"* (NLT). John 8:12 tells us that the light has come, and that light is Jesus: *"Jesus spoke to the people once more and said, 'I am the light of the world. If you follow me, you won't have to walk in darkness, because you will have the light that leads to life."* (NLT)

In Ephesians 5:8, Paul says, *"For once you were full of darkness, but now you have light from the Lord. So live as people of light!"* (NLT). First John 1:7 tells us, *"But if we are living in the light, as God is in the light, then we have fellowship with each other, and the blood of Jesus, his Son, cleanses us from all sin"* (NLT).

We are called out of the darkness of this world to live in light. Just as the citizens of Mount Pearl lived in the light of the greenhouses, we are called to live in God's light.

Father God, thank You for being the light of my life. May Your light shine through me so that others living in the darkness will see it. Amen.

JUNE 19

"Now faith is confidence in what we hope for and assurance about what we do not see" (Hebrews 11:1).

Is faith measurable? If so, how would you measure faith? God doesn't say you have to have a litre of faith, or a bushel of faith, or a ton of faith. He just says to have faith.

In Mark 11:22, Jesus tells the disciples to *"Have faith."* He doesn't quantify it. He just says to have faith. He does say in Matthew 17:20 that, *"... if you have faith as small as a mustard seed, you can say to this mountain, 'Move from here to there,' and it will move ..."* If a mustard seed of faith in God can move a mountain, what could you do with a sunflower seed of faith, or the largest seed in the world?

"For by this [kind of] faith the men of old gained [divine] approval" (Hebrews 11:2, AMP). They put their faith into action. Faith is measured by the results. So if you want to know how much faith they had, look at the outcomes and what was achieved.

> By faith these people overthrew kingdoms, ruled with justice, and received what God had promised them. They shut the mouths of lions, quenched the flames of fire, and escaped death by the edge of the sword. Their weakness was turned to strength. They became strong in battle and put whole armies to flight. Women received their loved ones back again from death. (Hebrews 11:33–35, NLT)

How much faith did they have? You tell me how much faith.

Father God, my faith at best is small. Please help me to put what faith I have into action. Amen.

JUNE 20

"I am a rose of Sharon, a lily of the valleys" (Song of Solomon 2:1).

I love flowers. Flowers touch my heart and make me smile. I love to see them grow in the garden, and I look forward to the first open buds of the season.

Why is Jesus called the rose of Sharon? Does this flower even look like the roses we know today? Maybe it's more like the wild roses. Do you remember the old-fashioned ones that our grandmothers grew in their gardens? Sharon is actually a place name in the Bible, meaning a field, plain, or valley. Maybe this type of rose grew there.

Of all the flowers that God made, most would agree that the rose is the loveliest. It's among the top ones that I prefer. Jesus's character could be compared to the qualities of the rose. It has a toughness but also tenderness. The rose, like Jesus, wears thorns. As well as being the most beautiful of all flowers, the rose is the most common. You can find it wherever you go, in all countries. It's the worldwide flower; it belongs to everybody.

But the Saviour also calls Himself the lily of the valley. What can we learn from this name? The plant has little white bells arranged in a row on a slim stalk. They almost hide under the broad green leaves. These delicate flowers can be compared to the humility of Christ. You wouldn't expect these plants to be hardy and thrive in spots where most other things don't. The lily also has many medicinal qualities. All parts of the plant contain a chemical similar to the drug digitalis, which is a heart stimulant. All these images remind us of the qualities of Jesus, and He's available to everyone and can change our hearts.

Father God, thank You for Your sacrifice on the cross and for giving me a new heart. Amen.

JUNE 21

"Eat honey, my son, for it is good; honey from the comb is sweet to your taste" (Proverbs 24:13).

"Oh, how I wish I had a bowl of chocolate icing to enjoy!" This was my childish way of thinking. Usually, I only had a scraping of the bowl or a spoon to lick, and most times, I had to share with my sisters.

One day I visited my Aunt Shirley next door, and as luck would have it, she had just baked a chocolate cake. She was in the process of mixing the most delicious looking chocolate icing. I waited around until she finished. Lo and behold, she offered me a taste. Hmm, it was delectable. The icing melted in my mouth, and my tongue was happy.

After she decorated the cake, it looked good enough for a picture on the cover of the *Herald*. Lucky for me, she didn't use all of the icing. There was a whole lot left in the bowl, and I eyed it hungrily. Much to my surprise and joy, Aunt Shirley said to me, "Would you like to have the bowl?" This was music to my ears. It was the most icing I'd ever eaten at one time. I shared a little with my aunt, but I had a good portion. It was sweet and chocolatey. But I ate too much and felt a little sick. I think she cured my craving for this tasty treat—at least for a time.

A childhood dream of mine was to be able to eat a huge amount of chocolate icing, but when that happened, I was nauseous afterwards. I know now that it wasn't good for me. The Bible tells us in 1 Corinthians 10:23, *"'Everything is permissible,' but not everything is helpful. 'Everything is permissible,' but not everything builds up"* (HCSB).

Father God, thank You for all the sweet and good things You have provided in my life. Help me to remember that not everything is good for me, and too much of a good thing is sometimes too much. Amen.

JUNE 22

"Those who are wise will shine like the brightness of the heavens, and those who lead many to righteousness, like the stars for ever and ever" (Daniel 12:3).

It's the day we get our report cards. I wonder what mine will say. I hope I get good marks and a lot of gold stars this year.

Do you remember getting report cards from school like this? We were graded with percentage marks, As and Bs, and stars. There were different coloured stars for different marks. Those were the good old days, when you knew exactly what your marks and grades were in school. These days you only get a report with a few numbers and comments.

I was thinking that stars on our report cards would be like the stars on our crowns in Heaven that we sometimes sing about. But the Bible doesn't specifically say anything about stars on crowns. It does say in the verse above that the righteous who win souls will shine like the stars forever.

Revelation 12:1 talks about a woman wearing a crown of twelve stars. Someday we'll find out what the meaning of the stars is. The most important thing is to work hard at whatever you're doing, whether in school, at work, or at home. The Bible tells us, *"And whatever you do, work heartily, as for the Lord and not for men"* (Colossians 3:23, WEB). Our goal should be to influence and teach others about God's love for them and, subsequently, lead them to Jesus.

Father God in Heaven, thank You for your promise of Heaven. I don't know if I'll shine as the stars, but please help me to do everything as though doing it directly for You. Amen.

JUNE 23

"With trumpets and sound of cornet make a joyful noise before the Lord, the King" (Psalm 98:6, KJV).

I was around thirteen years old when my Grandfather Rowe presented me with a shiny, new brass cornet to play in the Salvation Army band. There were a few people there who could play, and one of them offered to give lessons to the younger folks who wanted to learn. I was excited to learn, especially since I had my own instrument. Several of my friends took lessons too, and we all practised together. Just learning to blow into the mouthpiece so that a sound came out was the first step. After many lessons and much practice, I was able to play a song. It was so rewarding!

Pretty soon, we were invited to sit in the band and play along where we could. It was a learning experience just being in the band, and we tried hard to follow the more experienced players. I loved to play and make the sounds, especially in the upbeat hymns. The Bible tells us to play instruments and shout joyfully before the Lord.

Imagine the sound when King David said *"… four thousand are to praise the Lord with the musical instruments I have provided for that purpose"* (1 Chronicles 23:5).

We are to praise the Lord always and in every way we can. I've heard it said that "When the praises go up, the blessings come down." It's hard to pout and praise at the same time. Be joyful and praise God using all your talents.

Father in Heaven, thank You for the opportunity I had to learn the cornet and play in the band. I want to always praise You with all that I am. Amen.

JUNE 24

"Only fools say in their hearts, 'There is no God.' They are corrupt, and their actions are evil; not one of them does good!"
(Psalm 53:1, NLT)

Who or what is a fool? Webster's Dictionary says it's a person lacking in judgement. It doesn't say that the person is lacking in intelligence. Many fools are highly learned. My husband says they lack common sense.

In Psalm 14:1, the Bible describes a fool as someone who says there is no God. Why do they not believe in God? Are they covering up some dark secret in themselves, or are they making an excuse to continue in the same selfish and sinful lifestyle? Without God, there would be no restraint of the worst of the wicked sinners in the world. You might think the world is bad now, but just think what it could be like without God: no morals, no order, and no end to lawlessness.

Proverbs 12:15a says, *"Fools think their own way is right"* (NLT). Evolutionists and scientists are always looking for ways to explain away the creation story and how we came to exist. They talk about stars, solar systems, black holes, and nebulas, as though somehow life evolved from elements in space. But I ask you, "Who made the beginning elements of matter and life?" Man can make something out of something, but only God can make something out of nothing: *"By faith we understand that the universe was formed at God's command, so that what is seen was not made out of what was visible"* (Hebrews 11:3); *"I am the Lord! I stretched out the heavens; I put the earth on its foundations and gave breath to humans"* (Zechariah 12:1, CEV). Genesis 1:1 says, *"In the beginning God ..."*

Father God, I know that You alone are the Creator of all things. Turn the foolish people around so that they believe in You, trust in You, and give their lives to You. Amen.

JUNE 25

"Do not gloat over me, my enemy! Though I have fallen, I will rise. Though I sit in darkness, the Lord will be my light" (Micah 7:8).

Cancer. There was a time when I didn't know much about cancer, and I didn't know many people with cancer. Since I've gotten older, that has changed.

I've learned about breast cancer, prostate cancer, bowel cancer, kidney cancer, brain cancer, lymphoma, and uterine cancer. I've learned more than I wish to know. I've never known so many people before who died with or are battling cancer. I've lost friends, church family, coworkers, and my dad to cancer. Make no mistake, it's a battle. We throw everything at it. Cancer is fought by young and old, rich and poor, ordinary and famous—there is no distinction.

The Bible doesn't specifically mention cancer, as it wasn't known at that time; however, it does describe many diseases that could have been cancer. When Jesus was on earth, He healed all manner of diseases in people that could have included various types of cancer.

In our lifetime, we will experience health and sickness, life and death. We'll have many troubles of all kinds, but also many joys. I take comfort in knowing that my life doesn't end with death on earth. I have a hope to live eternally with God in Heaven. When I'm down and experiencing some of the hard times, I recite the verse above, and my spirit and resolve are strengthened.

Father God, thank You for Your promise to be my light through all of the dark times in my life. I can say to the enemy "Do not gloat over me." Amen.

JUNE 26

> *"At the moment I have all I need—and more! I am generously supplied with the gifts you sent me with Epaphroditus. They are a sweet-smelling sacrifice that is acceptable and pleasing to God"* (Philippians 4:18, NLT).

I drove the car into the driveway. I was a little tired, and my mind was busily going over the agenda and discussions of the meeting I'd just left.

I stopped, turned off the motor, and reached for my bag and papers. As I got out of the car, I noticed that the sky was almost dark. Everything was silent and still. I stood there taking in the quietness of the evening. After a few moments, a sweet fragrance filled the air; it was very pleasant to my senses. I breathed in and wondered where it came from.

I looked around the garden. The further I walked down the driveway, the stronger the fragrance. I realized it was coming from all the flowering trees in my neighbourhood and in our yard. There was no wind, and the air was heavy with the beautiful scent. I felt surrounded and very relaxed by it. I don't think any spa could compete with it. It cleared my mind from the busy thoughts and made me stop and appreciate my surroundings.

I thought about what the Bible says about a sweet-smelling sacrifice, given freely and not out of guilt or obligation. The Lord is pleased when we give from our heart and love for Him. It is to Him a fragrant offering. My thoughts went to God and the many blessings He has given me. I hope that my life can be a sweet fragrance of the life of Christ, and that I can influence others to follow Him.

Father God, just as the fragrance of the fruit trees was sweet-smelling to me and very pleasant, our prayers and praise are sweet and pleasing to You. Help me to remember to give You thanks in all things. Amen.

JUNE 27

> *"Therefore, since we are surrounded by such a great cloud of witnesses, let us throw off everything that hinders and the sin that so easily entangles. And let us run with perseverance the race marked out for us"* (Hebrews 12:1).

I remember when I was young, we had plastic bubble blowers shaped like pipes. We'd dip the pipe into the bubble solution and then blow into the pipe to have the bubbles come out at the end. When we used up all the bubble solution, we'd make our own from dish detergent. Most children I know love to blow bubbles and then run around to catch them. According to the Internet, the first patented bubble blowers date back to the 1920s, but references to bubble blowing go back centuries. Since then, many children have enjoyed this experience.

I liked to see the bubbles all around me in a cloud. As the light hit them, they shone with many different colours. When a big one would float by, I'd reach out my hand to catch it. Sometimes, it would even stay on my hand for a few minutes.

The verse above talks about being surrounded by a cloud of witnesses (figuratively speaking), referring to the saints of old and faithful believers that have already passed. I like to imagine that the ones I know are there watching and cheering me on. All of us should live every day as if we could actually see them there and hear their encouragement. We can be inspired by their confident example so that we can live faithfully and run the race for God. Never forget that you're not alone in your walk for Christ. Be encouraged and run your race with energy and determination.

Father in Heaven, thank You for this encouragement to persevere through troubles and to remember the faithful lives of the people from the past. Help me to live faithfully and run the race. Amen.

JUNE 28

"For the Holy Spirit will teach you at that time what you should say" (Luke 12:12).

Newfoundlanders love to talk about the weather more than anything else—even more than politics. In the morning, noon, and night we check the weather forecast on our televisions, radios, and smart devices. In between these times, we talk about it with our family, friends, and coworkers. This can be verified by the many weather phrases we use: *The fog is as thick as pea soup. It's a mauzy day. A nor'easter is blowing in. The sky is as black as your boot. The sun is splitting the rocks. Some day on clothes. It's blowing a gale.*

I thought that no one talked about weather as much as Newfoundlanders, but I was mistaken. I was surprised when I went to Florida for the winter to hear so many conversations about the famous topic. I wondered why this was the case. After some thought, I realized that the weather is a safe subject. It's a conversation starter when people are reluctant to share anything personal or controversial.

Some topics bring out emotional responses, and questions might be seen as too personal, so we stick to "What's the weather like there today?" Instead of asking about the weather, practise asking more direct questions about someone's day-to-day life. Sometimes it's just a matter of asking the right questions. Often you'll discover that they're just waiting for someone to care enough to ask and listen. What's wrong with asking, "Is your heart right with God? Does your soul belong to Him?"

Father God, help me to ask the right questions and have more meaningful conversations with the people I meet. Amen.

JUNE 29

"For God watches how people live; he sees everything they do"
(Job 34:21, NLT).

My cousin Bonnie and I wanted to hang out at the local snack bar and pool hall. As well, we wanted to stay out a bit later than normal, as it seemed that our friends had more freedom than we did. So I told Mom that my aunt was okay with it, and my cousin told her mother that my mother was okay with it. Well, Aunt Fronie saw through the whole lie and we were both grounded. Now we couldn't get out at all.

Aunt Fronie seemed to have a knack of discovering our true motives and actions. She always knew what we were up to. I'm sure she had spies everywhere. She kept her eyes on all us first cousins when we were together in Chance Cove. Her all-seeing eyes remind me of 2 Chronicles 16:9a, which says, *"The eyes of the Lord search the whole earth"* (NLT),

Just like Aunt Fronie had her eyes on us teenagers, the eyes of the Lord see everything throughout the earth. Nothing is hidden from Him. God sees our every move. He sees our true intentions and motives. You can lie to others, and you can lie to yourself, but you can't lie to God.

Be honest with yourself and God. Don't be afraid to tell Him everything. He already knows anyway, but He wants you to talk to Him about it. Trust God to take care of what concerns you. He knows all the things that affect you, and He knows your needs. He will guide your choices and give you peace of mind over all your circumstances. Talk to God today.

Father God, when I was a child, I learned many lessons. Today I'm still learning. Please help me to be true and honest in all my living. Amen.

JUNE 30

"And the blood of his Son Jesus washes all our sins away"
(1 John 1:7b, CEV).

"… he is able also to save them to the uttermost"
(Hebrews 7:25a, KJV).

This is the time of year for sprucing up the house. There are always things to do around the house, and it seems like we just finish painting a room and it's time to start another one.

One year we bought a cheaper paint on sale to paint the kitchen. But the paint we chose didn't cover very well. After applying three coats, I gave up. We usually buy paint that covers with one coat, and in some rooms if the colour is quite different from the previous one, we may need two coats of paint. Well, I learned my lesson that year, and I'll be sure to have better paint for the next project.

Since we're talking about full coverage, one of my pet peeves is not having the sheets tucked in at the bottom of the bed. I like to have the sheets and blankets covering me from top to bottom and tucked in at the foot. If I have a restless night from tossing and turning, I don't like to wake up in the morning with the bedcovers on the floor!

As the Bible tells us, Jesus's blood fully covers our sins. Don't doubt your salvation when you sincerely ask God to forgive you. God looks at us through the purity and sacrifice of His Son. When you're covered by Jesus's blood, you have full coverage. If Jesus says your sins are forgiven, you are forgiven indeed. God saves to the uttermost.

Father God, help me to remember that I don't need to worry about my salvation, because I have full coverage. Help me to spread the word of Your amazing love and grace. Amen.

JULY 1

"God reigns over the nations" (Psalm 47:8a).

"For the kingdom is the Lord's: and he is the governor among the nations" (Psalm 22:28, KJV).

On Canada Day, we celebrate our country. We celebrate being part of a great democratic nation. As Canadians, we're proud of our heritage. On this Canada Day, we're enjoying the day at Kona Beach Park. It's a sunny, warm day, and families are here to participate in the planned events. There are lots of fun activities for the kids to enjoy, and a variety of food and treats. After dark, there will be colourful fireworks to light the sky.

Do we give our country much thought? How did we get to where we are now? What can we learn from the mistakes of the past? What does the future look like for us? We have a lot to be thankful for in this part of the world: affluence, medical care, and access to education. We enjoy many freedoms that were hard fought for in World Wars. But are we free from immorality? All sorts of crimes and detestable acts are being committed.

The Bible tells us that God will judge the nations just as He will individuals. Psalm 110:6a says, *"He will judge the nations."* Billy Graham said, "Our greatest need—as individuals and as a nation is to turn to God and seek His forgiveness and mercy."[8]

Pray for our country and our leaders. In Romans 13:1b, Paul tells us, *"For all authority comes from God, and those in positions of authority have been placed there by God"* (NLT).

Father God, on this Canada Day, I'm more aware than ever that You are the ruler of nations. Thank You for this great country. Help us, Lord, to become a God-fearing and God-following nation. Amen.

---

[8] "Billy Graham 'My Answer,'" Billy Graham Evangelistic Association, accessed October 12, 2025, https://billygraham.org/answers/does-god-punish-whole-nations-as-well-as-individuals.

JULY 2

"If one of you is carrying some meat from a holy sacrifice in his robes and his robe happens to brush against some bread or stew, wine or olive oil, or any other kind of food, will it also become holy? The priests replied, 'No'" (Haggai 2:12, NLT).

If something clean brushes against something dirty, will the dirty object become clean, or will the clean object become dirty? Good question, isn't it? We can ask the same question of holiness. Will it rub off or not?

Try brushing against a dusty car door before getting in. You're sure to get the dust from the car on your coat or your clean black pants. Meanwhile, the car is still dirty. Just like the verse above says, holiness will not rub off on others, but contamination sure will.

Holiness means to belong to God. Easton's Bible Dictionary explains that personal holiness is a work of gradual development carried on under many difficulties. The Bible gives us many warnings to persist in prayer.

If your attitude is wrong, if your daily living is filled with wrong choices, if you harbour those little sins and are continually negative in your words and towards others, then you're likely not practising holy living. Your contamination will rub off on others.

Don't think that someone else's holiness will rub off on you or get you into Heaven. Holiness doesn't come from attending church either. Only repentance (being sorry for your sins and turning from them) puts you on the path to holiness.

Father God, help me to not be contaminated by the world around me. I want to live as You would have me live. Help me to be aware of these things and to always keep praying to make the right choices. Amen.

JULY 3

"... he spit on the ground, made some mud with the saliva, and put it on the man's eyes" (John 9:6).

One day as a child, I went raspberry picking with my mom and dad. The field was just off a wood's road near a local town. Dad found a good spot with lots of raspberry canes. It seemed like the perfect spot.

Unfortunately, while I was picking berries amongst the tall canes, I was stung by a wasp right between my eyes on the bridge of my nose. It hurt so much that all I could do was cry. Someone said "Get some black mud." Before I knew what was happening, I was wearing a blob of black mud on my nose. It was supposed to help with the pain and stinging, but it didn't look pretty.

It was such a painful experience that even now I carry around ointment for bites and stings. As soon as I get the first little bite, out comes the tube of Afterbite or Benadryl for the swelling and itching. When these things don't help, I mix baking soda with a little water to make a paste, which actually helps a lot.

Did you know that Jesus used mud when He healed the eyes of a blind man? He could have cured the man's eyesight without it, as He is God. But some people need something tangible that they can touch and see in order to believe. Why did He use the mud? I don't have the answer to that. But the Lord uses whatever methods He chooses to use to help someone believe and to bring Him glory. Restored health by any means—whether ordinary or miraculous—is always a gift from God.

Father in Heaven, thank You for all the common things You provide that cure our ailments. Help me to see You in the simple as well as in the magnificent things of the world. Amen.

JULY 4

"He covers the sky with clouds; he supplies the earth with rain and makes grass grow on the hills" (Psalm 147:8).

"He provides rain for the earth; he sends water on the countryside" (Job 5:10).

Is there anything more refreshing than summer rain? I love the brightness and the smell of the grass after a rain. It's like a brand-new canvas of colour that the artist just completed. When we'd camp in the summer, I'd love the sound of the rain on the roof of our camper. Sometimes it was like a loud crescendo of raindrops, and then it would taper off like a soft tinkle on a piano.

Sometimes in the evening while sitting on our patio, we can see the dark thunder clouds forming just below us in the rear of our property. When we see them coming, we get everything under cover. We can hear the thunder rumbling towards us, then we see the lightning streaking across the sky. When it starts, it's a downpour. Little rivers of water flow down our driveway to the garden. Pretty soon, the storm is over and the rain stops.

I think about the rain and how the earth would be parched without it. We wouldn't be able to grow food or have fresh water to drink. In fact, life couldn't exist without the rain. This life-giving water is a gift from God that we often take for granted.

The Bible tells us in James 1:17a that *"Every good and perfect gift is from above, coming down from the Father of the heavenly lights ... "* The perfect gift was God's Son, Jesus Christ. He came so that those who believed in Him could have eternal life. This is the gospel message: Jesus gave His life to pay the price for our sins.

Father God, thank You for all Your gifts to us. But most of all, thank You for Your Son, Jesus. Help me to never take this for granted. I want to let others know about this gift of salvation. Amen.

JULY 5

"But we had to celebrate and be glad, because this brother of yours ... was lost and is found" (Luke 15:32).

I went outside to check on the puppy, and he wasn't there. I felt a sense of panic rising inside of me. Somehow he'd gotten out of the little wire pen in the backyard and was missing. A Pomeranian puppy was on the loose. I dropped everything to look. I called out to Terry to help.

This was such a small puppy. He only weighed a pound or two and was just three months old. How far could he go? There were so many dangers: lots of traffic to run him over, bigger dogs to pounce on him, and strangers to take him. Terry and I frantically looked everywhere. He went in one direction and I went in another, searching in driveways and yards.

Finally, I saw a little boy coming down the street towards me with something in his arms. When he got up close, he held out the puppy and said, "I found him on my street and I was bringing him back." I was so happy and relieved. I thanked the boy, who was being very careful with my puppy. I felt like giving him a big hug and shouting for joy.

Can you imagine our relief and excitement? At last, my puppy was home, safe and sound. In the story of the prodigal son, the father felt even more relieved. He was filled with gratitude and rejoiced that his son had returned home. This is how God feels when we come back to Him. Jesus tells us in Luke 15:10, *"In the same way, I tell you, there is rejoicing in the presence of the angels of God over one sinner who repents."*

Father in Heaven, thank You for showing us how much You love us. Thank You that there is much joy in Heaven when a person finds their way back to You. Amen.

JULY 6

"Then Moses, Aaron, Nadab, Abihu, and the seventy elders of Israel climbed up the mountain. There they saw the God of Israel" (Exodus 24:9–10a, NLT).

Moses, Aaron, Nadab, Abihu and seventy leaders went to the mountain. There they saw God! All of them saw. All of them ate and drank with God.

Then God told Moses and Joshua to come further up the mountain to get the stone tablets of commandments to give to the people. According to online resources, to reach the summit of Mount Sinai on foot takes about two and half hours. Moses told the leaders to stay there and wait for him to come back and to consult with Aaron if they had a problem. Moses and Joshua were gone from the others for forty days and forty nights.

Exodus 24 tells us that's all the time it took for Aaron, the leaders, and the people to turn away from God. They forgot the covenant they'd made at the base of the mountain. They forgot their mountain experience with God when they ate and drank with Him. In forty days, they forgot their God and built an idol out of their gold.

Obedience to God seemed easy when they were on the mountain in God's presence. As soon as Moses was out of their sight again, the grumbling started. Their human weaknesses took over. Are we like this? Do we recognize God as being good only when things are rosy? When we face uncertainties and troubles, do we grumble against God instead of waiting for His direction and timing?

Father God, we're so quick sometimes to forget who You are and what You've done for us. Help us to be obedient to You and to always be on course with Your plans for us. Amen.

JULY 7

"As Jesus was walking beside the Sea of Galilee, he saw two brothers ... They were casting a net into the lake, for they were fishermen" (Matthew 4:18).

The dark green motorboat stopped just outside the narrow opening to the cove. The sea rolled lightly, and the little punt bobbed slightly in the water. The boat belonged to two brothers from the town. They fished together every day, and sometimes one or two of their sons helped when they were out of school. It looked like they were jigging, probably for squid.

When I was growing up in Chance Cove, the main occupation there was fishing. There were many fishermen, and in almost all of the boats, you'd find family members. Brothers fished together. Fathers fished with their sons, and sometimes wives fished with their husbands. Fishing was a family business.

They made and mended nets. They repaired their boats and tuned up the engines. They cleaned, salted, and dried the fish. They shared the work and the profit from the sale of the fish. Families worked together out of necessity and convenience. You could depend on your family during the good times and the rough times. They were resourceful people of strength and integrity.

Do you wonder why Jesus was drawn to the fishermen? Sometimes God calls ordinary people for extraordinary purposes.

Father God, thank You for the fishermen and families of my hometown who worked and fished together. Help us all to work together for You, no matter our background or past experiences. Amen.

JULY 8

"... and [she] extends her hands to the needy" (Proverbs 31:20b).

"Jesus, who rescues us from the coming wrath"
(1 Thessalonians 1:10b).

"Hurry up! Blow up the big tube. It's a perfect day for swimming."

My cousins and I were spending the day with our family at Bellevue Beach Park. All we wanted to do was swim, play, and have a picnic. I couldn't wait to get into the water. We had a truck tire tube to float on and play with.

We took turns playing and floating around on the big tube. When it was my turn, I jumped on the tube. *Plop!* I went right through the hole and down into the water. It was over my head and I swallowed some. I couldn't get to the surface, and I couldn't breathe. It all happened so fast that I could have drowned very quickly, because I went right out of sight. Then I felt someone's hands on me, lifting me out of the water. My older cousin Maxine was there, saw what was happening, and pulled me out. She may not even remember today what she did, but she definitely saved me from drowning.

I was scared, but not enough to stay away from the water. In no time at all, I was back in. It didn't seem like a big deal. When I think about what could have happened, I realize how close to death I came. God made sure there was someone there to rescue me. Maxine acted quickly and was God's hands that day. How many more times has God provided an escape for me? Too numerous to count, I'm sure.

Father in Heaven, just as Maxine rescued me from drowning at Bellevue Beach Park, thank You for rescuing me from the eternal punishment promised to those who don't believe in You. Thank You for forgiveness. Amen.

JULY 9

"The Lord wraps himself in light as with a garment; he stretches out the heavens like a tent and lays the beams of his upper chambers on the waters" (Psalm 104:2–3a).

One year when my father was working near Avondale, the family camped for the entire summer by a river just outside of town. Several families with fathers working for the same company camped there as well. There were travel trailers and hard top campers. Four girls around the same age slept in a large tent. I was one of them, and we pitched our tent on a field not far from the river. We had a lot of fun that summer and slept pretty well in our tent.

One night there was a terrible rainstorm. We woke up during the night to discover that the inside of our tent was very wet. The strong wind had blown our door open, breaking the zipper. The field was flooded—not enough to wash us into the river, but enough to make us very uncomfortable. What a night that was! Somehow, we managed to get the door fastened, and then we climbed on top of our mattresses and tried to sleep.

The next day, everything needed to dry out. The grassy field dried up in the sun, so, thankfully, we didn't have to move our tent.

This experience teaches that we're not free from storms. Our tents are fragile, and sometimes we put them in the wrong place. Psalm 104 reminds me of that night in the tent, as it speaks of a tent with the beams in the water. Our God is so great that He stretches the heavens like a tent and extends the beams to the waters of the earth. If you look out over the ocean where it meets the sky, you may see the beams reaching to the water.

Father God in Heaven, thank You for being a great God. Thank You for protecting us during the storms of nature and of life. From a thankful heart. Amen.

JULY 10

"Listen! I am standing and knocking at your door. If you hear my voice and open the door, I will come in and we will eat together" (Revelation 3:20, CEV).

Early one morning, I looked out at our back garden. The green grass had been freshly mowed the previous day, and the misty rain glistened on the short blades.

I noticed a very still robin looking intently down at the grass. Suddenly, his head dove down. He tugged and tugged until he pulled up a long earthworm. This reward for persistence and patience was his breakfast. I am amazed at their skill in finding food. The worms are beneath the surface of the ground, but the robin listens for their movement. His head tilts from side to side as he listens. Now I ask you, how much sound can an earthworm make? We have trouble listening even when someone is talking directly to us. But the robin is attuned to the tiniest sound. His life depends on listening.

I concluded long ago that the world is a noisy place. There's noise from the mechanical inventions that modern man uses. We put earphones in our ears to listen to videos, loud music, news broadcasts, podcasts, and so much more. No wonder people have a hearing problem—and not just a problem that requires hearing aids. We have a problem listening to God. How can we hear the still, small voice of God when we fill our ears with the noise of the world?

We need to have quiet time for listening to God. Put away all distractions. Turn off the noise, even if you have to wear earplugs. Focus on some scripture passage or a few verses, and then just listen. God is knocking on your heart, and He promises that when you open the door, He will join you there.

Father God, help me to have quiet time with You every day. Help me to focus on You, even when there are noises around me. Amen.

JULY 11

"So our faces are not covered. They show the bright glory of the Lord, as the Lord's Spirit makes us more and more like our glorious Lord" (2 Corinthians 3:18, CEV).

The small field outside our house was glowing yellow as the summer sun warmed the ground and caused the buttercups to bloom. I couldn't wait to go outside and run around the flowers with my friends.

When I was young, my friends and I often played in the garden by my house. Little yellow buttercups wove their way through the grass. The gardens glowed with the bright flowers, and they were so dainty and bright. I loved to look at them and pick them for bouquets. My friends and I would pick a bunch and hold them under each other's chin and say, "Do you like butter?" If your skin looked yellow, that meant that you liked butter. If the yellow of the buttercup wasn't reflected on your skin, then you didn't like butter. It didn't matter to us that on a sunny day, everyone's skin looked yellow against the bright buttercup.

As the yellow of the buttercups reflects off our skin, so God's love will reflect off us. Others will see that we have Jesus in our hearts and will say, "There's something different about that person; they have a glow about them." Who's looking at your life today? Who or what do they see reflected in you?

Do you like butter?

Father God, I'm often in situations where I'm not sure if Your likeness is seen in me. Please help me to be confident that You're always with me and living in me. Thank You for Your power in me that is greater than the one in the world. Amen.

JULY 12

"I want you to do whatever will help you serve the Lord best, with as few distractions as possible" (1 Corinthians 7:35b, NLT).

These days, it's so good to get outside in the fresh air and away from the non-natural noises in the house—especially the television. We spend a lot of time in the winter looking at and listening to the made-up productions coming from the TV. It's such an intruder into our thoughts and lives. Why can't we just turn it off and listen, think, or read? Why does the television always have to be on, loud, and opinionated? Sometimes it's rude, sometimes vulgar, sometimes selfish—actually, it's always selfish, because it demands our attention, minds, and time. Have we become a mindless people?

We're so dependent on the television and other electronic devices. Do we know how to spend time with other people in conversation or silence? What has the world become? If you let it, the noise of the world will keep you from hearing the voice of God. Our enemy is so good at distracting us that we don't even realize it until after the fact. He will try to distract the most devoted heart.

Beware of distractions. Have a close look at your daily activities and decide for yourself where the distractions are. What do you need to do to improve your attention to the Lord?

Father God, help me to recognize distractions and then to put them aside. I want to be more in tune with real people and with You. Amen.

JULY 13

"Cast your cares on the Lord and he will sustain you; he will never let the righteous be shaken" (Psalm 55:22).

My experience with water skiing took place at Thorburn Lake. It was my one and only attempt at this sport. For a whole week afterwards, the strained muscles in my legs felt rubbery, and I had trouble walking. This is how it went:

My sister Monique and I hopped into the speedboat with Dad and headed out over the cold water. We went out a little way and then got out of the boat. We wore life jackets and treaded water with our legs. She had the water skis in her hands, and I was trying to put them on. She gave me instructions: "Put one ski on first and then the other. Let the skis float a little. Keep them up straight. Sit in the water like in a reclining chair, with the footrest out." I tried to do what she was telling me, but the skis kept floating apart.

Monique held me in position, giving me instructions and encouragement. Finally, I had the skis on. We signalled my dad in the boat, and it took off at full speed. Suddenly, I lost my balance and fell into the water. We tried it repeatedly. Monique told me to make sure I let go of the pull rope when I lost my balance, so I did—many times. Finally, after several attempts, I was on top of the water, flying over the waves, with my dad at the helm of the speedboat. I was so excited, and I felt a wonderful sense of accomplishment.

Life is like that. Sometimes we experience several failures before success. However, God has promised to be with us and not let us stay down when we fall. We must not quit but keep on trying!

Father God in Heaven, thanks so much for all Your promises. Thank You for encouragement from others, and especially my sister. Amen.

JULY 14

> *"The flowers are springing up, the season of singing birds has come, and the cooing of turtledoves fills the air"* (Song of Solomon 2:12, NLT).

One time while my daughter was visiting on her summer holidays, we were sitting in the backyard enjoying the warm sunshine. It was a beautiful summer day, and we were very relaxed. Then we heard a bird singing. I said, "Listen! Do you hear that?" It was a beautiful melody. We watched the birds and tried to discover which one was singing. Was it the robin, the yellow finch, the grosbeak, the nuthatch, or some other bird that couldn't be seen? We thought it might be a robin or a colourful yellow finch, but we couldn't be sure.

Every day I heard the beautiful melody and still didn't know which bird was singing it. One day when I was in the front garden, I heard it again. I stayed still and tried to pinpoint the location of the sound. It seemed very close. Sure enough, right on the top of the tree by which I was standing, a bird was singing. I was very surprised to see that it was a plain brown sparrow.

The Bible makes special reference to the sparrow. Several verses talk about God watching over the sparrow, and in Bible times, the temple protected them. Even though sparrows were inexpensive to purchase, the Lord was concerned about their welfare. Jesus used the example of the sparrow to tell us how much God values us: *"Don't be afraid; you are worth more than many sparrows"* (Luke 12:7b). Never doubt your worth in God's eyes. He has a purpose for you. Remember, the sweetest song from a songbird is the one from the plain brown sparrow.

> *Father God, thank You for caring even for the most insignificant. Sometimes I forget that You have a purpose for me, even though I feel so unworthy. Help me to remember the sparrows' song. Amen.*

JULY 15

"Whether you turn to the right or to the left, your ears will hear a voice behind you, saying, 'This is the way; walk in it'"
(Isaiah 30:21).

One day after a very stressful week in St. John's, I found myself driving towards Pippy Park. I went to the Botanical Gardens and paid the fee to the receptionist. There were many nature exhibits inside the building, and I looked at all of them. The receptionist gave me a map of the park's trails, so I went outside and wondered which way to go. I looked at the markings on the map and went to the first garden. It was a Newfoundland medicinal plant garden. Signs on each plant explained what it was and its medicinal purpose. The lily of the valley, for example, is valued as a tonic for the heart.

I then took the trail over the hill. It was a beautiful, warm day, and I needed some time alone with God in nature. The trail wound this way and that, over boardwalks and marshy areas, through the trees and up the hills. I was totally at peace. Along the way, I sat on a bench. All I could see was a small portion of the trail, and the rest was forest. I wanted to stay and not move for a long time, but I looked at my watch and noticed that the park closed in one hour.

I walked along and came to a crossroads where there were signs telling me the name of the trails and their length. Because of the time, I took the shorter trail. Near the end, I came to the exquisite rock gardens. They were designed beautifully, with lots of interesting plants.

I left the garden feeling very relaxed and renewed. Not only the plants, but also the whole park was a tonic for my heart that day.

Father God, thank You for giving me exactly what I needed that day. I found my way around with the map, but it was You who led me there. Amen.

JULY 16

"His lightning lights up the world; the earth sees and trembles" (Psalm 97:4).

"Your thunder roared from the whirlwind; the lightning lit up the world! The earth trembled and shook" (Psalm 77:18, NLT).

The thunder rumbled and crashed as the lightning flashed across the sky just over the tops of our trees. I saw the dark clouds moving and forming together as they neared our house and garden. I watched through the window and felt the oppressive air filled with moisture. Suddenly, there was a loud thunder boom and a bang, like a gunshot. The house went silent. I knew the electricity had gone out. The lightning had hit a vital transformer that helped to deliver our power.

Several hours passed before the electricity was restored. During the wait, I enjoyed the absence of sounds from mechanical things. All I could hear was the occasional roar of thunder. As the evening darkened, I placed candles around the house and sat down with the soft light around me. This time of quiet and working with my hands was peaceful.

I worked by candlelight as I hand-stitched a block for a quilt project. I thought about what it may have been like in years past when the darkness was lit by lanterns and candles. By the dim lights, school children sat at the kitchen table to complete their schoolwork, women knit socks and mitts, and men repaired their fishing nets.

Jesus said, *"I have come as a light to shine in this dark world, so that all who put their trust in me will no longer remain in the dark"* (John 12:46, NLT). When we learn to trust Jesus, we are freed from the darkness of this world.

Father God, thank You for sending your Son, Jesus, to be a light for the world. Help me to trust in Your light and to be a light for others. Amen.

JULY 17

"Like water reflects a face, so a man's heart reflects the man"
(Proverbs 27:19, WEB).

One day during my lunch period at work, I went for a walk. It was a beautiful late-summer day. I loved to go to the park and stroll around the path there. I loved to sit on the bench and look at the little man-made pond.

I could see reflections of the surrounding houses, the church steeple, and the trees on the smooth surface of the little pond. The reflections were almost the perfect image of the real thing—the real McCoy. Once in a while, a slight breeze blew across the pond, and the reflections would have wavy lines instead of straight. They were almost perfect but not quite.

How I wish that when people look at me, they see Christ's likeness. I wish they see Christ's love for them through me. I suppose that when the winds of adversity blow on me, Christ's reflection is pretty wavy.

What do others see when they look at me? Do they see a stuck-up, snobby woman, or a woman who is confident and assured and who loves the Lord and wants to please Him?

I had a few quiet minutes by the duck pond as I stared at the scenery reflected in the water. I noticed that the clouds and wind marred the reflections. I pray that the clouds and winds of living don't mar Christ's reflection in my life. I want to reflect the qualities and character that people will recognize as Christ in me.

God, I know that my heart can only reflect Your love and goodness when I empty it of me. All of self—including self-centredness, self-absorption, and self-defensiveness—have to go. Help me to be a true reflection of Christ. Amen.

JULY 18

*"Simon Peter said, 'I'm going fishing.' 'We'll come, too,'
they all said"* (John 21:3a, NLT).

Mom woke me up at 6:30 and said, "Uncle Ed called and will be ready soon." I jumped out of bed and quickly dressed in my fishing clothes. I had some coffee and a slice of toast with jam.

I grabbed my cod fishing tackle and rod from the car, put on my short rubber boots, cap, and cotton gloves, and then walked the short distance to the wharf.

Uncle Ed helped me climb safely down the wharf's ladder to the boat. I breathed the salt air and felt relaxed. He made sure we had what we needed. Then he untied us from the pier and pushed away from the weathered wood. He sat in his chair and started the engine. It roared into life, and away we went. Uncle Ed watched the fish radar and looked around the shoreline and hills to get his markings. Then he said, "You can try here."

As the colourful fish lure descended nearly to the bottom, I felt the tugs on the line. "I got one on," I said to Uncle Ed. I braced my feet against the side of the boat and reeled in as the rod bent near the water. I let the rod go down and reeled in the slack in the line. Finally, I saw the large cod coming to the surface. Uncle Ed grabbed the gaff and pulled the fish aboard. It was a good size. We continued like this until we had our quota of five fish each. As we motored home, the eagles watched us from their rocky perches. We'd had a good day of fishing, and I hope they did too.

As I reflected on this fishing trip, I thought about the disciples. When they didn't know what to do or where to turn, they went fishing. Jesus knew when they needed His assurance and He appeared to them there by the shore.

Father God, thank You for the peaceful experiences of fishing on the ocean. Most of all, thank You for being in my life. Amen.

JULY 19

"Like cold water to a weary soul is good news from a distant land"
(Proverbs 25:25).

I saw some bees today—honey bees. I observed a bee colony in a large see-through hive on display at the Insectarium in Deer Lake. There were thousands of bees. Some were leaving for the fields, and some were returning.

I saw the honeycombs and was amazed at the worker bees tending to the young. I found the queen bee and watched her moving around the comb, laying more eggs. Then I saw a funny thing in the hive. A returning bee with its wings spread out was doing a little dance. She seemed to be very excited as she danced around in circles, turning this way and that way. Other bees surrounded her and seemed to be encouraging her dance. Her wings vibrated as she danced. She looked as if she was in a square dance following the directions of the dance caller.

Apparently, this is the bee's way of telling the other bees in the colony that she found a good place to gather rich nectar. She found just the right place where the flowers bloomed. She had good news to tell, and she didn't waste any time in telling it to all the other bees.

What news are you sharing? I want to tell the good news about God's Son, Jesus. He loved us so much that when He died on the cross, He took our sins to the grave. When you believe and accept Him into your heart, you receive an eternal home in Heaven. Now that's good news, don't you think?

Lord, as the honey bees return to the hive and tell the others the good news about the sweet nectar, help me to be a better witness about Your Son, the cross, the forgiveness of our wrongs, and the promise of eternal life with You in Heaven. Amen.

JULY 20

"So let's not get tired of doing what is good. At just the right time we will reap a harvest of blessing if we don't give up"
(Galatians 6:9, NLT).

I heard a *tap, tap, tap*. When I looked out the patio window, I saw a downy woodpecker pecking at the bird feeder post. The post was made of treated hardwood, so making a hole in it takes some effort. He kept pecking at it for quite a while. I wondered if woodpeckers suffer from headaches.

Later in the day, I could see a little hole in the wooden post. A suet seed block was hanging from the post, and I noticed the woodpecker pecking out a portion of it. Then I saw him stuff the seed in the little hole he'd made. As the days went by, he continued to make holes and store seeds there. I guessed he was putting away food for later. I wondered if he'd ever eat that food.

Fast forward a few months and, lo and behold, there's my woodpecker pecking the food back out of the holes in the post he'd made months earlier.

In the beginning, the woodpecker showed me the value of persistence as he worked so hard at making the holes and then putting away the food. Later, he showed me that by being persistent, he had a harvest of food when he needed it. Paul writes in Romans 2:7 that God will give eternal life to those who persist. Just like the woodpecker, if we're persistent in our work for God, there will be a time of harvest, even if it does seem like a long time away.

Never, ever quit working for the Lord.

Father God, thank You for this little lesson from the woodpecker. His persistence is a good example for me. When I feel like quitting, I remember his persistence and I keep going. Amen.

JULY 21

"In him we have ... the forgiveness of sins, in accordance with the riches of God's grace that he lavished on us ... " (Ephesians 1:7–8)

It was a hot summer day, and we were thoroughly enjoying camping at Kona Beach Park. In the afternoon, my daughter and I went to the beach to go swimming. The blue water was topped with huge swirls of white that reminded me of the frosting on a cake. The water, although inviting, was sending large waves to the beach, and many people were enjoying themselves in the refreshing surf. I decided to give it a try.

I carefully stepped into the water and walked out to my waist. I took my time getting used to the cool temperature. The waves were very strong and powerful against my legs. I stood up in the water, and before I had a chance to take the plunge, a powerful force caught me by surprise from behind. A giant wave washed over me and covered me with the foamy water.

You can imagine my shock and how it felt when the huge wave collided with my legs and knocked me over. The force of the wave and the cold water nearly took my breath away. I came up out of the water sputtering to catch my breath. It sure staggered me. I was more careful after that but did enjoy the rest of the time in the water.

When I asked God into my heart, I experienced grace like a giant wave. It seemed like my whole life passed in front of me. As it struck me with its full force, I realized two things: I was forgiven of my sins, and I hadn't done anything to deserve it. I have found that God's grace is more powerful and amazing than we can ever imagine.

Let God's grace wash over you.

Father God, Your grace astounds me. I love Your surprises and how You show up when I least expect it. Amen.

JULY 22

"Remain in me, and I in you. As the branch can't bear fruit by itself unless it remains in the vine, so neither can you, unless you remain in me" (John 15:4, WEB).

When the spiritual retreat weekend is over, does the thought of starting another week of busyness and mundane tasks leave you joyless? Unfortunately, we do feel like this sometimes. The dull, or humdrum, parts of our lives aren't always desirable, but it's in those times where we truly live. We can't always experience the mountaintop highs. We are called to abide, especially in the mundane.

When we worship with other believers through singing, reading the Word, and prayer, we enter into the place where God resides. We need these times of personal and corporate worship to help us focus on Jesus Himself. But what about the rest of the time? What can you do to stay in the vine during the bad days and mundane part of your life?

Lean into Jesus every ordinary moment of the day. Do it through prayer and reading the Word, and do it joyfully. Each of us in Christ has a life to live, and not all of us have glamorous, exciting lives. But in the everyday tasks, we can abide and produce fruit for Christ.

Hudson Taylor said: "Abiding not striving nor struggling; looking off unto Him; trusting Him for present power … this is not new, and yet tis new to me."[9]

Father God, I want to abide in You through every day, whether dull or exciting, sad or joyful, commonplace or extravagant. I trust You for the power I need to abide, and I know that when I do, the right fruit is produced. Amen.

---

[9] "J. Hudson Taylor's Spiritual Secret," Abide in Christ, accessed October 12, 2025, http://www.abideinchrist.com/messages/exchltay.html.

JULY 23

"When they had crossed, Elijah said to Elisha, 'Tell me, what can I do for you before I am taken from you?' 'Let me inherit a double portion of your spirit,' Elisha replied" (2 Kings 2:9).

The concept of the double portion has been used throughout history to refer to God's abundant blessing. Six times in the Bible, specific reference is made to a "double portion." When someone receives a double portion, he gets a gift twice as much as that given to others.

On a visit to Florida, I bought a pair of earrings that were very special to me, and I wore them frequently. They reminded me of my dad because they were fashioned to look like sailboats. You see, my dad's father owned a schooner, and my dad told many stories about it.

That summer, my sister and her family visited from Georgia, and I drove to my mother's house to see them. While I was driving there and wearing my favourite sailboat earrings, I had a strong feeling that I had to give away this cherished possession. I tried to ignore the voice that was telling me to part with them, but eventually, I said, "If I'm to give them away, I want a direct sign from the person who's supposed to get them."

I arrived at Mom's house excited to see my sister. She looked at me and said, "Oh Suzanne, I love your earrings!"

Well, that's it then, I thought. I took them off and said, "They're yours."

Later that summer my sister-in-law came for a visit and presented me with a beautiful pair of earrings plus a bracelet. I was certainly surprised, and I immediately thought about the double portion verse above. I don't know if it applies here, but it did teach me a lesson about giving. Giving away something special or costly is better than giving leftovers from our riches.

Father God, thank You for this lesson about giving to others. Help me to be a good giver from my heart. Amen.

JULY 24

"And I will compensate you for the years That the swarming locust has eaten, the creeping locust, the stripping locust, and the gnawing locust— My great army which I sent among you" (Joel 2:25, AMP).

Newfoundland has its share of insect plagues, especially when the black flies hatch. Dad used to say they could pick you up and carry you away. Thankfully, we don't have locusts.

Locusts are a plague of insects that resemble a mighty destroying army. The Bible says in Joel 2:3b that *"Behind them is nothing but desolation; not one thing escapes"* (NLT). Locusts eat every leaf, every stalk, and every part of the plant in their path. Nothing is left—not the fruit and not even the seed for next year's growth. The Bible uses the swarming locust, the hopper locust, the stripping locust, and the gnawing locust to describe our enemy—Satan. He comes to steal, kill, and destroy us spiritually, emotionally, and physically.

I mourned over the years I lost before I was a believer in Christ, but I realized that God could restore. The enemy stole my faith in God and my witness for Him. C.H. Spurgeon said, "The fruits of wasted years are gone, gone past hope. Yet, behold, the Lord … declareth that these long-lost spoils shall be restored! Is anything too hard for the Lord?"[10] God can still give me all that the locusts (the enemy) took from me.

Do you have lost years you want back? God promises to restore them if you confess that He is Lord, delight yourself in His Word, and repent of any unconfessed sin in your life.

Father God, help me to sow the seeds, and please bless the remainder of my life as I give You all the praise and glory. Amen.

---

[10] Charles Spurgeon, "Truth Stranger than Fiction," The Spurgeon Center, accessed October 12, 2025, https://www.spurgeon.org/resource-library/sermons/truth-stranger-than-fiction/#flipbook/.

JULY 25

"For my yoke is easy, and my burden is light" (Matthew 11:30).

As I walked along the road through the park where we camped, I saw a man pedalling a bike that had a bar at the back with a smaller bike attached, and a child sitting on that bike. I'd never seen anything like it before. I thought it was a good idea. Not surprisingly, the man pedalled harder and took the strain. When they passed by, I could see that the child was pedalling a little, but I was glad that the father was on the front bike.

Before I finished my walk, they passed me again. The child was clearly tired and didn't pedal at all. The burden on the child was light because the father took the strain up front and did all the hard work. As I looked at them, the meaning of the verse above became clear to me.

Sometimes we try to take charge and sit in the front seat. We end up taking all the strain and the burden. Some of us would rather do things ourselves than ask for help. We think we can do a better job than anyone else. I want to tell you that there's always someone who can do it better.

The yoke in the above verse was a double harness. The larger one was for the stronger animal, while the smaller one was on the one being trained. Jesus is saying that if you're tired, sit on the back seat for a while, and He'll pedal up front while you rest. Be yoked with Him.

Father God, this memory reminds me to rely on You when I'm tired or worrying too much. Thank You for always being there to take the load and give me rest. Amen.

JULY 26

"You should know this, Timothy, that in the last days there will be very difficult times" (2 Timothy 3:1, NLT).

I have never experienced hot weather in Newfoundland like this before. When I was growing up, air conditioning meant opening the windows to allow the ocean breeze to blow in. Today, I'm thankful for air conditioning units that cool the air in our home. The upstairs bedrooms would be intolerable without the cool air from the window unit we have installed. As it is, my energy level is very low because of the heat and humidity.

It seems that I'm less tolerant of hot temperatures and high humidity these days. According to climatologists, the world's climate is changing. I could have told them that. The weather is changing and the earth is heating up. The polar icecaps are melting at an alarming rate.

When I look at the world, I see that it is changing morally, socially, and spiritually too. People and society are more tolerant of certain behaviours and less tolerant of Christian principles. The climate is heating up there, too.

Paul tells Timothy *"The time is coming when people won't listen to good teaching. Instead, they will look for teachers who will please them by telling them only what they are itching to hear"* (2 Timothy 4:3, CEV). Are we experiencing that today?

Climate change is real, whatever environment you look at. If we don't change the way we treat the earth, it will one day be unliveable. If we don't change our heart and view of God, we will not have eternal life in Heaven.

Father God, help me to do my part to take care of the earth and also to tell others of Your love for them. Open their minds and hearts to receive good teaching from Your Word for them. Amen.

JULY 27

"He cuts off every branch in me that bears no fruit, while every branch that does bear fruit he prunes so that it will be even more fruitful" (John 15:2).

"Boy, oh boy, they taste good!" I exclaimed. Big, red, sweet raspberries—Pop's pride and joy. He'd just picked some from the garden, and I was there to share them with him.

Someone said the canes "were brought over" from England and the berries were "cultured." I wasn't sure what that meant, but I knew the berries were bigger and redder than any wild berries I'd ever seen.

Pop went to the garden every day to pick the ripened berries. The tall green canes produced large red berries. The canes didn't get that way without some help. A small brook wound its way down the hill by his house and brought fresh water to the garden. Pop tended the berry canes faithfully. In spring and summer, he removed the dead canes and the weeds. He fertilized the plants and tied up the canes that were drooping. Just like the vinedresser in John 15, he tended the plants to help them produce the most fruit.

These days, my husband and I grow raspberries in our garden. I've learned that to get the best yield, pruning is important. We cut off the tops and remove the dead canes to force the plants to grow more fruiting branches. This gives you a higher yield of fruit.

God does the same thing with us. He cuts out the things in our lives that spoil our Christian growth, allowing more room in our lives to concentrate on the things of God. In time, we produce more fruit for Christ than we would have before.

Father God, thank You for the lessons I learned from watching my grandfather. I know I'm like a branch and need pruning in order to produce the fruit that's important to You—the fruit that comes from abiding in You and living a Christian life. Amen.

JULY 28

"Jabez called on the God of Israel, saying, 'Oh that you would bless me indeed, and enlarge my border! May your hand be with me, and may you keep me from evil, that I may not cause pain!'"
(1 Chronicles 4:10, WEB)

In 1 Chronicles 4:9, we're told that Jabez's mother named him Jabez because his birth was painful. His name means "born in pain." How sad to be given a name with that meaning. I wonder if he was ridiculed by his brothers because of it.

Most of us like to know how we got our name and what it means. My name means "lily of the valley." I'm glad it doesn't have anything to do with pain. I'm sure Jabez must have known what his name meant, and I can't help but wonder what he thought about it.

His prayer included the request to keep him from evil so that he wouldn't cause pain. I find this version of the verse very interesting and logical. Jabez was more honourable than his brothers—thus, his request to not cause pain. The idea of pain appears twice in consecutive verses. It makes sense that Jabez requested this. Maybe he didn't want to cause any more pain than he already had. This verse tells me he feared God, put his future in God's hands, and asked for God's protection.

Regardless of the meaning of your name, trust your future to God. Just as Jabez requested, ask God to guide you, to bless you, and to keep you from evil.

Father God, thank You for this prayer of Jabez. It reminds me to put my trust in You no matter what the circumstances of my life. Amen.

JULY 29

"But when he had become powerful, he also became proud, which led to his downfall" (2 Chronicles 26:16a, NLT).

I was feeling very confident and exhilarated when my first book was published. I had to be very cautious not to let pride step in. God hates pride. When we become confident in our own abilities and accomplishments, we become very susceptible to sin. After great victories, and when our defences are down, Satan launches his attacks.

We must be extra vigilant and careful to give God all the praise and glory. Remember, God hates pride because it takes our worship from Him and focuses it on ourselves. Sometimes power leads to pride, and pride can lead to sin.

In 2 Chronicles 26:5, we read that *"… as long as the king sought guidance from the Lord, God gave him success"* (NLT). But then he became proud and sinned against the Lord by entering the sanctuary and personally burning incense on the altar. He refused to stop when confronted, and then leprosy broke out on him. He lived in isolation the rest of his life.

In Acts 12:21–23, we read about another leader who became powerful and proud. An angel of the Lord struck Herod with a sickness, and he died because he accepted the people's worship instead of giving glory to God. Give God the credit in everything, because He's the one who gives us success. Great blessings and power bring great responsibility and accountability.

How are you using the blessings and power He has given you? Are you taking the glory for yourself? Be very careful of who gets the recognition.

Father God, I want my life to be pleasing to You. Whatever success or accomplishments come my way, I give You the credit and the thanks. When I'm weak, help me to go forward with the strength I have because I know You are with me. Amen.

JULY 30

*"Our days on earth are like grass; like wildflowers,
we bloom and die"* (Psalm 103:15, NLT).

I love the relaxing days of the summer, especially while camping. I love the beach and the water. As I sat in my beach chair reading a book and sipping on cool water, I felt totally relaxed. With my sunhat and sunglasses on, I was prepared to stay there for a while. "This is the life," I said to myself.

Oh wow! As soon as I thought it, I realized immediately what was happening. I was becoming comfortable with what the world offered. Make no mistake, this earthly life is not the life I'm really looking forward to. Sure, it's pleasant here today with the warm summer wind and sunshine. Shorts and a tank top are the garments of choice today, which are much preferred to the layers of winter clothing. I reminded myself that this life on earth is temporary.

I sat by the lake for a while enjoying the scenery and the sound of children having fun in the water. Afterwards, I even swam in the cool, refreshing water for a spell. I felt lulled into a temporary peace of mind. Nothing is really wrong with that, as long as you remember the word "temporary." I felt the nudge that said, "Don't let all this fool you into a false state, and don't let your guard down."

Psalm 90:12 says, *"Teach us to use wisely all the time we have."* (CEV). If I live my life trusting and serving God, one day when I get to Heaven, I'll truly be able to say, "This is the life."

Heavenly Father, thank You for the pleasant days that are good for our mental health. Help us not to be lulled into a false sense of security, but to remember that our security is in You, and that our days here are short and temporary. Amen.

JULY 31

"It is of the Lord's mercies that we are not consumed, because his compassions fail not" (Lamentations 3:22, KJV).

When I read Lamentations 3, I realized that the despair and anguish in the first half of the chapter represent how most of us feel through times of discouragement. Sometimes it seems as though everything that could go wrong has gone wrong.

The writer describes feeling aged and broken; everywhere he turns, the way is blocked. He's a target for attack; he's being ridiculed and taunted and has no peace. He feels that his strength and hope have perished.

But just when bitterness almost overwhelms him, he remembers God's faithfulness. God is present, even if you're unaware of it. Lamentations 3:23 says that God's compassions *"are new every morning."* When you wake up in the morning, God is there. When others fail you, God will not.

I wondered why the word "compassions" is plural. Usually this word is singular. In this verse, it embraces mercy, pity, love, tender-heartedness, concern, and kindness. The word "compassions" covers all of this.

In remembering the attributes of God, the writer of Lamentations has hope. He says in 3:24, *"The Lord is my portion, therefore I will put my hope in Him"* (HCSB). The writer's instruction is to examine yourself, turn back to the Lord, and lift your hearts to God, because God is faithful (1 Corinthians 1:9). He shows us this by His protection (2 Thessalonians 3:3), His mercy (Psalm 89:2), and His love (Romans 8:35–39). We must cling to Him.

Father God, Thank You for Your compassions. I know that when we turn to You, Your mercy and love know no limits. Amen.

AUGUST 1

"I command you today ... to walk in his ways and to keep his commandments" (Deuteronomy 30:16a, WEB).

"Take two giant steps forward!" I lifted my foot and stretched my right leg as far as I could reach. Then I lifted my left foot and stretched my left leg as far as I could. The leader said, "You didn't say 'Mother May I,' so go back to the beginning."

"Oh, I forgot," I said.

We called this particular game "Mother, may I?" Someone would be the mother, or leader, and we'd all line up horizontally behind her. The mother would call out a command, such as "Take two giant steps forward!" If you stepped out without asking, "Mother, may I?" you'd have to go back to the starting line. Sometimes the command might be to take one giant step forward and a baby step backwards. Each time, though, before we moved, we had to ask the same question: "Mother, may I?"

Oh, the fun we had playing this and other childhood games. We played many outdoor games, such as tiddly sticks, hopscotch, spotlight, and red rover. I don't know where all the games came from, but I imagine they were passed down from previous generations. I learned them from my older cousins, and we certainly had fun while playing them.

Many games taught us life lessons to help us in our Christian walk. Mother, May I taught that before we take steps in a certain direction or make a major decision, we need to look for guidance and ask God for permission first. Should I move forward, or not? Father, may I?

Father God, thank You for childhood games. Thank You for lessons learned while having so much fun playing them. I pray that I will always ask You first before I step out in any direction. Amen.

AUGUST 2

"When they landed, they saw a fire of burning coals there with fish on it, and some bread" (John 21:9).

It was the day for our cook-up at Bellevue Beach Park. Aunts, uncles, cousins, Nan, Pop, Mom, Dad, and my sisters all went to the park. A couple of the sites had open-sided log shelters that we called cook houses. There was a woodburning cooking stove there and picnic tables.

We had a campfire outside, and the children liked to collect little pieces of wood to throw into it and then poke at with a long stick. Aunt Fronie said, "If you play with the fire, you'll wet the bed." I'm not sure how true this prophecy was. But it was so good to be with family and share food this way. There were many laughs and much fun.

The verse above talks about a time after Jesus's resurrection. The disciples were discouraged, to say the least. They didn't know what to do, so Simon Peter suggested that they go fishing. After a night on the water with no luck catching fish, they turned towards shore. Someone called to them from the shore and told them to put their nets on the right-hand side of the boat. They did this and caught so many fish, they couldn't pull in the net. When they got to the shore, they saw a fire burning, fish cooking, and bread waiting to be sliced. All of this was miraculously provided and prepared by Christ.

There's nothing like a cook-up in the outdoors and time with family and friends to dispel sadness and defeat. Jesus showed up when they needed to be fed, encouraged, and restored. Never doubt that He'll show up for you too.

Father God, thank You for Your Son, Jesus, who died on the cross for me. Thank You for forgiving me and restoring me when I fail. Help me to follow You and not worry about what others do. Amen.

AUGUST 3

"Life is short, and you love your wife, so enjoy being with her. This is what you are supposed to do as you struggle through life on this earth" (Ecclesiastes 9:9, CEV).

"May your fountain be blessed, and may you rejoice in the wife of your youth" (Proverbs 5:18).

Who can say what makes a good and a long marriage? Is it love alone? I think it comes from growing up and a growing together. You must commit to each other and be willing to seek the good of the other person. In other words, you must try to put the other person above yourself. When each person does this, you'll have a strong marriage. That's not easy to do all the time, but we should strive for that.

Use the words "I'm sorry," and be quick to say them when you're wrong. Always be ready and willing to forgive the other person. Don't hold on to hurts or grudges.

Spend time together doing what the other person likes to do. It can't always be your way. You'll be surprised just what new things you learn.

In addition to all of this, love each other deeply, warts and all. The Bible says that *"love covers over a multitude of sins"* (1 Peter 4:8b).

There is so much more to marriage than what I've mentioned. Even after many years, couples have more to learn. God gave us this gift of companionship and love. Sadly, many marriages fail these days. If you don't know God, ask Him into your heart and into your marriage. With God, all things are possible.

Father God, thank You for my marriage. Help me to be the spouse You would have me to be. Amen.

AUGUST 4

"After He had dismissed the crowds, He went up on the mountain by Himself to pray" (Matthew 14:23a, AMP).

What a beautiful sunny morning at Kona Beach. Terry and I have a campsite at the park for the months of July and August. This morning, I woke up to another glorious day. Before lunch, my friend Melvina asked if I'd like to hike at Goodyear's Cove, which takes you up the side of a mountain. I said that I'd love to, so off we went with sneakers, comfy clothes, hats, water bottles, and our phones. You never know when you'll want to take a picture.

There were many steps to the top, and we had to rest several times. We took that time to take a few pictures. Up we went. My legs burned, my knees ached, and my feet hurt, but I kept on going. We made it to the top, and I was pleasantly surprised that I'd done it. What a view! The path opened up to a treeless mound of low shrubs. The sky and the ocean filled my sight.

The blue was framed by a rocky shoreline, where spruce trees filled in the border. In the distance, I could just see the coloured houses on the hills and a few small boats on the water. Seabirds used the wind currents like aerial highways while they searched for food on the ocean.

The peace I felt there was amazing, and for a while, we couldn't even speak. I can see why Jesus went up on the mountain to pray. I love this quotation by Frances Ridley Havergal: "A toilsome ascent leads on to a wide and glorious view!"[11] I think Heaven will be like that.

Heavenly Father, I'm so grateful for this day and the beauty You created here. I'm so glad I was able to make it all the way to the top of the mountain. I felt Your presence in the quiet of my surroundings. Help me to remember this day and the peace You gave us there. Amen.

---

[11] "Compensation," Havergal Trust, accessed October 12, 2025, https://www.havergaltrust.com/updates/compensation/.

AUGUST 5

"... follow the tracks of the sheep and graze your young goats by the tents of the shepherds" (Song of Songs 1:8).

I'm sure you've seen animal tracks while berry picking, trouting, or camping. From the tracks, you can determine the size and type of animal. You can tell if it was walking or running, and even the direction it went.

For a while, my husband and I raised German Shepherd dogs. We learned many things about them. One thing we learned is that they sometimes single track. That means that on a perfect trot, the hind paw lands in the print left by the front paw. It's something to see when the dog is in good shape and well trained. He practically floats off the ground as he majestically moves in a flying trot, with his hind paw landing where the front paw was. With his black face, alert expression, pointed ears, muscled legs, and regal stance, he is something to behold. He is fearless and loyal.

As Christians, we should be single tracking—not in our own tracks, but in the footprints of the Lord: *"... you should follow His steps"* (1 Peter 2:21b, WEB). Following in the footsteps of Jesus means that He leads, not you! We should be studying Jesus's example and asking ourselves, "What would Jesus do?"

Jeremiah 31:9b says, *"I will cause them to walk by the rivers of waters, in a straight way in which they won't stumble"* (WEB). When you're on the right track, you'll stand fearlessly and not fall.

Father God in Heaven, thank You for leaving Your footsteps for us to follow. Like stepping stones in a stream, all we have to do is place our feet on the stones in order to have a safe crossing. Lord, help me to walk in Your footsteps. Amen.

AUGUST 6

"a time to weep and a time to laugh, a time to mourn and a time to dance" (Ecclesiastes 3:4).

Like most children of my generation, I loved to skip rope. I remember getting a new skipping rope in the spring from my grandmother's shop. Usually, they were bright-coloured with wooden handles. There were short ones for single skipping, but you could get the longer ones for double skipping with your friends. Most times, I skipped using a single rope, as did my friends.

Sometimes we used a longer rope, with a friend turning on each end, and one or more jumping as the rope went around. Skipping is a lot more fun with friends, and we'd sing along with the jumping.

Strawberry shortcake, gingerbread and tart,
Tell me the name of your sweetheart.
A, B, C ...

One time, my Great-grandmother Sarah Rowe jumped rope with us. At the time, she was in her late eighties. The only smooth surface around for skipping rope was in the middle of the road. We didn't worry about safety, because at that time, there was very little traffic. On one particular day as she crossed the road from my nan's house to Uncle Sam's house, she joined us and jumped in the rope a few times. We were surprised, and she laughed as she went on her way. She lived well into her nineties. Maybe her long life came from taking time for fun and play as well as serious living.

Father God, thank You for providing a time to play. I remember many times like these. Thank You for the gift of laughter and for giving us the direction to put aside the seriousness of life sometimes and have fun with our friends. Amen.

AUGUST 7

"For as lightning that comes from the east is visible even in the west, so will be the coming of the Son of Man" (Matthew 24:27).

It was a warm night and raining very heavily outside. Laurieann, Tiffany, and Sherri were in the bunk beds, asleep. Terry and I were chatting with his parents in the living room area.

All of a sudden, flashes of lightning lit the sky, and a few seconds later, the thunder boomed. It rumbled across the valley. The lightning flashed again, and then the thunder rumbled. Again, the lightning flashed, and then the thunder boomed right overhead. The cabin shook, and the girls came running out of their bunks, frightened half to death. We held them and calmed them down until the lightning was less visible and the thunder sounds were far away.

We were staying for a few days with Terry's parents at their cabin nestled right under the Long-Range Mountains in Codroy Valley. The storm was intense because it funnelled down through the valley between the mountains. I have never seen a storm as grand in its light show and sound effects as that one.

The Bible tells us that when Jesus comes again, He'll be visible to the whole earth. Our lightning storm was only visible to the people who live in the valley, but Jesus will be seen by all the people on earth. Make sure your heart is right with God so that you're prepared for that day.

Father God, thank You for showing us Your power in nature through the lightning and the thunder. Help us to be ready for Your return. Amen.

AUGUST 8

"Make your light shine, so others will see the good you do and will praise your Father in heaven" (Matthew 5:16, CEV).

I want you to do something for me. Get a pen and paper, and draw a large circle on the paper. Then write in the circle the names of all the people in your life with whom you have any sort of contact. Start with your family, your friends, your neighbours, and then people at the stores, at your workplace, at the doctor's office, and so on. What does that circle look like? Is it filled with names? However many you have, this is your *circle of influence*. This is your mission field for the Lord.

Your circle of influence is comparable to the ripples on the still water of a pond. When you throw in a rock, the circle starts small and then expands to wider and wider circles. Everyone has a circle of influence. We influence people every day by our actions, attitudes, and words, and it isn't always a positive influence. You see, you can have a positive or a negative impact.

As Christians, it's very important to be aware of our influence. No matter whose company we're in, we must always protect our witness for Christ. Never let your guard down. Never say or do things secretly or with certain people that you wouldn't do in front of others. You are a representative of Christ to the world. You are the Christ that unbelievers see.

In your circle of influence, be a sweet fragrance of Christ that is expanding out to all within your reach.

Father God, I often think of my witness for You and how I want it to be better. Help me to be a positive influence and a sweet fragrance for You in my circle. Amen.

AUGUST 9

"I, Jesus, have sent my angel to give you this testimony for the churches. I am the Root and the Offspring of David, and the bright Morning Star" (Revelation 22:16).

One time when my oldest daughter was in the hospital for major surgery, she developed internal bleeding and complications after the operation. One of these complications required another trip, late in the night, to the operating room. I paced the floor in front of the OR, and then I sat in the waiting area. I was lonely for Christian companionship. I prayed, "Lord, I know I can talk with You, and I thank You, but it seems so long since I talked to another Christian. Is there another Christian person in this hospital? Father, could You let me know that I'm not alone?"

I took out my Bible from my bag and started to read. A few minutes later, I saw an elderly couple turn the corner and walk up the hallway towards where I was sitting. When they walked past me, I heard the man singing in a strong, clear voice "He's the lily of the valley, the bright and morning star. He's the fairest of ten thousand to my soul!" The woman looked at me and smiled. Isn't that awesome? God answered my prayer faster than I hardly had time to breathe. I was instantly overjoyed, overwhelmed, and peaceful. I was suddenly aware that God was with me. That's why He's called the lily of the valley. He is the lily in our valleys. I don't know who that couple was, but I really want to meet them some day.

You see, God was telling me, "I am in the valley with you, and you are not alone." Acts 12:11b says: *"Now I know without a doubt that the Lord sent his angel and rescued me ..."*

Father God, thank You for letting me know that I am not alone. You are the bright spot in the dark moments. Help me to remember the lesson of the lily. Amen.

AUGUST 10

*"For you know that it was not with perishable things ...
that you were redeemed from the empty way of life handed down to
you from your ancestors, but with the precious blood of Christ ... "*
(1 Peter 1:18–19)

I grew up listening to conversations about power. My grandfather had a generator that he operated to supply power to the shop and the house. There was enough power for electric lights and for freezers in the shop. The power was vital so that the food wouldn't spoil.

Later on, my dad worked for the Newfoundland Power Commission, and then he worked for Newfoundland Light and Power, which later became Newfoundland Power. He talked about kilowatts and megawatts of power. He played an active role in the installation of the first power substations on the Island. He knew what power was all about. Despite all that power, there is more power in one drop of Jesus's blood than all the power generated worldwide.

The Bible tells us in 1 John 1:7b that Jesus's blood has *cleansing* power: *"... the blood of Jesus, his Son, purifies us from all sin."* In Ephesians 1:7a, Paul tells us that it's *redeeming*: *"In him we have redemption through his blood, the forgiveness of sins ... "* Hebrews 13:12 tells us that Jesus's blood is *sanctifying*: *"And so Jesus also suffered outside the city gate to make the people holy through his own blood."* Revelation 12:11a tells us Jesus's blood is *conquering*: *"They triumphed over him by the blood of the Lamb ... "*

We sing a song that asks, "What can wash away my sins? Nothing but the blood of Jesus." Do you have that power in your life?

Father God, there is power, wonder-working power, in the blood of the Lamb. Thank You for Your Son. Help me to live each day with Your power in my life. Amen.

AUGUST 11

"O house of Jacob, come ye, and let us walk in the light of the Lord"
(Isaiah 2:5, KJV).

Have you seen that blue lately? You know the blue that I mean? The blue that you glimpse once in a while through the cloud-filled sky. I saw that blue today. It was the brightest blue I ever saw. It was there right overhead, and I almost missed it with my head hanging down looking at the ground. I glanced up, and then I saw it. It was so bright and blue against the dark clouds. The gold and orange trees were a beautiful contrast with the blue. I would never think of mixing those colours together, but God did.

I'm glad I didn't keep my head down like I wanted to. It felt so heavy as I trudged along with my shoulders slumped and my feet dragging. But something nudged me to look up. As I glanced at the sky, I expected to see more of the dark clouds that were the order of the day. I did see clouds, but right overhead in the middle of them was a patch of bright blue sky, and all of a sudden, the sun's rays came shining through. Just for a moment, it was bright and sunny.

My mood changed. I continued my walk with my head up and my shoulders back. Everything seemed much clearer now, and I didn't give the dark clouds another thought. Imagine! I almost missed the blue.

Oh God, forgive me when I walk through some days with my head down, with my thoughts swirling around the problems I tend to see. Remind me to look up to see the blue, to see that You are there amongst the dark clouds. Amen.

AUGUST 12

"So he got up and ate and drank. Strengthened by that food, he traveled forty days and forty nights until he reached Horeb, the mountain of God" (1 Kings 19:8).

In this chapter of 1 Kings, Elijah, who was a prophet of God, goes to Mount Horeb to meet with God. In the preceding verses, we learn that God had given Elijah two great victories over the evil King Ahab. But when Queen Jezebel threatened Elijah's life, he became afraid. In fact, the Bible tells us that he ran for his life.

Consequently, he fell into a depression. He travelled into the wilderness and sat under a tree. God let him rest for a while and provided food for him to eat. Eventually, God called him to a meeting to set him back on his mission as God's prophet. Elijah's work wasn't over.

All of us go through periods of feeling down or feeling like a failure, especially after great accomplishments, victories, and spiritual experiences. It's okay to rest for a while, but not too long. We must remember that God's purpose for our life is not over yet.

In 1 Kings 19:11–12, we learn that God's voice wasn't heard in the windstorm, earthquake, or fire. It was heard after the turbulence. When Elijah was ready to listen, God came as a still, small voice.

Why was all this necessary? Often this is God's way to get our attention. And when God wants your attention, you better listen.

Father God, thank You for times of rest. Help me to get back on my feet and to remember that You have a purpose for my life. Amen.

AUGUST 13

"There is a time for everything, and a season for every activity under the heavens" (Ecclesiastes 3:1).

This is the conversation I had with the leaves. "No, it can't be! What are you doing on the ground? You're supposed to be on the trees. It's only August, for goodness' sake."

The other day, I took a break from my workday. During my lunch time, I walked around the beautiful central park of my town. As I neared a stand of trees that was about halfway around the trail, much to my dismay, I saw that the ground was littered with brown, decaying leaves. I was shocked to see signs that the summer could be ending so fast. I wanted it to last for at least another month. Sometimes it seems like the things we look forward to take a long time to come, and then they end before we know they're there.

This morning the temperature dropped from the twenty-degree mark to twelve degrees, and there's a frost warning for tonight. My inner voice cries and says it's too soon; I'm not ready for the cold, the shorter days, the black nights, and all the extra activity that comes with winter.

Ready or not, here I come! I remember this phrase from my childhood when playing hide-and-seek. I knew that as soon as the finder said this, I had better be in my hiding place. Sometimes, if I wasn't ready, I'd be found right away. Ready or not, time passes and new seasons begin.

Am I ready for another winter season? Are you?

Father God, this year I lost my dad. There's supposed to be a time for everything. Is there time for grieving too? Have I had enough time before the busy season starts again? Lord, please help me to be ready to greet each day with energy, hope, and enthusiasm. From a thankful heart. Amen.

AUGUST 14

"Let no one on the housetop go down to take anything out of the house. Let no one in the field go back to get their cloak" (Matthew 24:17–18).

When God tells you not to go back or look back, then don't do it. Your life may depend on it.

In Genesis 19:17b, Lot and his family were told to, *"Flee for your lives! Don't look back, and don't stop anywhere in the plain!"* But in verse 26 we read that Lot's wife looked back and became a pillar of salt. Why did she look back? She was likely reluctant to leave her former life and looked back with longing. She was told to leave everything behind, but she couldn't let it go.

There's a true story of a woman who was told to leave her house immediately because a hurricane had caused huge waves to form that would soon sweep her home out to sea. But she went back to retrieve something in the house just when the wave smashed the house and dragged it out to the ocean. Regrettably, she lost her life, while the people who'd left the house were safe. It's better to leave it all behind and get out with your life.

Jesus said, *"No one who puts a hand to the plow and looks back is fit for service in the kingdom of God"* (Luke 9:62). God wants us to give Him our full attention. He doesn't want part-time loyalty. Some people may want to follow Jesus but are hindered because they care for other things. Attachment to our old life will cause us to lose our eternal life with God. Let go and let God lead you.

Father God, help me to follow You and not look back. I have a new life with You, and I let go of the past. Amen.

AUGUST 15

"You are radiant with light, more majestic than mountains rich with game" (Psalm 76:4).

"Wake up! It's time to get up. We have to go before all the best spots are taken."

When I heard Terry's voice, I opened my eyes. It was dark. "What time is it?" I asked. He said, "Four o'clock."

Boy, oh boy, I am not a morning person. I thought about the promise of big trout that were just waiting to get on my hook. I pulled myself out of the sleeping bag, stretched my arms to the sky, and then got dressed.

It was August, and we were camping by a river canal system in the wilderness. What a beautiful place! We quietly put the boat in the water and loaded it with the fishing gear. We got aboard and pushed off from shore. We wanted to get to the best fishing spot before any other fishermen, so we were being very quiet and used the paddles first instead of the outboard motor.

The only sound the paddles made was a little *plop* when they entered the dark water. It was barely daylight. As we slowly made our way along the narrow river canal, we listened to the sounds of the rippling water and the birds singing their wake-up calls. By the time we arrived at the best fishing place in the river, the early morning mist cleared and the sky was brighter. I will never forget that glorious morning. It was a special gift. I wondered if there was anywhere more peaceful or majestic. I can imagine God saying, "You think this is nice, wait until you see Heaven."

Father God, thank You for Your gifts of sight and sound so that we can appreciate the beautiful world You made. Help me, Lord, during the busy, noisy days to remember these peaceful snapshots in time. Amen.

AUGUST 16

"But don't just listen to God's word. You must do what it says. Otherwise, you are only fooling yourselves" (James 1:22, NLT).

"If anyone among you thinks himself to be religious while he doesn't bridle his tongue, but deceives his heart, this man's religion is worthless" (James 1:26, WEB).

These days the store shelves are full of generic brands. Even when you get a prescription from the doctor, the pharmacy dispenses a generic brand-name drug and not the original.

All over the Internet, people are selling and buying knockoff brand names. They're made to look exactly like the original brand. Designer brands are expensive, but knockoffs (fakes) are cheaper, and the imposters make money. Some people are fooled by the knockoffs and pay full price, as if it was the original.

Personally, I don't want to be generic in anything I do or profess to be. I don't want to be an imitation. I don't want to be like the crowd. I want to be the real deal and have real faith. I want to be authentic in my talk and walk with God. In Luke 6:46, Jesus asks, *"Why do you keep on saying that I am your Lord, when you refuse to do what I say?"* (CEV).

Are you a generic Christian? Are you just repeating the same old words and actions without putting your heart into it? Use your talents and gifts to be a genuine, brand-name Christian in your walk with God.

Father God, help me to be real and authentic in my Christian walk. May I always look to You for truth. Amen.

AUGUST 17

"Look at the birds of the air; they do not sow or reap or store away in barns, and yet your heavenly Father feeds them ..."
(Matthew 6:26)

I am hopeful that I've learned to take one day at a time and to appreciate the small stuff, like a hot cup of tea, a good night's sleep, a day without aches and pains, a good meal, and time with visitors and friends. Most of us, though, tend to live in the future and worry about what will happen to us tomorrow.

One day while camping, I walked on the beach and strolled along the boardwalk trail until I came to a large, flat rock. It was peaceful, so I sat down. The sun was shining, and there was hardly any wind, just a gentle breeze. The waves were calmly rolling to the beach and splashing on the rocks. The sky was blue with little white lines, like a person with a few streaks of grey in their hair. I felt the soft touch of the sea breeze and smelled the freshness of the air.

As I looked out over the ocean, I noticed one lone gull close to the rocks where I sat. He was idly floating on the blue water and seemed to be relaxing and enjoying the sun. He stayed in the same place close by me. He didn't look for food or fly away. He certainly wasn't in a hurry to leave or worried about getting something to eat. I thought, *He's not worried about tomorrow—what the weather will be like or where his next meal will come from.* If God can provide for him, surely He can provide for my needs.

I read a story that sums this up perfectly: Said the robin to the sparrow, "I should really like to know why these anxious human beings rush around and worry so?" Said the sparrow to the robin, "Friend, I think that it must be that they have no Heavenly Father such as cares for you and me" (Anon).

Heavenly Father, thank You for this reminder of Your constant care. Amen.

AUGUST 18

"I sleep and wake up refreshed because you, Lord, protect me"
(Psalm 3:5, CEV).

"In peace [and with a tranquil heart] I will both lie down and sleep,
For You alone, O Lord, make me dwell in safety and confident trust"
(Psalm 4:8, AMP).

Did you know that human beings spend one-third of their lifetime sleeping? If you're seventy-five, that means you've spent twenty-five years asleep. Well, some people may not sleep that much if they're poor sleepers. I know many people like that.

Some people have trouble falling asleep or staying asleep. This seems to be an epidemic in our country today. How many people have to take sleeping pills, alcohol, or other drugs to help them sleep?

Many people are unable to shut down their thoughts. Their nights are restless periods of tossing and turning. Sometimes, I have trouble sleeping. I'm either too warm or too cold, my feet are aching, my muscles are cramping, or some noise wakes me up. Other times, I may stay awake worrying about someone in my family, or a financial situation, or something else entirely.

What you eat or drink can affect your sleep as well. Too much caffeine or a heavy meal before you go to bed can disturb your sleep. There are many reasons for poor sleep, and if you've tried all the common remedies but still can't sleep, you should see your doctor to rule out a physical problem. In addition to whatever the doctor recommends, we should spend time with God by reading His Word and then giving all our concerns to Him in a prayer. Ask Him for peace of mind and a restful night.

Father God, You alone should fill my thoughts as I lie down to sleep—not the worries of the day. Help me to relax my mind and body to receive a restful sleep. Now I lay me down to sleep. Amen.

AUGUST 19

"Our mouths were filled with laughter, our tongues with songs of joy. Then it was said among the nations, 'The Lord has done great things for them'" (Psalm 126:2).

Uncle Eric arrived at my grandparents' house in Chance Cove driving a new convertible. It was a thing of beauty to our teenage eyes. My cousins and I thought he was the coolest uncle anyone could have. I think it was the first convertible I ever saw in Chance Cove.

Uncle Eric was so much fun to be around. He was a kid at heart and indulged us young cousins by taking us for a ride around the lower and upper coves of Chance Cove. We sat in the seats with the top down, the wind blowing through our hair, and joy on our faces. We sang songs at the top of our voices, laughed at each other, and waved to everyone we saw. We drove around and around, cruising up and down the roads. I never forgot that day and the time we had with Uncle Eric. It was certainly a time to laugh and have fun. Thank you, Uncle Eric, for that memory.

Proverbs 15:13a says that *"A joyful heart makes a face cheerful"* (HCSB). That's so true for Uncle Eric because he had a joyful heart. The Bible tells us to be cheerful and joyful. Even Nehemiah (8:10) told the people that joy in the Lord gives strength. It's good to laugh, have fun, and be joyful. It strengthens your heart physically and spiritually.

Father God, thank You for this memory of Uncle Eric. It always reminds me to look for the joy in every circumstance of my life. Amen.

AUGUST 20

"My enemies turn back; they stumble and perish before you"
(Psalm 9:3).

The Bible talks a lot about enemies. I always thought that an enemy had to be someone that I crossed paths with in my daily life. But I've learned that there are many types of enemies.

Sometimes our enemies are the things within us that keep us from succeeding or moving forward. Maybe it's a memory of a hurtful or tragic circumstance. Maybe it's unforgiveness. Maybe it's bitterness over losses, disease, or financial burdens. Do you have these kinds of enemies? These things are like chains holding us back.

Fear, doubt, and worry are enemies too. Do you feel like the ones in Luke 8:37, where it says that a great wave of fear swept over them? Sometimes I'm fearful of what the future holds, but then I remember that God is already in my future. Fear is an enemy that keeps me from having faith in my heavenly Father.

Throughout the Old and New Testaments, God tells us not to fear. In Luke 8:50b, Jesus says, *"Don't be afraid. Only believe, and she will be healed"* (WEB).

When we feel overburdened with these enemies, we need to tell God how we feel and ask Him to bring us out of it. Psalm 9:10, 12 tells us that God never abandons anyone who searches for Him, and He does not ignore those who cry to Him for help. Keep on trusting and never give up. Give fear the boot. It has no place in your heart.

Father God, I bring all my fears and worries to You. Bring to my mind Your promises of victory over my enemies. Amen.

AUGUST 21

"The Lord wraps himself in light as with a garment; he stretches out the heavens like a tent" (Psalm 104:2).

As we were eating lunch, we looked out the trailer window at our view of the tent section of the campground across the park road. We watched a young couple who had just come in. They were preparing to set up their tent. Terry said, "Just look at them, so young, and they have two little girls—one still in diapers. The mom looks something like you did, with the same brown hair and with two little girls like us."

There were tears in our eyes. I thought back over my life, my marriage, and our two daughters. For a brief moment, I wished I could do it over. I wished I could undo all the mistakes and follow God's plan much sooner than I did. I suddenly understood that we only get one chance to raise our children in the light of God's love before they're adults. Now more than ever, the world needs Jesus. People need Him in their hearts, homes, families.

I felt that I'd missed the mark. I could have done it better. But I can't do it over. What's in the past is done and gone. I wasted so much time on worldly things, and I made wrong choices. But I made a right choice too—to believe in Jesus and put my life in His hands. This choice outweighs all of my bad choices combined. God promised in Zechariah 10:6a, *"... I will restore them because of my compassion"* (NLT). I hold God to that promise. Max Lucado wrote, "One good choice for eternity offsets a thousand bad ones on earth."[12]

Father God, thank You for all the experiences of my life—the good and not so good. Thank You for watching over us and giving us our beautiful family. Amen.

---

[12] "One Good Choice," Max Lucado, April 11, 2017, www.maxlucado.com/listen/one-good-choice/.

AUGUST 22

"... you received the Spirit of adoption, by whom we cry, 'Abba! Father!'" (Romans 8:15, WEB)

"Because you are his sons, God sent the Spirit of his Son into our hearts, the Spirit who calls out, 'Abba, Father'" (Galatians 4:6).

One time when I was visiting my sister, I woke up in the middle of the night hearing my niece call out, "Daddy, I need you. Daddy, I need you. Daddy, I need you." Just then, her father came running out to her bedroom to see what she needed. He talked to her, calmed her down, and stayed with her until she went back to sleep. That's exactly what our heavenly Father does for us when we call out to Him. He stays with us and fills us with His peace.

Everyone wants a father who loves them, who will scoop them up in his strong arms, protect them, and help them through the struggles of life. Unfortunately, not everyone has a perfect earthly father. But our heavenly Father is perfect and wise. He is our Father God.

If we give our children what's best for them because we love them, won't our heavenly Father do the same for us? He loves us and wants us to love Him back. In Romans 8:15 and Galatians 4:6, Paul says that the Spirit in us tells us to call God "Abba Father," which means Daddy. We can talk to Him anytime, anywhere. As Christians, we become children of the heavenly Father.

Do you see God as your heavenly Father? John 1:12 says: *"But to all who believed him and accepted him, he gave the right to become children of God"* (NLT).

Father God, thank You for being my heavenly Father and for always giving me what You know is best. Amen.

AUGUST 23

"And, 'I will be a Father to you, and you will be my sons and daughters, says the Lord Almighty'" (2 Corinthians 6:18).

I don't have a specific nickname, but one of my cousins called me Sam. Over the years, I've answered to Suse, Suzy, and Susan. There was an elderly man in our church who couldn't remember my name, so I told him to remember the song "Oh Susanna, Won't You Cry for Me." Maybe your friends have a nickname for you.

Did you know that God has many names too? In the Old Testament, God is the Creator, the God Most High, the God Who Sees, the Lord Will Provide, and the Lord Is Peace. The most remembered name is probably the Lord Who Is My Shepherd. We're all familiar with that name because of the well-known Psalm 23, which says, *"The Lord is my shepherd; I shall not want"* (v. 1, KJV).

In the New Testament, Jesus introduced a new name for God. He called Him Father. Jesus used this name when He prayed to God, and He invites us to use "Father" when we talk to God. We should talk to God plainly, as we'd talk to our friends.

Just stop and think about that for a moment. The God who created everything in the heavens and the earth, who is all-knowing, all powerful, and present everywhere at once, tells us He is our heavenly Father. We can call Him Father and talk to him anytime or anywhere. Isn't that amazing?

Oh God, knowing that I have a heavenly Father who is always there for me fills me with strength and encouragement. Thank You that I can talk to You anytime. Amen.

AUGUST 24

"The Lord loves the gates of Zion more than all the other dwellings of Jacob" (Psalm 87:2).

When I grew up in Chance Cove, many of the houses had little front yards with a picket fence and gate around the whole property or the front garden. This was to keep unwanted animals out and other animals in, such as the sheep or horses.

Gates come in many shapes, sizes, and designs. One particular gate that had special meaning to me is the gate to my grandparents' front yard. It was just a wooden gate that creaked when it opened, but it was no ordinary gate. It was special not because of its material, shape, or workmanship, but because it opened to my grandparents' home. I loved that place. It was a place of love and warmth.

I've always thought that opening a gate is like opening a book. What will I discover inside? I have many memories of my grandparents' yard and home, especially from my childhood days. I spent countless hours playing there. The big tree is still in the yard. It's perfect for climbing. You can sit on a branch and watch the people walking by, or swing from the branches or hang upside down. It wasn't a fancy yard, but it was an extraordinary, special place. Do you have memorable gates in your life?

A lot of living occurs inside a gate: playing with friends, greeting people, saying goodbye to people, laughing, celebrating, and reflecting. Inside the gate is a very special place. Even the Lord has a love for gates. The gates of Zion allow us entrance into the presence of God. Be sure your heart is right with God so you can enter the most important gate of all.

Father God, thank You for special gates like the one to my grandparents' yard. Thank You for Your promise that one day I'll go through another gate—the gate to Heaven. From a thankful heart, in Jesus's name. Amen.

AUGUST 25

"You will drink from the brook, and I have directed the ravens to supply you with food there" (1 Kings 17:4).

I caught my first trout in Gut Brook. You see, I was a little girl who loved the outdoors. I played along the shores of the brook and under the old wooden bridge. I often watched older teenagers fishing there and thought that I'd like to try to catch one too.

I went there one day with an old bamboo fishing pole. I baited the hook with worms I'd dug by my grandfather's barn, and I tied a little red and white bobber to the line. I threw the line into the water many times but with no success. I watched that red and white bobber to see if it would go under the water, but no trout tugged on my hook.

I tried fishing at a deeper pool by the concrete bridge. I'd watched other people fishing there in the past and tried to imitate what I remembered seeing them do. I threw my line into the water over and over again. All of a sudden, the bobber dipped below the top of the water. I jerked the line and pulled with all my might. In came my line, my hook, and a trout. It was small, but the size didn't diminish my excitement. I ran home and proudly displayed my prize to my mother. I had a wonderful sense of accomplishment.

I'll never forget the day I caught my first fish, and I've loved fishing ever since. I often found peace and quiet for my thoughts and soul there. What a place to rest from troubled times! I understand why God directed Elijah to go to the brook. It's described in 1 Kings 17 as a place of rest, a hiding place, and a place of nourishment both physically and spiritually. Let's go to the brook.

Father God, thank You for the love of outdoors that You gave me. Thank You for the peace You supply when I look with amazement at all You created. Amen.

AUGUST 26

"When you reap the harvest of your land, do not reap to the very edges of your field or gather the gleanings of your harvest" (Leviticus 19:9).

It was a beautiful sunny day—very quiet and no wind. I went to the garden to walk around and sit for a while in the sunshine. We had just harvested the root vegetables, and the rows seemed empty.

I walked up and down the rows and noticed a little bit of orange here and there poking through the ground. I was wearing my garden gloves, so I reached into the soil and felt around. Lo and behold, I pulled out a good-size carrot. The carrots were hidden in the ground because during the harvest, some of the stalks had broken off when we were trying to pull them up.

I continued until I had checked all the rows. As I walked along, stooping down and checking the soil, I thought about the verse above and also the reference in Ruth 2:2 to Ruth gathering enough food by going through the field after the harvesters. That's the meaning of the word "gleaning." The Bible gives us specific instructions to leave the gleanings for others. I think I dug out another seven or eight kilograms of carrots. We may not have people gleaning in our fields today, but God still expects us who have more to look after the less fortunate.

Gleaning was practised because God wanted to make sure that the poor, the homeless, and widows would be taken care of. The landowners weren't to take all the harvest but to leave the fields with some crops. God has given us a way to look after the poorer in society and still help them keep their dignity. They get to work the farm and enjoy a harvest too. Always think of ways to help others without destroying their self-respect. One day you may be in need like them.

Father God, thank You for Your provision for us and the reminder to take care of the less fortunate in our society. Amen.

AUGUST 27

"During those peaceful years, he was able to build up the fortified towns throughout Judah. No one tried to make war against him at this time, for the Lord was giving him rest from his enemies" (2 Chronicles 14:6, NLT).

Times of peace are so nice. I love them. You know the times I'm talking about: when the family is getting along, when no one is sick, when vacation time is coming, when the weather is cooperating with our plans, when work is going well and our world is just right. These times are refreshing and renewing. We can rest easy and regain our strength. But we shouldn't rest for too long. During these times, we should also prepare for times of trouble. They're a time to rebuild our resources, our strengths, and our relationships.

Today's verse speaks of such a time. Asa was king in Judah. He pleased God by doing what was right. He tore down the idols and pagan places of worship. He commanded the people to obey God's commands and teachings. Consequently, God gave him rest from his enemies.

During this peaceful time, Asa didn't stay idle but rebuilt the defences of the cities of Judah. He knew that it would be too late if he waited until he was attacked. When the trouble eventually came, he was prepared—and he prayed: *"… O Lord, no one but you can help the powerless against the mighty! Help us, O Lord our God, for we trust in you alone"* (2 Chronicles 14:11a, NLT).

From this passage we learn that during the peaceful times, we should prepare for trouble. Make decisions thoughtfully and calmly, and build your defences now. When the time of trouble comes, you will withstand the attack. Pray to God for help, and trust in the Lord.

Father God, I love the times of peace, but I know that they won't last. Help me to be prepared for the times when trouble comes. Amen.

AUGUST 28

"… they hid from the Lord God among the trees of the garden. But the Lord God called to the man, 'Where are you?'" (Genesis 3:8b–9)

Someone helped me out of the boat and onto the beach. We were at a little cove just down the coast a short distance from Chance Cove. We'd come in Pop's motorboat. He was there, along with Nan, Mom, Dad, Aunt Fronie, a few cousins, and maybe others whom I've forgotten. As I walked from the beach towards the little valley, I couldn't believe my eyes. In some places, the grass was as tall as I was, and in other places, it was taller.

We came by boat to this place because it wasn't accessible by road. It was a good place to pick berries and have a picnic. When the adults walked over the hill to pick the berries, the children stayed in the valley to play hide-and-seek in the tall grass. You couldn't even see the tops of our heads as we walked through. My cousins and I had so much fun that day while the adults were berry picking.

All day long, we took turns hiding in the grassy field and searching for each other. Sometimes we called out "Where are you?" When someone answered, we followed the sound of the voice until we found him or her. We spent the entire day playing. I will never forget that day, the tall grass, or the excitement we felt when we found who we were looking for.

Where are you? Are you hiding from God? God wants to talk to you and have a relationship with you. He is continually calling, and I'm sure He'll be excited when you respond with "Here I am."

Father, I'm so happy that You didn't stop searching for me. So many souls are hiding, just as I did in the tall grass when I was a child. Lord, some of them are afraid to come out of hiding. Don't stop calling to them until they do come to You. Amen.

AUGUST 29

"'What do you see, Amos?' he asked" (Amos 8:2a).

What do I see? At first glance, I saw the dark, choppy water. The strong wind stirred the water on the lake until white foamy edges appeared on the waves. Next, I noticed that the mountains surrounded the lakeshore like the scalloped edge of a country quilt. The various greens dotted throughout the hills turned to shades of black in the late evening sky. I looked up. The threatening clouds covered the sky like a blanket and were darker in the distance.

But something else is there. What am I overlooking? Oh, I see it now—a round, orange buoy about thirty feet from shore. It didn't belong in the picture. It stood out against the dark, stormy colours. The buoy wasn't moving from its place, just bobbing in the waves. It was attached to a rocky anchor, and although the wind blew and the waves beat it around, it stayed where it was supposed to be. This one lone orange ball kept its place in a stormy, dark world because of its anchor. It was a bright, easy-to-see marker for anyone passing by.

As Christians, we're placed in a world that's sometimes dark and full of trials. However, we don't have to be moved by these trials, because we're firmly attached to the Rock, who is Jesus. When someone passing by looks at us, we should stand out like the bright orange buoy in the lake. We should stand out as someone who isn't like the world around them. We should be a marker that says, "Through the storms of life, I will not be moved, because I am fully attached to the Rock." Zechariah 5:2a asks, *"What do you see?"*

> *Father God, help me to not be moved by storms and trials. Help others to see You through me in all areas of my life. Amen.*

AUGUST 30

"The pride of your heart has deceived you, you who dwell in the clefts of the rock, whose habitation is high, who says in his heart, 'Who will bring me down to the ground?'" (Obadiah 1:3, WEB)

Is your security in wealth? From the time we start school until we complete all our education, we're pushed to go for the highest-paying career. The more money you make, the better. Then there are the lotteries advertised as the answer to all your problems. They try to get us to pay our money and take a chance on winning millions. You could be set for life, they say. People talk about winning the lottery and what they'd do with the money. Are the rich happier than the poor?

This mindset sets us up to believe that gaining money and possessions is the most important goal of life. Paul wrote, *"But people who long to be rich fall into temptation and are trapped by many foolish and harmful desires that plunge them into ruin and destruction"* (1 Timothy 6:9, NLT). How much material wealth do you need to feel secure? Can material things give lasting security? For the poor it may be little, but for the rich, it may be a lot. Many of us feel secure when we have money in the bank. We think that nothing can bring us down. But we fail to remember that this type of security has no eternal value. Only God can give true security.

Instead of teaching our children to pursue money and possessions above all else, we should be teaching them first of all to pursue a godly life. In 1 Timothy 6:17 Paul writes, *"Charge them that are rich in this world, that they be not highminded, nor trust in uncertain riches, but in the living God–…"* (KJV). It also says, *"Tell them to use their money to do good"* (1 Timothy 6:18, NLT).

Father God, I don't want to put my trust in possessions and money. Help me to use what You've given me to help others. Amen.

AUGUST 31

"Be cautious and hide when you see danger—don't be stupid and walk right into trouble" (**Proverbs 27:12, CEV**).

One time while berry picking, I sat in an ants' nest. This is how it happened. A couple of my sisters, a few of my friends, and myself went berry picking. We headed towards Trout Pond, which was on the trail over the hills not far from our house. On the way there, I saw a patch of blueberries right by a mound of rocks, just off the path a little way. I stopped, went right over, and sat down. I wanted to get them all, and I hoped no one else would try to pick berries in the same spot. I picked and picked. I tasted a few. Boy, oh boy, they were delicious!

Suddenly, I felt something on my leg, and then the other leg. When I looked down, I saw that an army of red ants were covering my legs. I screamed, jumped up, and started dancing around while blueberries went flying through the air like big blue raindrops. All my hard work was for nothing. The container was empty.

It was my own fault for being selfish. I had been so excited to see the berries that I didn't look very carefully, and I didn't see the danger. I just sat down and picked with no regard to where I was. Consequently, I lost all the berries in my bucket. Because I wanted to pick more than my friends did, I didn't pay attention to the threat. Oh yes, when we think of ourselves first instead of others and greedily try to get the most, we often get into trouble.

Father in Heaven, it was a lot of fun picking berries, but the ants weren't much fun. I realize now that I was greedy and careless. Lord, help me to apply this lesson to my life today. Help me to be less selfish and more aware of the consequences of thinking only of myself. Amen.

SEPTEMBER 1

"He took them along and withdrew privately to a town called Bethsaida" (Luke 9:10b, HCSB).

"... he withdrew by boat privately to a solitary place ..." (Matthew 14:13)

This beautiful, sunny fall morning, as I sit at the table drinking coffee, I try to concentrate on my reading, but I'm constantly being interrupted. Terry is listening to the news on TV; the radio is on; car doors are banging; our neighbour returned something to the backyard; and the dogs are barking. After a little while, the TV and radio are off. Terry has gone to the store, and the dogs are quiet. I settle in again to read, but then the phone rings.

Sometimes finding a quiet time is frustrating. I take a few deep breaths, whisper a prayer, and sit at the table again. When I look at my notes, I see this verse: *"He will bring you quietness with His love"* (Zephaniah 3:17b, HCSB).

Interruptions are part of life, aren't they? Even Jesus faced interruptions when He tried to have a quiet time. Our plans, even in the small things, don't always unfold as we'd hoped or thought. Psalm 37:7a says, *"Be still before the Lord and wait patiently for him ..."*

Finally, it's peaceful, and I'm enjoying watching the little birds feast at the feeders just outside my patio. It reminds me to feast on God's Word and enjoy what He provides.

Father God, thank You for these quiet times when I can read Your Word and what You have to say through the verses. Help me to not get frustrated when I'm interrupted but to wait on You for the right time. Amen.

SEPTEMBER 2

"The harvest is past, the summer has ended" (Jeremiah 8:20a).

"He made the moon to mark the seasons, and the sun knows when to go down" (Psalm 104:19).

Today I thought about how much I love summer. All through the winter months, I long for summer. I think about the snow melting, the leaves coming on the trees, the flowers and the grass growing. Mostly, I like to feel the warmth of the sun. I like the days of summer for walking on the beach, having campfires, sitting in the garden, and just relaxing with family and friends.

Another summer has ended. Most of our garden has been harvested. Did summer meet all my expectations this year? Probably not. We make lots of plans, and sometimes they don't always unfold the way we thought they would.

Then the thought came to me that I live my life for the seasons, especially summer. By doing this, I miss out on what the other seasons offer. Who doesn't like the beautiful colours of fall—the reds, oranges, and yellows? And the cooler sweater-days are more comfortable for walking and working outside.

And what about winter, with the sun shining on a fresh snowfall? I know people who prefer winter. They enjoy winter activities such as skiing, skating, and snowshoeing. Come to think of it, I do like to walk in the snow when it's new and white.

In spring I look forward to new life beginning and the new buds breaking open. We plant our seeds in starter pots and plan what to grow in our garden. We also plan for vacation periods and trips. Each season has its beauty and purpose, and I'll look for the beauty in each moment.

Father God, forgive me for forgetting that each day is a gift. Help me to appreciate every day that You give me. Amen.

SEPTEMBER 3

"When you believed, you were marked in him with a seal, the promised Holy Spirit" (Ephesians 1:13b).

Oh no, it's that time of year again when I spend hours washing, cutting, and boiling. It's harvesting time, and things will be *put up* (preserved) for the winter months. It isn't too bad, though—except for the mess I make. Mom always said I dirty every dish and pot in the kitchen.

At the end of summer and in early autumn, I make preserves to store in the cellar for the winter. Sometimes I make pickled beets, jelled beets, berry jellies, jams, and bottled moose and rabbit. I preserve all of these items in jars that have lids lined with a rubber ring that seals the bottle and keeps the food from going bad. Without the proper seal, my hard work is wasted.

One year, I bottled pickled beets and put them in the cellar. But there was something wrong with the seals, and a few of them blew their tops. What a mess! I had beet juice everywhere. It took quite a while to clean it all up! Obviously, my seals were either defective or I didn't use them properly.

The verse above says that when you put your trust in Jesus, you're sealed with the Holy Spirit. I think that's a unique way of wording it. When I read this verse, I thought of preserving foods in bottles. If we want our food to keep a long time, we need a good seal.

The Holy Spirit lives in us to encourage us to make right decisions and be a good influence on others. The Spirit corrects us, guides us, comforts us, and intercedes for us when we don't know what to pray. With the help of the Spirit, we can live a productive and meaningful Christian life. Are you sealed like this?

Father God, thank You for the help of Your Holy Spirit. He guides me daily with gentle nudges and comforts me by His presence. Thank You for the promise of Heaven with You. Amen.

SEPTEMBER 4

"The Kohathites will come and carry these things to the next destination. But they must not touch the sacred objects, or they will die" **(Numbers 4:15b, NLT).**

Wow! That's some dangerous work. Newfoundlanders know about dangerous work. Fishing on the ocean is just one example. In my grandfather's day, they fished from wooden schooners and sailed to the Labrador coast and the Grand Banks without GPS or any of today's modern tools. Many men were lost when schooners ran aground or sank in stormy weather.

Men who work on power lines have a very dangerous job. People who work in search and rescue, firefighters, miners, soldiers, bomb disposal specialists, and, recently, medical personnel exposed to deadly viruses all do dangerous work. I'm sure there are more you can add to this list.

In the passage above, a group of people are assigned to carry the most sacred objects that God set apart for the Israelites to use in worship in the Tabernacle. Only Aaron and his sons are to take care of these holy objects. Before the objects are moved, everything is covered with cloth and put on carrying frames. Poles are inserted in the frames, and then the Kohathites of the Levite tribe, who were chosen by God, transport the items to the next destination. Only the Kohathites can do this, and they're warned not to touch the sacred objects or they will die. They can't go into the tabernacle alone or even look at the objects without Aaron and his sons present.

These were the safety measures designed to keep the workers safe. If they followed the protocols, they'd be unharmed.

Father God, sometimes people die in unsafe working conditions. Help workplaces today to ensure the safety of all personnel. Be with each person who has dangerous work to do and protect them. Amen.

SEPTEMBER 5

"Then he said to them, 'Watch out! Be on your guard against all kinds of greed; life does not consist in an abundance of possessions'" (Luke 12:15).

In the early years of our marriage, Terry and I had a Dodge Dart that we'd bought new in 1975. We kept the car for several years. Eventually, through normal wear and tear, parts wore out. One evening, I was driving to my college when the car filled with smoke. I pulled over to the side of the street, rolled down the windows to let the smoke out, and continued on my way. Apparently, a few wires had burned off in the dash.

Another day, I was driving my daughter Laurieann to school when the car's chassis collapsed on top of the wheels. There was a lot of rust underneath that had to be fixed.

Finally, something gave out in the starting mechanism, and the key wouldn't start the car. I had to open the hood and use a screwdriver against two terminals to start the car. Whenever I'd go out on a quick errand, I wouldn't turn off the engine, especially if it was raining. I knew that thieves could easily steal a car left running, but it was an old car, and I thought no one would want it anyway. I definitely wouldn't advise leaving a car running these days.

When I look back at the experience, I laugh at it, even though at the time it wasn't funny. I was thankful that at least I had a car to drive. It was a valuable life lesson about appreciating the material things that we did have and realizing that there were blessings in life that are far more valuable than the best material things.

Father God in Heaven, thank You for providing everything we need, not everything we want. Help us to appreciate the real blessings of life. From a thankful heart. Amen.

SEPTEMBER 6

"Jesus said to them, 'I am the bread of life. Whoever comes to me will not be hungry, and whoever believes in me will never be thirsty'" (John 6:35, WEB).

Bread is such a simple food, but it's necessary for our well-being. Even when we don't have a lot of food, we usually have bread.

In our local neighbourhoods and around the world, plenty of people are starving physically. You only need to watch the news or commercials about world hunger to know that this is the case. And all over the world, people are also starving spiritually. Jesus said to them, *"I am the bread of life. Whoever comes to me will never be hungry, and whoever believes in me will never be thirsty."* Does this mean that once we become a disciple of Jesus, we'll never doubt again? Does it mean that once we experience God's love, we'll never feel loneliness again? Does it mean that we're free from those difficult experiences, that we're finished with anxiety and will never struggle with our faith again? It would be nice if it worked that way. But I don't know of any Christian who describes their life like that.

Maybe Jesus is trying to tell us that His love for us is enough to see us through the darkest moments in our lives. He doesn't leave us to face those moments alone. He's always present with us and constantly reaches out to us.

Trusting in Jesus means that we have faith in the One who can fill the void—if not with easy solutions, then with peace and grace.

Father God, thank You for being the constant presence in my life. Thank You for Your grace in every situation I face. Amen.

SEPTEMBER 7

"Fearing that we would be dashed against the rocks, they dropped four anchors from the stern and prayed for daylight" (Acts 27:29).

Indian Tickle on the Labrador coast was a good place for fish. However, it was located on a rough shore that made it very dangerous for schooners to moor up. Not only was it windy, but there was also a terrible swell from the ocean.

One such night after the fish were all cleaned away and the men had turned in for the night, the wind rose to gale force, with a heavy swell from the ocean. Suddenly, the skipper called all the men to the deck. The two main anchors were deployed, and then the skipper decided to also deploy an extra anchor, called the *ketch anchor*, to try and steady the *Fronie Myrtle*, the schooner my grandfather owned.

The *Fronie* was holding her own, and my grandfather figured they were going to be okay. But in the darkness, another schooner drifted right into them. The schooners tangled together. The men scurried around trying to free the other schooner. Both schooners were dragging their anchors and drifting. With a great effort from the crew, the schooners were separated, and the *Fronie*, with the extra anchor held her mooring until the storm passed.

The next morning the schooner that came down across the Fronie was in on the beach with three or four others with them. All their catch was scattered along the shore and all hopes for a successful year were gone. The 'Fronie' with her Ketch anchor had held on during the storm. During your storms, do you deploy your 'ketch' anchor and pray for daylight?

Father God, thank You for the many times You watched over my grandfather and crew. He deployed the schooner's ketch anchor, and I'm sure he trusted You as the ultimate anchor of his soul. Amen.

SEPTEMBER 8

"You Gentiles are like branches of a wild olive tree made to be part of a cultivated olive tree. You have taken the place of some branches that were cut away from it. And because of this, you enjoy the blessings that come from being part of that cultivated tree" (Romans 11:17, CEV).

One of my sisters and her husband have many apple trees on their property. When they bought their house, the apples trees were already there, having been planted by previous owners. They have more than one kind of tree, and up to three different types of apples on one of them.

These trees have some branches that were grafted into the main trunk of the tree. Grafting is a procedure that joins two plants into one. Usually, an opening is created on the trunk of one of the trees, and a branch from another tree is inserted into it. It's secured in place until they grow together. This is done to combine the best features of two plants. Usually, a more tender plant is grafted to a stronger root and bottom part of another plant.

The verse above refers to grafting. Some of the Jews rejected Jesus as God's Son and didn't believe the message of salvation. They were cut off, and the Gentiles (anyone who was not Jewish) were joined to the vine to share in the gift of eternal life through Jesus.

In John 15:5, Jesus says, *I am the vine, and you are the branches. If you stay joined to me, and I stay joined to you, then you will produce lots of fruit. But you cannot do anything without me"* (CEV). We can't accomplish anything in our Christian life without being in the vine.

Father God, thank You for the strength and nourishment I get when I stay connected to You. By daily prayer and reflection, I remain in Your love. Amen.

SEPTEMBER 9

"That person is like a tree planted by streams of water, which yields its fruit in season and whose leaf does not wither—whatever they do prospers" (Psalm 1:3).

One day as I was looking out my window at the garden, I saw a blue jay in the big tree closest to the patio. I heard him calling to other blue jays, and one by one they flew to the tree to perch on the branches. I realized that I wouldn't hear the jay's song if the tree wasn't there.

Then I remembered a trip we took to Western Canada. As we drove through the farmlands of the prairies, I took note that there weren't many trees. I thought it was so sad. Compared to Newfoundland, the prairies looked a little bare. But I noticed that the trees they did have were planted in special places, such as around farm homes for shade, along a driveway for a windbreak, and also as fencing along farm borders. They provided shade and protection from the sun for the cattle and horses.

The Bible references trees numerous times. In the Psalms, they're a symbol of strength, stability, and righteousness. Trees are also used to represent people and their spiritual state. The righteous person is compared to a tree that is firmly planted, produces fruit, and does not wither.

When I hear of this type of tree, I think of the tall aspen trees we have on our property. Their leaves dance in the breeze, and they make a musical sound. They are straight, strong, and able to withstand wind, rain, sun, and drought. These are my favourite trees and the type of tree I would want to be.

Father God, thank You for all the different types of trees that You created. Help me to stand tall like the aspen trees and have my roots deep in You. Amen.

SEPTEMBER 10

"The people complain, 'Spring and summer have come and gone, but still the Lord hasn't rescued us'" (Jeremiah 8:20, CEV).

The harvest around Jerusalem lasted from April to June. After that came the summer, which was the fruit season. When the harvest was bad, they hoped for a good crop of fruit in the summer. But when all this failed, they were in despair.

This was the case with the Israelites who continually turned away from God. They worshipped handmade stone and wood images instead of the living God. It seemed that God had forgotten them. They spoke the words above when they were in exile. They had hoped to be rescued by another nation but were not. Their hope was crushed.

The Israelites had a long history of forgetting God and ignoring His instructions. Judges 2 tells the story of the Israelites turning from God and then God allowing them to be taken by their enemies.

How are we any different from these people? We make promises to God and follow Him when everything is going well. But the danger of prosperity and blessing is that after a while, we become complacent and forget where it came from. Our hearts fill with pride, we forget to pray, we forget to be thankful, we forget to be generous, and we forget to worship the living God. Sometimes, we turn away from God and worship the things He gave us. They become our idols.

We must be very careful to keep our promises to God. We must not become as the Israelites did and risk losing God's protection and blessings.

Father God, thank You for Your great mercy. Many times, I have failed to keep my promises, but You bring me back and forgive me. Help me to never forget where You brought me from and how You have blessed me. Amen.

SEPTEMBER 11

"Then Moses climbed the mountain to appear before God"
(Exodus 19:3a, NLT).

When I was growing up, we climbed the hills around Chance Cove, and we walked up Church Hill every day. There were no high mountains around us, but it was so nice to get to the top of the hills and look out at the ocean and all around the harbour. We saw everything at once—the boats coming and going, the people at work on their boats, men cutting wood, and women hanging clothes on the lines. We saw them, but they couldn't see us. We had a bird's-eye view.

In the Bible, Moses went up and down the same mountain three times. It was a mile-and-a-half hike to the top. He must have been in good shape for a man who was eighty years old. Moses reminds me of mountain climbers today. They make it their mission to climb the highest mountains in the world. Many have tried to climb Mount Everest (the tallest mountain) but failed on their first attempt. Even so, many keep trying to get to the top.

But why go to the mountaintop? Some go for the view, some for the challenge, some for the accomplishment, and some for the praise. But Moses went up to meet with God.

An unknown author said, "When everything feels like an uphill struggle, think of the view from the top." John Maxwell said, "Everything worthwhile is uphill."[13] Max Lucado wrote, "Don't measure the size of the mountain; talk to the One who can move it."[14]

> *Dear God, it seems as though being on the mountaintop gives us the best view. We have good experiences on the top of the mountain, but everyday living takes place in the valley below the mountain. Help us to remember the mountaintop while living below it. Amen.*

---

[13] "Nothing That's Worthwhile Comes Easily," Change That Up, accessed October 7, 2025, https://changethatup.com/articles/nothing-thats-worthwhile-comes-easily/.

[14] Max Lucado, *Traveling Light: Releasing the Burdens You Were Never Intended to Bear* (Nashville, TN: W Publishing Group, 2001), 102.

SEPTEMBER 12

"When you come, bring the coat I left at Troas with Carpus. Don't forget to bring the scrolls, especially the ones made of leather" (2 Timothy 4:13, CEV).

I thought that after years of travel and lots of practice packing, unpacking, and repacking that I'd finally perfected the art of not leaving anything behind. Much to my dismay, I just discovered that on a recent trip to visit my mother, I left behind my camera. I have an excuse, though, because when I arrived at my mother's house, there was such a crowd staying there that I decided to put my camera in a safe place. You know what they say, "Out of sight, out of mind." I broke my own rule: Don't put things out of sight, or you may forget them when repacking.

What did you leave behind on your travels this year? Did you leave a coat, like Paul did? I'm sure you have stories to tell of things left behind in hotel rooms, houses, airplanes, and maybe even at home. Clothing, medicines, and electronics are all examples of things left behind.

Remember the movie *Home Alone*, in which the little boy is left at home while the rest of the family go on a Christmas vacation? It's a very funny movie, but it wouldn't be so funny if it happened to us. One time, I went to St. John's for meetings. When I got there, I discovered I'd left my work clothes at home on the hangers. It was a perfect excuse to buy more clothes.

In life, there are things that should be left behind: past mistakes, regrets, poor choices, childishness, bad living, hurts, and unforgiveness. I once read that "Freedom is not found in the things we hold but from the things we leave behind."

Is God asking you to leave your things behind?

Father God, thank You for leaving behind Your Holy Spirit, Who is my helper. Help me to leave behind the things that hinder my influence for You. Amen.

SEPTEMBER 13

"One Sabbath Jesus was going through the grainfields, and as his disciples walked along, they began to pick some heads of grain"
(Mark 2:23).

My dad let me sit in the wooden box on the back of his red cab truck as he drove to each fisherman's shed. He collected their dried salted codfish to take to the bigger market for sale. At each stop, the piles of fish got higher and higher.

It was great fun to sit on top of the piles and feel the wind in my face as we went along the road. Sometimes I'd peel a little of the flesh off and snack on it. It was deliciously salty from the curing and drying in the sun.

Collecting the salt codfish from the fishermen's sheds and then snacking on that food reminds me of the verse above, which tells us that Jesus and the disciples picked some grain in the fields to eat as they walked along, even though it was a Sabbath. All people are under moral laws that we must follow regardless of the end result. But the disciples were hungry, and even though the Jews followed ceremonial laws that forbade them to pick grain on the Sabbath, they ate out of necessity, which takes precedence over this type of law. They didn't violate any moral laws.

When I ate the salt cod, I didn't think about any type of law, even though I shouldn't have damaged the prepared salt cod. And I certainly wouldn't have starved without the fish. I hope the fishermen didn't lose too much value on the fish because of me.

Father God, sometimes there seems to be an over-abundance of laws. Help me to live morally and to follow the laws of the land as best as I can. Amen.

SEPTEMBER 14

"One of those listening was a woman from the city of Thyatira named Lydia ... When she and the members of her household were baptized, she invited us to her home. 'If you consider me a believer in the Lord,' she said, 'come and stay at my house'" (Acts 16:14–15).

Do you show hospitality? The dictionary.com definition of hospitality reads, "the friendly reception and treatment of guests or strangers."

During the COVID pandemic, hospitality changed. We couldn't entertain most family members or close friends, let alone strangers. Post-pandemic times found us desperately trying to get back to where we'd been pre-pandemic. For a long time after the pandemic, we wondered when we'd ever feel totally comfortable.

Before Jesus's death, He and the disciples travelled from place to place, and many people opened their homes to them. Back in those days, people relied on the hospitality of strangers, as there weren't many inns available.

Hospitality is an important part of the Christian life, especially when shown to strangers and those in need. The Bible tells us to be hospitable: *"Cheerfully share your home with those who need a meal or a place to stay"* (1 Peter 4:9, NLT).

Our opportunity to show Christian hospitality was limited during the pandemic, but we did find ways to safely practise it.

Father God, even though the pandemic caused our hospitality to suffer, thank You for helping us to get back to opening our homes again. Amen.

SEPTEMBER 15

"'Sir,' the invalid replied, 'I have no one to help me into the pool when the water is stirred. While I am trying to get in, someone else goes down ahead of me'" (John 5:7).

One time while staying at our cabin at Thorburn Lake, several of us walked to the river and over a steep hill to get a good look at the waterfalls there. Going down wasn't too bad, but then we had to get back up the steep, muddy slope. My father, who was leading the way, was sure-footed and nimble like a mountain goat, but some of us weren't so agile and got left behind—me included. Actually, I was the last one in line. I thought I'd never get up that slope. My legs were rubber, and I was out of breath. Just when I thought I'd been forgotten, Uncle Ed reached down his hand and pulled me all the way to the top.

Often what people need is a hand to help them get up: to get up in the morning, to get up out of debt, to get up out of addictions, to get up out of abusive relationships, to get up out of unemployment, and to get up out of a negative way of life.

One day, Jesus went to the pool of Bethesda in Jerusalem. Sick people gathered there because they believed the water could heal them. Jesus spoke to one of the men lying there and asked him if he wanted to get well. Of course, he did. Who doesn't want to be well? Jesus told him to get up, pick up the stick he was leaning on, and walk. The man's problem had become a way of life. It was his crutch. He had no one to help him. He had no hope, and he had no desire to help himself. Jesus made him realize that he did want to get well, and at Jesus's words, he did get up and walk.

Reach out to a hurting person today. You may be just what they need to get back up.

Father God, I don't want to lose hope because of any hardship. Help me to get up and rise above my hurts so that I can help others to get back up. Amen.

SEPTEMBER 16

"... arm yourselves likewise with the same mind ..."
(1 Peter 4:1, KJV)

Me (with the phone in my hand): "Hello, hello!"
Person on the other end: "Hello, hello!"
Me: "Arlette, I just picked up the phone to call you. I never even got a chance to dial the number."
Arlette: "I just dialled your number, and it didn't even ring."

Does that ever happen to you? You pick up the phone to call someone, and before you got a chance to dial the number, that same person is saying, "Hello, hello." They thought of calling you at the same time that you thought of calling them. Somehow, the telephones connected before you heard the rings. When you're very close to someone and they're on your mind, there seems to be a telepathic communication between you.

That is the way it is with our heavenly Father. Every time we pray, our mind and thoughts link with God. We have a spiritual, telepathic link to Him. He knows we're going to pray before we even close our eyes, and He knows what we'll say even before we say a word. In fact, He's already working on our prayer request. Isaiah 65:24 tells us, *"Before they call I will answer; while they are still speaking I will hear."* Isn't it wonderful to have a friend like that? He knows our request before we ask.

Father God, thank You for being such a good friend and helper. Thank You for knowing my prayer before I even say a word. Even so, I know You love to hear my voice, as I love to hear Yours. Amen.

SEPTEMBER 17

"The Lord remembers us and will bless us: He will bless his people, Israel; he will bless the house of Aaron" (Psalm 115:12).

The fields were flooded in Codroy Valley, and the houses close to the river were in danger of falling in and turning over. I'd never seen so much water there. Fields where cattle grazed and crops grew were now totally underwater.

On the way back home, I saw where the water was receding and parts of the fields poking up through the water. The fields were again reclaiming their space as the water flowed downstream or sank into the ground. It reminded me of the Great Flood account in the Bible.

Before the earth flooded, Noah built an ark (a large boat) to save his family and the animals. For a long time, they floated on the waters. But God remembered them and blessed them. After the rain stopped and the water receded, they saw dry land again. What a joy it must have been for Noah and his family to see land finally showing above the water!

So much is beyond our control, because nature seems to have a will of its own. Although we try to control it, we can't. We must remember that God controls all things for His purpose. We can be sure of one thing—God is a good God. After the storm, dry land will appear again.

Sometimes it seems as though God is far off and distant from us. We wonder if He's even listening to our pleas for help. In these times, remember the promise in the verse above. God remembers us and will bless us.

Father God, thank You for this promise that You remember us. Forgive me when I forget this and start to doubt and fear. I know that You will lead me along my life's path. I look forward to the rain ending and dry land appearing. Amen.

SEPTEMBER 18

"Abraham looked up and there in a thicket he saw a ram caught by its horns" (Genesis 22:13a).

I watched a television program one morning with my husband. It was about a hunting guide who worked in the Brooks Range in Alaska. This particular video told the story of a hunt for a mountain ram called a Dall sheep.

After ten days of only seeing one sheep two miles away, and after walking over seventy-five miles, they finally saw a big ram on the side of a mountain. The hunter took his time to get the sight and then aim. He was finally able to get a ram.

The guide related that on the night before, he'd read John 14 in his Bible. In that chapter, Jesus says that when all the glory goes to God, you can ask anything in His name and you will receive it. He prayed that if God would allow them to get the sheep, he'd be sure to give God all the glory on his video, which he did. When I listened to his experience, I was reminded of the story of Abraham and Isaac. When Isaac questioned his father about having an animal for the sacrifice, Abraham told him the Lord would provide.

The guide recounted that his life was forever changed by the experience. He gave his life over to God and shared his experience on the video and with others.

We must be careful not to take the glory for ourselves for something that God has accomplished and provided. Proverbs 16:3 tells us to commit all our plans to God and we will succeed.

Father God, You are the great Provider. All honour and glory belong to You. Help me to give You the praise for every experience and every blessing in my life. Amen.

SEPTEMBER 19

"… be patient, bearing with one another in love" (Ephesians 4:2b).

I have an Uncle Ed. I think everyone should have an Uncle Ed. If I were to pick one word to describe him, it would be "patient." I grew up with Uncle Ed living next door to our house. He was a schoolteacher and taught me in grade six in the little two-room school in Chance Cove. When I went to grade nine in Arnold's Cove, he was teaching there too, and I was in a few of his classes. He certainly was patient with me, and I didn't get into too much trouble.

My friend Norma and I travelled with him every day from Chance Cove to the high school in Arnold's Cove. He drove a Volkswagen Beetle, which he expertly manoeuvred over the twists and turns, hills and potholes of our community.

I would be eating my breakfast or getting ready when I'd hear *burmpt, burmpt*. That was him honking the horn. Mom would say, "Hurry up, Uncle Ed is here; you're going to be late." I'd think, *Oh no, I'm late again. Another morning when I didn't get out of bed in time.* It was hard to keep me on time because I loved to dally and daydream. I guess you could say I wasn't a morning person.

Uncle Ed was very patient, as I was often late. He'd wait for me and then stop for Norma. I don't know how he put up with me. He drove me to school for two years.

Uncle Ed retired from teaching, and eventually along came the grandchildren to keep him busy. He's a patient man with them as well. Maybe waiting for me was good practice. Ha! Just joking! Love you, Uncle Ed. *"Whoever is patient has great understanding"* (Proverbs 14:29a).

Father God, thank You for my Uncle Ed. He is a man of great understanding. Thank You for his example in my life. Amen.

SEPTEMBER 20

"Don't be fooled by those who try to excuse these sins, for the anger of God will fall on all who disobey him" (Ephesians 5:6, NLT).

There's a cost to disobedience. I remember the times as a child when I was disobedient. My parents were quick to put a stop to it and to punish me. I would sometimes go against what they were telling me for my own good. I'd get my feet wet in the cold saltwater at the beach. I'd play too close to the edge of the wharf. I'd climb the rocks around the shore. And on and on.

As I grew up, I sometimes hung around with the wrong people. I didn't study as much as I should have. I stopped going to church. The cost of disobedience for me was being away from God for many years. I missed out on all the years I could have been living a Christian life.

There are many biblical accounts of people disobeying God and suffering the consequences. For example, in Genesis, we read about Adam and Eve, who disobeyed God and were banished from the Garden of Eden. In Daniel 4, we read about King Nebuchadnezzar, who exalted himself above God and was humbled when God made him like an animal eating grass. In 1 Corinthians 10:21, Paul writes that there were believers in Corinth who were disgracefully known for civil disobedience and sexual immorality. Because of this, he told them that they couldn't partake of the cup of the Lord Jesus Christ.

Even believers in Christ will reap the fruits of disobedience if they don't repent.

Father God, help me to be obedient to You and be quick to repent when I'm not. I don't want to lose Your blessings because of unrepentance. Amen.

SEPTEMBER 21

"Once more Jesus put his hands on the man's eyes. Then his eyes were opened, his sight was restored, and he saw everything clearly" (Mark 8:25).

I received my first pair of glasses when I was eight years old. Shortly after I got them, the earpiece on one side broke off while I was playing outside during recess. Over the years, I've had many pairs of glasses, and many have broken. I remember putting tape on the earpiece when the hinge broke and on the middle bridge part when that broke in half.

I didn't want to wear glasses, even though they improved my eyesight. I didn't appreciate the gift of sight they gave me. I hated wearing them because I didn't think they were fashionable. I put up with some jokes and funny names, but overall, it wasn't too bad.

I had one pair that were purple with rhinestones on the rims. They were shaped like cat eyes and curved up at the sides. It was very fashionable at the time! When I was a little older, I liked the simpler frames, and when I was in my late teens, I wore the small gold-wire frames. They were the fashion for the hippie types. I wasn't really a hippie, but I loved the bell bottom pants that most people wore.

These days I wear contact lenses most of the time. When I read the verse about Jesus healing the blind man, I thought how amazed he must have been to see. Even though my eyesight isn't perfect, I can't imagine being blind.

Miracles happen all the time. Everything that happens to restore sight is a miracle, and I think that God is behind every medical advancement. He has given us the gift of modern medicine to perform modern-day miracles.

Father God, thank You for modern-day medicine that restores sight. Amen.

SEPTEMBER 22

"Even the sparrow has found a home, and the swallow a nest for herself, where she may have her young" (Psalm 84:3a).

There once was a little sparrow living in an airport terminal in Toronto. I was surprised to see this little bird as I sat waiting for my flight. It startled me at first when I caught the movement out of the corner of my eye. It must have flown in through an open gate.

It pecked at the plentiful supply of food crumbs that littered the floor of the waiting areas. As I watched it, the sparrow hopped closer. I threw out a few seeds from my multigrain sandwich bread.

I wondered where it would get a drink. I hope it found water at the various drinking fountains placed around the building. This little bird seemed to be used to the hustle and bustle of people and luggage as it quickly flew and hopped around.

I felt sad for the sparrow living without trees to perch on or other little birds for company. It was out of its natural environment; it was entirely alone in a foreign land. Sometimes we may feel like this when certain life events happen. When you get to an unfamiliar place and you don't know how you got there, remember Luke 12:6–7.

> What is the price of five sparrows—two copper coins? Yet God does not forget a single one of them. And the very hairs on your head are all numbered. So don't be afraid; you are more valuable to God than a whole flock of sparrows. (NLT)

Father God, I'm so thankful for this reminder that I am important to You. Not only do You care for the sparrows, but You care for me too. I need not be afraid. Amen.

SEPTEMBER 23

"Be always on the watch, and pray that you may be able to escape all that is about to happen" (Luke 21:36a).

One time I was driving Mom's car to take her to an appointment in St. John's. We stopped at the supermarket on the way out of the city to buy a few groceries that she needed. When I pulled out of my parking spot, I almost hit a woman who was walking into the store. Even though I'd looked both ways, she was in a blind spot caused by the frame on the side window. I didn't see her until it was almost too late.

I got a severe fright and realized that tragic accidents can happen very quickly. You have to be absolutely certain that there's no one in your path when you're behind the wheel. The driver is responsible for controlling where the vehicle goes. You need to turn your head and look all around. Even then, I've had a few close calls and near accidents while driving.

Driving and not being able to see your blind side can cause an accident. The same is true for our spiritual walk. If we're not careful to ensure that we can see around the blind side, we could be swiped by Satan. We must always be on the alert. We must always check every side, in front and behind—not just with our mirrors, but we must make the extra effort to turn around and check for ourselves. Only then can we avoid those blind attacks. Be diligent in your study of God's Word, and don't neglect prayer.

Do you have a spiritual blind side? *"Never stop praying, especially for others. Always pray by the power of the Spirit. Stay alert and keep praying for God's people"* (Ephesians 6:18, CEV).

Heavenly Father, help me to be always watchful and alert for any blind spots in my physical life as well as in my spiritual walk with You. In Jesus's name. Amen.

SEPTEMBER 24

"So Joshua asked them, 'How long will you put off entering to take possession of the land which the Lord, the God of your fathers, has given you?'" (Joshua 18:3, AMP)

Procrastinators' motto: Why do today what you can put off until tomorrow?

The Israelites put off taking possession of the land that God had promised to give them. They were given an inheritance but didn't take ownership of it or move into it. There could be several reasons for their delay: they feared resistance; they felt it was too much work; they wasted time; they weren't motivated; or they lacked leadership. Their delay kept them stuck where they were. They didn't grow in their faith because they were reluctant to advance to the next step. They wanted the safety of where they were.

Are we like this sometimes? God promises to be with us in everything we do for Him, but we're hesitant to put it to the test. Has God given you a promise for something that you haven't claimed yet? Are you afraid to move from where you are and take hold of it? What's holding you back? Examine your life. What changes can you make to get unstuck and to experience the growth and plans God has for you?

First, write out the promise, just as the Israelites mapped out the land. Second, break it down into smaller, achievable segments, just as they divided the land into sections. Last, enlist help when you need to, just as they helped each other possess their allotted portion. Encouragement and teamwork go a long way in helping to accomplish a mission.

Remember, if God has given you a promise, He expects you to complete your part of it. Don't put it off any longer.

Father God, help us to move ahead in our walk with You and not stay stuck in one place. Grow our faith, Lord. Amen.

SEPTEMBER 25

"But the Lord is in his holy temple: let all the earth keep silence before him" (Habakkuk 2:20, KJV).

"Be silent, all flesh, before Yahweh; for he has roused himself from his holy habitation!" (Zechariah 2:13, WEB)

Are you a good listener? A few years before my retirement, I went to a training course about how to listen. It was very informative, and I learned that not everyone can master the art of listening. We learned techniques to help us be better listeners. I'm guilty sometimes of not listening attentively. But when I am in a conversation, I try to put into practice what I learned.

I was given a talking stick. I could hold the stick and talk until I was sure the other person understood what I was saying to them. They had to remain silent until I was finished. Then they had to repeat back their understanding of what I'd said. When I thought they understood, I passed the stick to that person so they could have their turn to talk.

Using the talking stick is a good way to improve communication and relationships with people. We have to remain silent and focus to really hear what they want us to understand. We were taught not to think about our response while they are talking but to listen with the goal of comprehending what's being said. Imagine the things you learn about people when you really listen to them this way.

When we're in God's presence, do we have silent periods of listening so that He has an opportunity to tell us something? Do we pay attention, or do we continue to talk?

Father God in Heaven, I know You have much You want to tell me. But often I spend my time with You talking and asking for things instead of listening to what You may be saying to me. Help me to be silent and listen to You. In Jesus's name. Amen.

SEPTEMBER 26

"Anyone who does not remain in Christ's teaching but goes beyond it, does not have God. The one who remains in that teaching, this one has both the Father and the Son" (2 John 1:9, HCSB).

My approach to most things is to study the facts and do my own research so that I know the truth about the matter.

When we were young, we enjoyed fooling our friends with practical jokes. It was fun as long as it didn't go too far. We especially enjoyed April Fool's jokes. We read in 2 John 1:7 that many deceivers have gone out into the world. But there's a difference between practical jokes and the type of deceiving the Bible is referring to.

There are a few examples in Scripture of deceivers. Jacob put on a goatskin to make his father think he was the older brother so that he could get the blessing and inheritance instead of Esau. But the biggest deceiver of all is Satan, who makes false statements about our faith, God, and the Bible. How can you know if someone is trying to deceive you? You know it's a lie if it doesn't match up with God's Word, or if certain sins are presented as acceptable today.

Would you believe someone if they said the earth is flat, or that storks bring babies? Obviously not, because you've learned the truth. The same is true of spiritual things. Spend time reading the Bible even if you don't feel like it. Start digging into the Word to build a firm foundation in your belief.

Father God, thank You for preserving the Bible for us to study and learn about You. Help me not to be deceived with false statements but to remember what You say and to teach the truth to others. Amen.

SEPTEMBER 27

"He performs wonders that cannot be fathomed, miracles that cannot be counted" (Job 5:9).

Miracle Whip made its debut in 1933. It's a salad condiment or a sandwich spread. It got its name because of the way the manufacturer blended together all the ingredients by using a patented "emulsifying machine." We use Miracle Whip almost every day on sandwiches or in salads and sauces. We don't think of it as a miracle—just a name on a jar of food.

We're surrounded by miracles every day. Some seem small and insignificant, and some are much grander, like the miracles of creation. The Bible tells us that we are fearfully and wonderfully made (Psalm 139:14). Just think about your eyes giving you sight, your ears with so many parts that enable you to hear sounds, and your lungs that expand and contract to bring in the air you breathe.

There are the miracles of the rain, the sunshine, and every created living thing. I think of the miracle of birth, of learning, and of growing. We sometimes take for granted the miracle of love and family, or even health—until we're sick.

The biggest miracle of all is the miracle of salvation. Jesus gave His life to save us from our sins. He arose from death to live in Heaven again. When we believe, repent of our sin, and ask Jesus to forgive us, we're assured of salvation. This is the miracle of grace.

What miracles are present in your life?

Father God, You perform miracles every day—many that we aren't even aware of. Thank You for the miracle of saving my soul. I look forward to spending eternity with You in Heaven. Amen.

SEPTEMBER 28

"So Christ has truly set us free. Now make sure that you stay free, and don't get tied up again in slavery to the law" (Galatians 5:1, NLT).

Can anyone really understand grace? What does it mean to live under grace? All our lives we live under laws and rules. Do this and don't do that. That's the way it was with the Jews. They had to follow many laws to satisfy their religious way of life. They lived under the umbrella of the law, and they were slaves to the laws that they had put in place themselves.

Then along came Jesus, who upset their whole way of life. Jesus taught repentance and forgiveness. He offered salvation as a free gift to those who believe. Saul, who became the apostle Paul, understood that free gift better than anyone. He was a Jew to the bone and practised all the laws to the letter. Then he met Jesus and his life and beliefs changed. He found grace. He found that undeserving, unmerited favour of God.

Once you find grace, you're no longer the same. We live in a world with rules and laws, and you have to earn your way. Not so with grace. It's a free gift from God, but it's so overwhelming that some people fail to believe or accept it. Even some Christians still have trouble accepting grace.

Grace enables you to live forgiven and to forgive others. Look for grace. It's a great treasure. Once you find it, live as one who's been forgiven. You'll be surprised where God will take you.

Father God, thank You for the grace You've given me. Help me to live my life under the umbrella of grace. Amen.

SEPTEMBER 29

"I will give thanks and praise to You, for I am fearfully and wonderfully made" (Psalm 139:14a, AMP).

I was present when my grandson was born. When the baby was given to me, wrapped in a blanket, I was speechless, overwhelmed, and awed. Tears filled my eyes as I thanked God for the miracle.

In this world where there seems to be so much tragedy, pain, and evil, we can easily find reasons not to celebrate. There are wars, hurricanes, earthquakes, and tsunamis. We probably don't need to look outside our own family to find sickness, financial problems, housing problems, marital problems, rebellious teens, addictions, and on and on. We could become very negative and depressed. Fortunately, the Bible tells me: I am a child of God (John 1:12); I am the apple of His eye (Deuteronomy 32:10); I am Christ's friend (John 15:15); I am chosen by Christ (John 15:16); I am a new creation (2 Corinthians 5:17).

I read a story about an old preacher who told some of his Sunday school boys what he'd be preaching on in the next Sunday's sermon. Wanting to trick him, the boys took his Bible and glued some of the pages together. The next Sunday, the preacher stood to read his text. As he got to the bottom of the page, he read, "When Noah was 120 years old, he took unto himself a wife, who—turning the page, he continued—"was 140 cubits long, 40 cubits wide, built of gopher wood, and covered with pitch inside and out." The minister paused with a puzzled expression on his face. He said, "My friends, this is the first time I've ever seen this in the Bible, but I take it as evidence of the fact that we are fearfully and wonderfully made!"

Heavenly Father, I celebrate because I am Your daughter. I know I can trust You with every detail and moment of my life because You have plans for me. Amen.

SEPTEMBER 30

"Anyone who believes in me may come and drink! For the Scriptures declare, 'Rivers of living water will flow from his heart'"
(John 7:38, NLT).

I'm at the Health Science Centre sitting with my dad. It's midnight, and I'm here for the night shift. The last few days have been hectic and sometimes tiring. There isn't much quiet time when you're around family in close quarters.

Yesterday afternoon, I had a chance to spend a few moments in the Garden of Hope, just outside the hospital's main doors. The sun was warm on my face. I sat down by the pool and fountain. It was peaceful, and for a few minutes I could put all the hospital noises in the background. I talked to God and then heard the soft tinkling of wind chimes. Then a gentle breeze moved the leaves on the trees. I looked around and saw colour. Lots of colour. The garden was filled with colour and many different shapes. I thought, *The presence of God is here.*

The pool in the Garden of Hope reminded me of the account in John 5 about the crippled man waiting for someone to help him into the pool for healing. Many people came to the pool at Bethesda for healing. It was said that the angels would stir the water, and when they did, it had healing properties. If I stirred the water in the pool, would Dad be healed? The man waited by the pool for years but couldn't get to the water. One day Jesus came to the pool and saw the man. He asked him if he wanted to be healed (John 5:6). The man said yes, and Jesus healed him.

That day in the Garden of Hope, I was the one at the pool waiting for Jesus. An hour later, I left the garden, fully restored and at peace.

Father God, I know I'm here for a reason, but I'm not sure what that is yet. Lord, thank You for this quiet time. Amen.

OCTOBER 1

"You came to greet him with rich blessings and placed a crown of pure gold on his head" (Psalm 21:3).

Knock! Knock! Knock! It took Hattie a long time to get to the door. She was severely crippled with arthritis, and her knees were swollen. Her hands were so deformed from the disease that her fingers formed right angles. I wasn't in a hurry, so I waited. Then I heard her voice: "Who is it?" I answered, "Mrs. Wheeler, your neighbour." The door slowly opened, and she pushed a stuffed animal door cozy out of the way.

When she saw me, she smiled and said in a raspy voice, "Come in. Come in." As she led me to the kitchen, we passed a small front room with very old furniture and a tiny television. The kitchen table was covered with odds and ends. There were dishes waiting to be put in the cupboards, unopened mail to read, and gift items from her Regal Catalogue to sort. She sold items from a mail-order company, and her home was full of assorted trinkets.

We sat at the table and she talked. She told me stories about growing up in old St. John's and about her teaching days. She described what our neighbourhood on Allandale Road looked like when they built the first houses. She asked questions about my family, too. She never talked about her illnesses or her pain. She was interested in her visitors' lives and could draw out their stories. You could forget for a moment your worries and busy life. I loved to visit her.

I never met anyone quite like Miss Harriet Freeman. She had no family of her own, but she left a legacy of friendships. She was a kind woman loved by all her neighbours and friends.

Father in Heaven, thank You so much for Hattie, who taught me that people and relationships are important, and that no matter what our circumstances, to always be thankful for everything. Amen.

OCTOBER 2

"When the Lord saw her, his heart went out to her and he said, 'Don't cry'" (Luke 7:13).

Once in a while, I have a pity party and think to myself, *I don't have much to offer. I don't have many talents, and I'm not making much of a difference.* When I feel discouraged like this, I reflect on some of the women in the Bible who made small contributions but are still a part of the story of Jesus. You might say they were supporting characters. If their small part was important to Jesus, then maybe mine is, too.

They were ordinary women, much like us today. They had housework to do, and sometimes they worked outside of the home. They had families; they got sick; they felt tired; and they struggled with worry and fear. Some made bad life choices. They shopped and admired nice clothes, pretty jewellery, and fine perfume. They travelled, entertained guests and friends in their homes, helped the poor, and volunteered their time. Does this sound familiar? They had needs and wants. Jesus saw them for who they were and where they were in life. They were important to Him. You are important to Him.

Several women in the New Testament aren't named, and they went unnoticed, but not by Jesus. He noticed them. He saw their need. I think these women remained unnamed because their issues are common to women everywhere and at any time in history. They could easily be us today.

Do you feel unnoticed sometimes? Be assured, you are noticed by Jesus. He came and died for us.

Father God, thank You for noticing me. Help me to continue to be part of Your story and to help other women be part of the story too. Amen.

OCTOBER 3

"While he was still a long way off, his father saw him ... "
(Luke 15:20)

There's a story in the Bible about a son who left home to find his way in the world. He didn't live very well; in fact, he lived a wild life. He wasted everything his father gave him. After a time, he decided to come home.

I can imagine the father watching the highway, waiting for his son to return. I remember that when my children took the car around town or travelled on the highway, I imagined every mile of their journey while I waited for them to come home safely.

My mother watched for me to come home. She looked out the window and listened for my footsteps and the sound of the porch door opening. Just as my mother watched for me, I watched for my daughters to come home, and I couldn't rest until I knew they were home safe.

When my youngest daughter was eighteen, she attended night school and drove the family car to class. One night while I waited for her to come home, the phone rang. A man's voice introduced himself as a constable, then he said, "I'm at the Health Science Centre with your daughter. She's okay, but shaken up. There's been an accident."

A parent's worst nightmare. I rushed to the hospital. Thankfully, she wasn't harmed. No wonder the Bible tells us to *"Devote yourselves to prayer, being watchful and thankful"* (Colossians 4:2).

Father God, I am so thankful that You watch out for my children too. I'm sure that You have protected them from many dangerous situations. I pray that You will continue to watch out for them. Amen.

OCTOBER 4

"Then, calling the crowd to join his disciples, he said, 'If any of you wants to be my follower, you must give up your own way, take up your cross, and follow me'" (Mark 8:34, NLT).

I've heard the saying many times that "everyone has a cross to bear" or "that's my cross to bear." But when Jesus said to take up your cross, He didn't mean it the way we do now. We understand it to mean putting up with unpleasant circumstances. But in Jesus's day, taking up your cross meant that you were heading for a cruel death—crucifixion. When Jesus said it, He wanted you to be ready to die for Him.

Today we can say that taking up our cross means to die to self—to die to our own agendas, our own pride, and our own selfishness. Even before Jesus died on the cross, He told people that in order to follow Him, they must take up their cross. We must give all of ourselves to follow Jesus. We must be willing to endure whatever challenges may come.

Are you willing to endure criticism, to face the tricks and schemes of evil and to deal with the doubts and accusations of your closest people? Are you ready to die because of your faith in Christ? Maybe we've been taking this verse too lightly.

What does it mean to you to take up your cross?

Father God, You sent Your Son, Jesus, to die for me. Help me to put aside my selfishness and fully commit to Him. Amen.

OCTOBER 5

"Keep me as the apple of your eye" (Psalm 17:8a).

"He shielded him and cared for him; he guarded him as the apple of his eye" (Deuteronomy 32:10b).

I went into my nan's shop, and there behind the counter was a large wooden barrel. When I looked in, I couldn't believe what I was seeing. There in the barrel were the biggest, reddest apples I'd ever seen. One apple was too big for one person. It was the perfect size to share with a friend. One end of each apple had five round points. My nan said they were the five-point barrel apples you could only get at that time of year. My first taste of this delicious looking apple did not disappoint. It was sweet, juicy, and not too hard—and the scent filled the store.

Do you remember eating apples like these that came in a wooden barrel? They were red and shiny. You could almost see your reflection in them, just like sometimes you can see your reflection in the pupil of someone's eye. In ancient days, the pupil of the eye was referred to as the apple of the eye.

God tells us that we are the apple of His eye. He values us so much that He holds us close to Him, and we're always in His sight. He tells me that I am his daughter. In Mark 5:34, Jesus says, *"... Daughter, your faith has healed you. Go in peace and be freed from your suffering."*

Paul says that when you give your heart to God and follow Him, God promises that *"I will be a Father to you, and you will be my sons and daughters ..."* (2 Corinthians 6:18). If you're a daughter of the King of kings, He sees when others want to harm you, and He is not pleased with them. Woe to them who would cause you hurt.

Heavenly Father, keep me always before You as Your daughter and watch over me. As the light is reflected on the shiny apple, let Your reflection be seen in me. In Jesus's name. Amen.

OCTOBER 6

"One day Moses said to his brother-in-law ... 'We are on our way to the place the Lord promised us, for he said, "I will give it to you." Come with us and we will treat you well, for the Lord has promised wonderful blessings for Israel!'" **(Numbers 10:29, NLT)**

Everyone makes choices in life. Some choices might not be life-changing, while others can be life-altering. Even small decisions can affect us significantly.

We may choose to eat at a restaurant instead of cooking supper. We choose what to wear when we get up. We choose what cable company to use for our television and Internet service. We choose whether to buy a new car or keep the old one. These are common, everyday choices, and we don't expect them to change our lives in a big way.

One day you might choose whether to go to college or university, and what career to work towards. Eventually, you might choose a spouse and where to live. All of these are major life choices. Someone might ask you to participate in something that's not good for you. This type of choice could affect the rest of your life in a negative way.

In the verse above, Moses asked his brother-in-law, Hobab, to come with him to the land that God had promised them. In other words, he asked him to leave his former life and put his trust in the living God. He answered Moses with, *"No, I will not go; I am going back to my own land and my own people"* (v. 30b). We're not told what happened to Hobab.

Many people are given the same choice. I'm asking you today, "Will you come, leave your former life, and give your heart to God?" The Lord has promised wonderful blessings for you.

Father God, thank You for the choice to follow You, and thank You for accepting me. Amen.

OCTOBER 7

"Through the tender mercy of our God; whereby the dayspring from on high hath visited us" (Luke 1:78, KJV).

When I read this verse, I wondered to myself, *What is the dayspring?* I discovered that "dayspring" means the beginning of the day, the first appearance of light, and the dawn of the morning.

One year I went on a moose-hunting trip with my husband, Terry. My father-in-law and my mother-in-law came along for the trip as well. We drove all the way to Main Brook on the Northern Peninsula and parked our trailer on an old wood road.

We had to get up very early in the morning. We ate our breakfast, dressed in warm clothing, and most importantly, put on our orange caps. We were ready to go hunting!

One morning we left while it was still dark. We parked the truck on a hill overlooking a recently cut area that still had woods in the background and waited patiently for the morning light to reveal the silhouette of a moose. The sky gradually lightened, but there wasn't much colour. Everything was still a shade of grey, except for an orange tint starting at the bottom of the sky by the tree line. We saw the edge of the sun and then more orange sky as the sun rose. Colours started to deepen in the hills, and we saw the trees and stumps more clearly. We anticipated every second of the coming light, when the night's blackness would fade and everything would be revealed by the light. That is the dayspring.

In the Bible, Jesus is referred to as the Dayspring. He's like that first light in the morning that pushes back the darkness of the night. Jesus pushes back the darkness in our lives.

Father God, thank You for shining light on the darkness of this world. Thank You that Your light in my life reveals things that once I didn't understand. Amen.

OCTOBER 8

"God blessed the seventh day, and made it holy, because he rested in it from all his work of creation which he had done" (Genesis 2:3, WEB).

I have many childhood memories of Saturday, the day before the Sabbath Day. On Sunday, all work stopped and we went to church, but Saturday was a different story.

Saturday was preparation day. We cleaned the house from top to bottom—scrubbing floors, dusting furniture, and sanitizing the bathroom. Mom made the dessert for Sunday dinner, and she freshened and pressed the Sunday clothes.

Saturday night we'd soak in the bathtub, wash our hair, shake on talcum powder, and put on clean flannel pyjamas. Mom wrapped my hair in rags in order to have curls for Sunday. After the bath, there was time for play. Dad would get down on the floor on his hands and knees, and the three of us—Nancy, Arlette, and I (Alexia and Monique hadn't been born yet)—would get on his back. He'd gallop all around the floor while we were laughing and falling off.

I have so many Saturday memories and all the things we did to prepare for Sunday. The Bible says to *"Remember the Sabbath day by keeping it holy"* (Exodus 20:8). This is the fourth commandment.

For some people, there's nothing special about Saturday or Sunday. They go about their lives and pay no attention to God. These are the days they devote to themselves and what they want to do. One day is just like another. People don't look at Sunday as a holy day. They say that times have changed. How can we keep Sunday holy in these changing times? What do you think?

Father God, help us to remember to put one day a week aside to focus on You, our Creator. Thank You for childhood memories of preparing for Sunday. Amen.

OCTOBER 9

"For you are the fountain of life, the light by which we see"
(Psalm 36:9, NLT).

Do you remember when people wrote with fountain pens? Some of you aren't old enough to have had that experience. Still, I'm sure you've probably seen a picture of one.

When I first went to work for the government, we kept fountain pens around for signatures on letters and official papers. These days, fountain pens are rarely used, and usually just for special documents. The writing from a fountain pen looks very elegant when done properly.

In my early school days, students mostly wrote with lead pencils and ballpoint pens. There may have been a few fountain pens around, too. The desks even had a place for the bottle of ink. I can imagine the mess when a student spilled the ink. The older fountain pens required you to dip your pen in the ink, write a little, and then dip again. Later, there were pens that you could fill up by opening a lever on the pen to suck up the ink and store it inside. This was a messy affair as well. Today, you can get fountain pens with pop-in ink cartridges. No more bottles of ink. No matter what kind of pen you use, they're all useless tools without ink. You can't write a word without it.

The Bible tells us that God is the fountain of life. Make sure you keep your Christian life worthy and useful by going to the fountain often.

Father God in Heaven, thank You for the lesson of the fountain pen. So often, I try to do things without being prepared by You. Please fill me with Your living water so that I can do and be all You planned for me. Amen.

OCTOBER 10

"You have shown contempt by offering defiled sacrifices on my altar"
(Malachi 1:7a, NLT).

The day after Thanksgiving is leftover day. The turkey we enjoyed this year was a broad-breasted, farm-raised bird from a farmer in our area. There seemed to be no end to the white meat as Terry sliced it for serving. As good as it was, there was still lots left over for the next day, and the next, and probably the next. I planned to have cold turkey with salads, then cold turkey sandwiches, and then turkey soup. As I planned the week's menu, I hoped the leftovers would soon be gone.

Leftovers are good for a day or so to serve the family, and it gives me a break from cooking, but the family wouldn't like it if I only gave them my leftover time, leftover conversation, leftover gifts, leftover affection, or leftover attention. My family needs more from me than just leftovers.

Today's verse was a message from God to the Jews, delivered to them by the prophet Malachi. The Jews were bringing their leftovers to God. They offered blind, lame, and diseased animals to God. They dishonoured God by offering imperfect gifts. God deserves our best in everything we give and do. Our true thoughts about God determine the type of gifts and services we give. Don't give God your leftover time, money, and energy. Don't keep the best and the most for yourself.

Malachi asked, *"But when you bring that kind of offering, why should he show you any favor at all?"* (Malachi 1:9, NLT).

Father God, forgive us when we fail to give You the best of us. We come to You sometimes when we're too tired for anything else instead of when we're awake and fresh. Help me to seek You before anything else. Amen.

OCTOBER 11

"Jesus answered, 'I am the way and the truth and the life. No one comes to the Father except through me'" (John 14:6).

"It's not fair!" We've all said that at least once in our lives. When we don't get our own way or something that we really want, or when we don't receive the recognition we think we deserve, we might think it's not fair. Where is it written that life is supposed to be fair? Do you know what? Life's not fair.

By whose standards do we determine what's fair or not? Usually, it's our own standards. We think that if we're good enough or work enough, we'll get lots of rewards—everything life can give us. But no matter how hard we try, bad things happen. There's no guarantee that you won't have health problems, financial difficulties, or relationship challenges.

We often apply the same rule to our spiritual life. If we work hard enough, we'll earn a place in Heaven. We often look at someone and say, "If she doesn't get to Heaven, then no one else will" or "She's going to Heaven for sure. Look at what she's done." When it comes to our spiritual security and a place in Heaven, the Bible tells us to believe in the one God sent—Jesus, God's Son. Jesus said, *"... This is the only work God wants from you: Believe in the one he has sent"* (John 6:29, NLT). Paul wrote, *"Abraham believed God, and it was credited to him as righteousness"* (Romans 4:3).

Father God, in our human nature, we think we deserve certain rewards in this life and the next. But the truth is, we're all sinners in need of Your forgiveness. Help us to accept your free gift of grace and to live our lives for You alone. Amen.

OCTOBER 12

"Like autumn leaves, we wither and fall, and our sins sweep us away like the wind" (Isaiah 64:6b, NLT).

Today I heard the sound of a leaf falling. I was sitting on the bench underneath the tall aspen and birch trees in the garden. It was peaceful and still. I thought about maybe lighting a fire in the pit, but it was so quiet, I just sat there listening. Then I heard a little snap and a fluttering as a leaf let go of the tree branch that had nourished it all summer. It gently floated to the grassy floor to finish its purpose as enrichment for the soil.

This is a reminder to me that as trees shed their leaves in the fall, I should let go of all the thoughts and things that weigh me down. I should let these burdens fall to the earth and wither away like the yellow and brown autumn leaves. Maybe I should make a new commitment to trust God and let go of all the unnecessary thoughts. But how do I do that?

Paul tells us in Romans 12:2a to change our thought process: *"Do not conform to the pattern of this world, but be transformed by the renewing of your mind."* You do this by focusing on the truths in God's Word. Review what God tells us about His provision and protection. Don't let negative thoughts control your life.

I can't remember ever hearing a leaf fall that way. It's easy to miss it if you're focused on something else, or if you let the noise of the world disturb the silence. Maybe God's still, small voice is like the sound of the leaf falling. I hope this has taught me to listen better for God and to give Him all my problems.

Father God, thank You for quiet times of listening. Sometimes I'm surprised by what I hear. Hearing the leaf fall was a reminder to be listening for Your voice. Amen.

OCTOBER 13

"Don't look out only for your own interests, but take an interest in others, too" (Philippians 2:4, NLT).

I was lying in my hospital bed at the old Grace Hospital in St. John's. It was the second or third day after my surgery, and I still couldn't keep much food in me. I was on the seventh floor, and it wasn't very warm there. It seemed as though the cold wind blew throughout the whole floor. The nurses covered me with warm blankets to keep out the chill.

My sister Alexia called to tell me she had some time off to visit me and wondered what I wanted her to bring. I said I wanted homemade bread toasted with Cheez Whiz spread on it. Sure enough, later that day she came by. She toasted the bread in the little kitchenette and put the spread on it. It was delicious and just what I needed. I never forgot about it. It's the most significant thing I remember about that whole experience. Her thoughtfulness and kindness helped to get me on the road to recovery.

There are many important jobs in the medical environment, from housekeeping to office workers to doctors. They're all needed for the smooth operation of the facility. The patients need them to perform their duties as best they can.

The role of the visitor is important as well for the overall well-being of the patient. I was grateful for all the staff who took care of me, but I was even more grateful for my sister. Sometimes it's the little things that are most appreciated. Never forget to help others, even if it seems very small.

Father God, I'm so grateful for all the good people You put in my life. I'm even more thankful for my family. Bless them and protect them. Amen.

OCTOBER 14

"So then, each of us will give an account of ourselves to God"
(Romans 14:12).

There's a lot of talk in government about being accountable—the importance of it, the expectations of the public, and the roles and responsibilities of a public servant. What's the meaning of the word "accountable"? The online Cambridge dictionary defines an accountable person as someone who "is completely responsible for what they do and ... able to give a satisfactory reason for it."

I was a government public servant in my secular job. In that position, I was accountable to my employer. There were certain expectations attached to the job description that I agreed to when I took the job. I was accountable to my director. I served the public, so I was accountable to them. And I was accountable to my coworkers.

While I was growing up, I was accountable to my parents. As a wife, mother, daughter, and sister, I'm accountable to my family.

We're accountable to our friends, to keep confidences, to treat them fairly, to be there for them. We're accountable to other people—especially non-Christians, who expect us to be somewhat perfect and never make a mistake. The way we behave can either turn others to Christ or away from Him. We're also accountable to the laws of the land.

We're accountable to many people. But don't forget that when our lives are over, we are accountable to God. How will you live so that you will have a good account before God?

We are accountable!

Father God, I'm sometimes overwhelmed by all this accountability. Help me to be all that You want me to be. Fill me with Your Holy Spirit so that I can have courage and power to live the way You want me to live. In Jesus's name. Amen.

OCTOBER 15

"Philip went to look for Nathanael and told him, 'We have found the very person Moses and the prophets wrote about! His name is Jesus, the son of Joseph from Nazareth'" (John 1:45, NLT).

What is the proper way to introduce someone? My sisters usually say, "This is my oldest sister, Suzanne." My mother says, "This is my daughter Suzanne." My daughters say, "This is my mom, Suzanne." My husband says, "This is my wife, Suzanne." Some Newfoundlanders might say, "This is da wife." How you introduce someone usually depends on your relationship with them.

Have you ever been in a situation where you wanted to introduce someone but forgot their name? That's embarrassing! Here's a way around that. Introduce yourself first. Most likely, the other person will then introduce themselves. Or take a step back and say, "Please introduce yourselves." If you meet someone you know, you could start the introductions by saying, "I'd like you to meet" or "May I introduce" or "Hello. It's nice to see you again." These are all good introductions.

John the Baptizer in John 1:29 introduced Jesus as *"The Lamb of God, who takes away the sin of the world!"* (NLT). Andrew told his brother Simon that Jesus was the Messiah (John 1:41). Now when Philip met Jesus, he told Nathanael that Jesus was the one that Moses and the prophets wrote about (John 1:45). Nathanael said in John 1:49, *"... you are the Son of God—the King of Israel!"* (NLT).

Have you met the one called Jesus? Will you introduce Him to your friends?

Father God, I'm so glad that I met Your Son, Jesus. He's all that the prophets wrote about and more. He is my Redeemer and my Friend. Please help me to introduce Him to others. Amen.

OCTOBER 16

"Let us not become weary in doing good, for at the proper time we will reap a harvest if we do not give up" (Galatians 6:9).

"Let perseverance finish its work ... " (James 1:4)

He took aim and then pulled the trigger. Terry shot the moose. It went down some distance away on a cutover section of forest behind a stand of trees. Terry told us to stay where we were as he walked towards the area to check on the bull moose. Just when he got close to the animal, it jumped up, ran further into the woods, and disappeared. Terry and his nephew Stephen went through the woods, following the path where the moose had headed, but they couldn't find him. Finally, they had no choice but to come back to the road.

He hated to leave an injured animal, so we drove further down the road to see if we could intersect the moose. We got out to look around, and suddenly, we spotted the moose walking slowly along the edge of the woods. He had his head down, so we knew he was injured. Terry was happy to catch up with this animal and complete the hunt. I was glad that he didn't give up, as some might do. His patience and perseverance paid off.

This was a lesson to me on not giving up. Sometimes what we're doing seems pointless, so we're tempted to throw in the towel. But the Bible tells us not to give up or get tired of doing good. Perseverance produces endurance and character. You'll reap the benefits if you don't give up.

Father God, thank You for this lesson about not giving up, even when I'm tired or it seems futile. Help me to persevere to the end. Amen.

OCTOBER 17

"Make every effort to live in peace with all men and to be holy; without holiness no one will see the Lord" (Hebrews 12:14).

Sometimes, no matter how hard we try, we're unable to live in peace with some people. It seems as though they were born to cause a racket. They know how to push your buttons. There are peacemakers, and there are strife-makers. My nan used to say, "Don't be a strife-maker."

Maybe you have to work with a person like that. You might have an unruly neighbour. Maybe you struggle with someone in a volunteer group, or even a family member. It could be anyone.

Of course, we can't change how other people act. So what do we do about it? What does the Bible say about this? Jesus shows us different ways of approaching this issue, depending on the situation. Sometimes He remained silent. Sometimes He asked questions. Sometimes He told a story, and sometimes He pointed people to Scripture.

Proverbs 20:3 tells us to avoid strife and quarrels if possible. Sometimes, though, we can't avoid dealing with difficult people. We have to be careful not to respond from our own hurt feelings or in anger. Remember to treat them as you would want to be treated. Show them the same love and patience that God gave you. Treat them with respect and gentleness. Remember, *"A gentle answer deflects anger"* (Proverbs 15:1a, NLT).

One thing for sure, when I cross the line from Earth to Heaven, strife cannot cross with me. I am so looking forward to leaving that part of my life behind.

Father God, thank You for Your example of how to react to difficult people. Help me to follow it and to remember to respond to them with love and kindness. In Jesus's name. Amen.

OCTOBER 18

"When he arrived and saw the grace of God, he was glad and encouraged all of them to remain true to the Lord with a firm resolve of the heart" (Acts 11:23, HCSB).

His name means *Son of Encouragement*. He was among the first Christians. His name was Barnabas, and he was an encourager to other Christians. I feel positive that many people became believers because of this. He even encouraged the apostle Paul. Imagine if Paul hadn't had this encouragement. Would he have written the major part of the New Testament that we read today?

Everyone likes to be around encouragers. They make us feel that we can accomplish anything, that we're of value, and that our life has a purpose. Where would we be without encouragers? I've had many encouragers in my life who have helped me accomplish things that I wouldn't have done on my own.

I've had criticizers too—sometimes helpful, but most times not helpful. Some have helped me to achieve more and to do things in a different way. Others have not. You have to be very careful about giving criticism. Never criticize the person; instead, encourage the correct behaviour to see the best results.

Many people around me would benefit from encouraging words. Sometimes, we're tempted to just point out where they went wrong. But you'll find that encouraging words help them more. Not many people are accepting of criticism, and it has to be tempered with a lot of love. Unless they know you want the best for them, it won't be accepted or useful.

Encourage someone in their belief and Christian walk today. Make a phone call, send a message and acknowledge their positive accomplishments.

Father God, thank You for all the encouragers You placed in my life. Help me to be an encourager to other people so that their faith is encouraged. Amen.

OCTOBER 19

"I tell you for certain that we know what we are talking about because we have seen it ourselves" (John 3:11a, CEV).

My father had a fantastic memory for storytelling. He remembered exact details and conversations. When he told a story, you felt as if you were there too. I listened to my dad tell accounts of things that happened to him as well as stories told to him by his father. He told stories about trips on the fishing schooner, the men in the logging camps, his work at various power companies, and his family.

He described the weather, where they were, what they said, and how they laughed or cried. He didn't leave out any details. His stories were about real people and real events. Some of them were firsthand accounts, and others had been told to him. Dad told the stories with the same feelings as when they happened. If it was funny, he laughed, and if it was sad, he cried.

We often rely on firsthand testimonies and accounts of events. We believe the stories because the witnesses are reliable and trustworthy. They're telling the accounts of real events, exactly as they happened.

The first chapter of Acts tells us that Jesus showed Himself to the apostles over a period of forty days before He ascended into Heaven. Jesus said to them, *"… you will be my witnesses in Jerusalem, and in all Judea and Samaria, and to the ends of the earth"* (Acts 1:8b). Jesus gave them many convincing proofs that He was alive. In this way, the apostles became reliable witnesses. The Bible records all these events from their accounts.

Lord Jesus, thank You for the reliable witnesses You chose to tell us about You and all the things You taught them. Thank You too for the witnesses of today who tell us about Your presence in their lives. Amen.

OCTOBER 20

"Be brave and strong! ... The Lord your God will always be at your side, and he will never abandon you" (Deuteronomy 31:6, CEV).

I confess that I've always wanted to be physically stronger, and I used to think that I should join a weightlifting program. To be physically strong, you need to follow the proper diet and participate in strength training exercises. Can you be weak one day and strong the next? Of course not. Building up physical strength takes time and practice.

What do you have to do to be mentally strong? I don't know if stubbornness counts. If it does, I have that. I know we need to exercise our minds with reading, solving problems, and challenging thinking. We need to feed our minds with positive things. Can you be mentally weak one day and strong the next? Of course not. It takes time and practice.

What do you have to do to be spiritually strong? Dig into the truths in God's book, the Bible. Persist in prayer and trust God to fulfill His promises. Can you be spiritually weak one day and strong the next? Of course not. It takes time and practice.

God promises that His strength will see us through anything. Philippians 4:13 says, *"I can do all things through Christ who strengthens me"* (WEB). The strength He gave yesterday was for yesterday's problems. Ask for a fresh supply every day, and He will give it.

There are no shortcuts to being or living strong. Growing in strength is a continual process that takes time, persistence, and patience. Remember Psalm 73:26: *"My flesh and my heart may fail, but God is the strength of my heart and my portion forever."*

What does the word "strength" bring to your mind?

Father God, I know there are no shortcuts to living strong. Help me to follow Your ways, and fill me with strength for each day. Amen.

OCTOBER 21

"In the same way, let your light shine before others, that they may see your good deeds and glorify your Father in heaven"
(Matthew 5:16).

When I was growing up in Chance Cove, some activities took place on the same day of the week every week. We didn't have to write them down, because everyone knew what they were and when to do them. For instance, every Monday was washday. Everyone in the cove washed clothes on Monday, and all of it was hung on the outdoor lines.

Wednesday night was the Home League meeting at the church for the women. You wouldn't find a woman at home that night. Saturday, though, was the day for pea soup and housecleaning.

After the pea soup lunch, there was housecleaning. Every Saturday, the floors were scrubbed, waxed, and shined by hand. We used buckets, scrub brushes, mops, and paste wax.

My mom scrubbed and dried the tiled floors. Then she rubbed on the paste wax with a soft cloth. When the wax dried, she went over the whole floor again with another cloth to buff it to a glossy finish. My sisters and I helped by putting on our wool socks and sliding around on the floor. We buffed the dull wax until the floors shone and you could see your reflection in them. Keeping the floors clean and shiny was hard work.

Keep your walk with God as shiny as possible so that others will see your light. Dust off the Bible, scrub your mind of unholy thoughts, wax your prayers, and shine up your good deeds. Isaiah 2:5b tells us to *"walk in the light of the Lord."*

Father in Heaven, sometimes it's hard for others to see the light within us. We become dull when we neglect to talk to You and read the Bible. Forgive our neglect and help us once again to be shining examples of Your love. From a thankful heart. Amen.

OCTOBER 22

"This encounter took place in Bethany, an area east of the Jordan River, where John was baptizing" (John 1:28, NLT).

God is so gracious. He speaks to us individually according to our unique personality. God speaks to us in ways that He knows we will see, hear, and understand.

If you're a nature lover, He may speak to you through experiences in the woods, such as exploring the trails, hunting, fishing, or maybe when you're in your garden. If you're a musician or just love to listen to music, He may speak to you when you play the instrument, sing a song, or write a song. If you're an artist, He may speak through the producing of the art, or when it's finished.

He may speak while you're quiet, walking, cooking, doing chores, sewing, or cleaning. He may speak through a child or another godly person. Most of all, He speaks through His Word while you read and study the Scriptures.

Many people in the Bible encountered God in unusual and extraordinary ways. There was Moses and the burning bush that didn't burn (Exodus 3:2); Elijah when he was on the mountain (1 Kings 19:11–12); John the Baptist encountering Jesus at the Jordan River (John 1:29); and Saul meeting Jesus on the road in a blinding light (Acts 9:3–4).

Many of us would like to meet or hear God in an extraordinary way, and maybe some of us do. But the important thing is that we're listening, ready to hear and do what He says. So be alert, because you never know when or where you'll have an encounter with God.

Father God, thank You for Your small voice when I read the Bible. Sometimes, I feel Your presence when I'm quiet in nature. The hymn says, "In the rustling grass I hear Him pass, He speaks to me everywhere." I know You are always with me. Amen.

OCTOBER 23

"... narrow is the way, which leadeth unto life, and few there be that find it" (Matthew 7:14, KJV).

It was the middle of the day. After eating the lunch that my mom had prepared, and after helping with the dishes, I left my house to call on my friend Norma. The main road was at the end of our driveway. It was wide with plenty of room for me and cars, if any came by while I walked. This road led to a new concrete bridge that crossed the gut. It was smooth with only a little turn and a small hill.

When I turned and looked towards the beach, I saw the old, narrow road and decided to go that way. It was just a well-worn footpath and very rocky. Although two people could walk side by side, in some places, the sea had washed some of the path away, and in other places, there was kelp and driftwood washed up from the ocean.

A fence was on one side of the path. It leaned a bit and was taller than me because it was on higher ground. As I walked, the sun shone brightly through the openings. My eyes would blink, because one moment it would be bright, and the next moment it was not. Over the old road I went. I walked around a turn past Alfred Rowe's house, and then I came to the old wooden bridge. The rails were gone. The old wooden beams were weather-worn, and openings were starting to show through the boards. I slowly crossed over the bridge, being careful of the dangers. Before me was a steeper hill, but at the top of the hill and down another steep path was my friend's house. I walked and walked and walked. Whew! I made it. It was worth it. This was the road less travelled, but I made it safely to my destination.

Father God, thank You for Your promise that if I believe that Jesus is the Son of God and follow His path, I will have a home in Heaven with You. Amen.

OCTOBER 24

"But we are citizens of heaven, where the Lord Jesus Christ lives. And we are eagerly waiting for him to return as our Savior" (Philippians 3:20, NLT).

A long time ago, I worked for the Federal Unemployment Insurance Commission (U.I.C.). People who were out of work would come to my office to apply for benefit payments to sustain them until they had work again. I'd advise them and then help them fill out the paperwork and submit it for payment. There was always a waiting period before payments would begin.

I thought about this the other day while I was listening to a song on the radio about Heaven. That's what my life on earth is—just a period of waiting for the full benefits. The words to the song say, "This world is not my home; I'm just passing through."

Sometimes it's hard to wait, isn't it? It's especially hard when you're waiting for important things, like a paycheque to cover the bills, or a doctor's appointment for a serious illness, or the resolution to a crisis situation. Every day we're waiting for something.

The Bible speaks to this in the Psalms: *"Wait for the Lord; be strong and take heart and wait for the Lord"* (Psalm 27:14); *"With all my heart, I am waiting, Lord, for you! I trust your promises"* (Psalm 130:5, CEV); *"Put your hope in the Lord. Travel steadily along his path. He will honor you by giving you the land …"* (Psalm 37:34, NLT).

Waiting requires patience, but it also has benefits. It produces great trust in God and leaves room for God to work. Are you waiting on something? Be assured that anything we wait for on earth is only temporary. Put your hope in God and wait for Him.

Father God, sometimes the waiting is hard. Help me to put my trust fully in You in all situations. I look forward to the time when this waiting period is over and I receive the full benefits of eternal life with You. Amen.

OCTOBER 25

"I pray not that you would take them from the world, but that you would keep them from the evil one" (John 17:15, WEB).

Do you pray for your children? If so, what do you ask for? What are your top priorities? What are your most repeated requests? Do you pray for health, good education, godly friends, a satisfying job, a loving spouse, and a home of their own? These are all good things, and I pray for these things for my children.

But when Jesus prayed for the followers God had given Him, He asked that they be kept from the evil one. He asked that they be pure and holy and know the truth (John 17:17), and He asked that they be one just as He is one with the Father (John 17:21).

We mainly ask for material things. But Jesus didn't ask for riches or anything the world offers. He asked for His people to be safe from evil. He wanted them united in their love for God and each other. He wanted them to be pure-hearted and holy by knowing God's truths.

These are not things of the world but things of God, and they have eternal value. It's fine to ask for good things for our children, but our top priorities should be the same as Jesus's requests: keep them from evil; give them pure hearts; make them holy; keep them in unity; and teach them God's truths.

Father God, it blesses me when I read that Your Son, Jesus, prayed for His followers, which includes me. I want the same things for my children too. Help me to keep them as top priorities in my prayer requests. Amen.

OCTOBER 26

"They will be like a tree planted by the water that sends out its roots by the stream. It does not fear when heat comes; its leaves are always green. It has no worries in a year of drought and never fails to bear fruit" (Jeremiah 17:8).

On an autumn day, I walked with the leaves. Side by side we walked, fast and then slow. The wind helped us. It directed me and the leaves to dance to nature's caller in a circle like a jig.

I'll tell you how it happened. It was a beautiful fall day. In the afternoon, I went for a walk on our street. On my return, I met the leaves swirling around my feet. As the wind blew, they followed me for a while. For a brief moment in time, my attention was diverted from the world as I danced with the leaves.

The next season is winter. In the winter, our trees look so bare. I wonder how they can look so lifeless and still be alive. Beneath the surface, the roots spread out and sustain the trees during the cold, dark winter. They are resting and preparing for a new season of growth.

Sometimes in our lives, we have long, dark winters when it seems our lives have no life, such as during a mourning period or after stressful events. Our days are mundane as we struggle to survive by just doing the next thing. We feel stuck, and there's nothing new in our days. But if our roots go deep in the truths of the gospel, our faith will sustain us until the next growing season. Then we can again dance joyfully with the leaves.

Father God, thank You for the promise to sustain us during the dark times of our lives. Help us to remember that seasons change and a new season of growth and joy will come again. Amen.

OCTOBER 27

"Then they plotted among themselves, 'Let's choose a new leader and go back to Egypt!'" (Numbers 14:4, NLT)

People like to offer advice, don't they? But sometimes we really don't want advice. We've already made up our mind on what we want to do or what we believe will happen. We think we're right and are making the right decisions. Even though other people may see it differently based on their experiences, we don't want their two cents' worth.

When I look back over my life, I can now see that as a teenager, I was a bit rebellious. I liked to do things my own way and in my own time. Some of my decisions weren't based on good advice but on my own wilfulness. Thankfully, I completed my education, entered the workforce, and had a wonderful family of my own.

Don't be too quick to reject advice you don't like. The cost to you could be higher than you want to pay. Joshua and Caleb told the Israelites that the land they looked at was good, and God would bring them safely there if they trusted in Him. Joshua said, *"but the Lord is with us. Do not be afraid of them"* (Numbers 14:9b). When the Israelites rejected this advice, they lost the right to enter the land God had promised them: *"not one of these people will ever enter that land."* (Numbers 14:22a, NLT).

Think through all advice carefully and compare it to God's Word. God has a plan for us, and it's the best plan for our life. Remember, *"The Lord is the one you and your followers are really revolting against"* (Numbers 16:11a, NLT).

Father God, when I'm rebellious, I'm so thankful that You are forgiving. Thank You for Your patience and mercy. Help me to weigh the direction and advice of others in light of Your Word. Amen.

OCTOBER 28

"The Lord is slow to anger but great in power; the Lord will not leave the guilty unpunished" (Nahum 1:3a).

If God is so loving and powerful, why doesn't He punish the wicked in the world? I'm sure all of us have wondered this at times. The book of Nahum in the Bible talks about this issue. The story is about Judah and its enemy, the Assyrians. No one could stand against them. The Assyrians conquered many nations, stealing all the wealth for themselves.

Nineveh was the capital city of Assyria, and God judged it for its oppression of the people they conquered, for its idolatry, and for its excessive lifestyle. Psalm 103:8 tells us that *"The Lord is merciful and gracious, slow to anger, and plenteous in mercy"* (KJV), but He will punish the wicked.

Nahum was a prophet who brought a message from God to the Assyrians and to Judah. To the Assyrians it was a message of doom: *"The Lord is a jealous and avenging God; the Lord takes vengeance and is fierce in wrath. The Lord takes vengeance against His foes; He is furious with His enemies"* (Nahum 1:2, HCSB). To Judah, he said, *"I'll snap your chains and set you free from the Assyrians"* (Nahum 1:13, CEV). In due time (some scholars say a few decades), Nineveh was destroyed, and the Assyrians were defeated.

Even though there are evil doers in the world, judgement will come. It might not happen right away, because God allows time for even them to come to Him. If God punished sin right away, we wouldn't be here. Be assured that evil will be destroyed in God's time. God rules over all the earth, good and bad. Place your confidence in the all-powerful God.

Father God, I wonder why there's so much evil. But I'm confident that You're in control and that one day there will be no more fear or wickedness. Help me to trust You for the future. Amen.

OCTOBER 29

"But he abandoned the counsel of the old men which they had given him, and took counsel with the young men who had grown up with him, who stood before him" (2 Chronicles 10:8, WEB).

In this story, we have a young King Rehoboam, son of the wise King Solomon. Too bad he didn't inherit his father's good sense to ask God for wisdom. When a situation came up that required perceptive and delicate handling, he rejected the advice of the experienced older counsellors. This was his downfall. Why did he accept the opinions of the younger men instead? Why do we accept bad advice? I think we do it for a number of reasons:

- Because it suits what we already believe and want.
- We may not be fully committed to God and we reject His ways, plans, and purpose.
- We resent the people who have been advisers and leaders for a long time.
- We want our friends to like us, so we support their views.
- We're more concerned for ourselves than for the good of the whole group.

It's important to seek wise counsel but even more important to follow that counsel. We have to put our preconceived ideas and feelings aside and ask how the decision will affect others. The Bible tells us to *"Get wisdom; develop good judgment. Don't forget my words or turn away from them"* (Proverbs 4:5, NLT). Ask God for wisdom and He will give it.

Father God, give me Your wisdom when I'm faced with important decisions. I want Your counsel in all my life situations, whether it comes directly from You or from experienced counsellors. Amen.

OCTOBER 30

"If you say, 'The Lord is my refuge,' and you make the Most High your dwelling, no harm will overtake you, no disaster will come near your tent" (Psalm 91:9–10).

We stopped for the night at Jonestown KOA Park in Pennsylvania. It was a beautiful park, and they gave us a drive-through site. It was a well-established park with lots of mature trees, trails, and a meandering river. It was windy when we went to bed that night, but we were expecting some wind, as the forecast had called for it. That was why we'd decided not to drive further but to stop there for two nights.

I was in a deep sleep when I suddenly woke up to a loud sound, like a train. The trailer started rocking side to side, and the bathroom door swung open and closed again. Terry and I looked at each other and said, "Is that the wind?" We heard crashes outside, like someone was throwing rocks at the trailer. It got worse, and I didn't know what to do but pray and pull the blankets over my head. I thought we'd tip over, but we had nowhere to go, so we stayed inside.

Then just as suddenly as it started, it stopped. It was still windy, but only a normal wind. When daylight came, we went outside. We saw destruction all around us. When I saw the extent of the debris, I cried. The trailer next to us was heavily damaged, with a big tree on the roof. Broken branches were all around our trailer. Our wooden picnic table had been broken in two pieces by a falling tree. Trees had broken off on one side of us, flown over our trailer, and damaged the one next to us. We were not harmed. Not a scratch on our trailer. Words can't express how grateful we were. I thanked God over and over again. *"He protected us on our entire journey and among all the nations through which we traveled."* (Joshua 24:17b).

Father God, thank You for protecting us and our tent during this storm. From a thankful heart. Amen.

OCTOBER 31

"Where there is no vision, the people perish"
(Proverbs 29:18a, KJV).

"But they delight in the law of the Lord, meditating on it day and night" (Psalm 1:2, NLT).

People need hope, but they also need a vision for the future. Without them both, we fail to flourish and may even dip to the lowest state of depression.

Proverbs 29:18a says that *"When people do not accept divine guidance, they run wild"* (NLT). This means that anything goes. Without vision, people will either withdraw into depression or run wild. This is happening in the world today. Depression is at an all-time high, and there seems to be no restraint on the evil things some people are involved with.

All of us need to hope for and look forward to something. We need to be able to see it in our mind and heart. We need assurance that there's a greater power than us that gives purpose to our lives

What we need is *First Choice Vision*—and not the kind referred to in the name of the local optical business. We need direction for our daily lives, and the Word of God is where to get it. If you want direction and vision for your life, look into God's Word. Psalm 25:5 says, *"Guide me in your truth and teach me, for you are God my Savior, and my hope is in you all day long."*

Father God, I'm so thankful that I can look into Your Word and get direction for my life. You give me hope for the future. Help me to point others to You. Amen.

NOVEMBER 1

"Can God really spread a table in the wilderness?" (Psalm 78:19b)

"What a spread they had at that supper!"

I grew up in a small community where people went to church, weddings, funerals, and times. For those of you who are a bit younger or not familiar with Newfoundland slang, a "time" is a social gathering, like a soup supper, concert, or even a dance (usually held in the school). It's pronounced "toime." What a time we'd have at the toime!

All the family went to the time. There were games, stories, songs, and food—lots of food. I especially remember the soup, which was usually meat and rice soup. It was really good, served with fresh homemade rolls that were shaped like crescents or clovers. Afterwards, we'd enjoy delicious homemade jam tarts and sweet tea.

Since we're talking about food, I'm convinced that there wasn't any bottom in my grandmother's boiler (big cooking pot). It seemed to me that no matter what she cooked, there was always enough for whomever dropped by. I think all of us know someone like that. It just seems like some people can feed the multitudes. My nan was one of those people. You could always get a slice of bread or a lassy bun.

The Bible gives us many examples of God putting out a spread. He provided for people who couldn't find food or water. God says, "Come to my table. I will provide." You can be sure that when you come to His table, there will be fresh meat soup, lassy bread, jam tarts, and sweet tea. But most important of all, there is *grace*. What a spread! Won't you come and dine?

Father God, thank You for providing all we need. Help me to come to You, especially during the downhearted times. Amen.

NOVEMBER 2

"Then I heard the voice of the Lord saying, 'Whom shall I send? And who will go for us?' And I said, 'Here am I. Send me!'" (Isaiah 6:8)

These are the things I remember my mom saying:

"Is anyone going to the post office today?"

"Will you go down to the mill and get your father for supper?"

"Go to your grandmother's and bring in an armload of wood."

It is funny that I never had trouble hearing these things, but when it comes to God, sometimes I'm not paying attention.

Isaiah was taken to Heaven in a vision and heard *"Whom shall I send? And who will go for us?"* But this wasn't just said for Isaiah's benefit. He overheard the continuous voice of God calling. Had I been in Isaiah's place, I'd be paying attention too. God is always calling. But how can we make sure that we hear Him?

In Isaiah 6:6–7, Isaiah realizes the greatness of God's holiness. Consequently, he's overwhelmed by the enormity of his own sin. In verse 1, he saw the Lord seated on the throne in Heaven. In verse 2, he witnessed the heavenly beings around the throne worshipping God. The Bible says in verse 4 that the doorposts and the thresholds shook, and the place filled with smoke.

I don't know about you, but I'd be paying attention after witnessing that! Isaiah was ready to hear God's request. Are you listening and receptive to God's voice? Have you heard the continuous voice of God calling you?

Father God, I want to be receptive to Your calling. Help me to be quick to listen and to obey Your voice. Amen.

NOVEMBER 3

"My times are in your hands" (Psalm 31:15a).

Tick-tock, tick-tock goes the big wall clock in our living room. Then it *donged* for half past ten o'clock.

Some people say the sound of a ticking clock is annoying. But when I hear the ticking of the clock at night, it reminds me that the other noises are winding down. They are quieter than they were all day as they retreat into the night. The occasional hum of a passing car or the revving of a motorcycle replaces the constant sounds of the day. I like this time of day the most. The television is off, the phone is silent, and all I hear is the *tick-tock*.

I wonder how we can hear God when there's so much noise around us. The only time I notice the ticking of the clock is when everything else is off. This is the best time to hear God too. The day is done. Whether it was sunny, fair, cloudy, or drizzly, it's finished. Whatever I did, said, or thought—or didn't—is done. I can't get it back or change a single moment. It was a good day. It was a day made by God. It was a gift the Lord made and gave to me to spend as I wish. Did I waste this gift or spend it wisely? I don't know. God willing, I'll have another day tomorrow and a new chance to do it better.

Why should He give us another day when we waste so much of our lives? Because He loves us. He gives mercy in spite of our actions, and grace to forgive as we start again with each new dawn. Psalm 118:24 says, *"This is the day which the Lord hath made; we will rejoice and be glad in it"* (KJV).

> *Father God, thank You for each new day, with its fresh supply of love, mercy, and grace that You provide to us. Help me, Lord, to live each day knowing that in a moment I could be in Heaven with You. Help me to simplify my busy life and concentrate on kingdom work. Amen.*

NOVEMBER 4

"God's word is alive and powerful! It is sharper than any double-edged sword. His word can cut through our spirits and souls and through our joints and marrow, until it discovers the desires and thoughts of our hearts" (Hebrews 4:12, CEV).

Some people's words are commanding and powerful. When they speak, everyone jumps. I'm sure all of us know someone like that. My Grandfather Rowe falls into that category. When he spoke, we trembled.

There's a story in Luke 7 about a centurion (Roman soldier) who sent someone to bring Jesus to heal his highly valued servant. When Jesus was partway there, the centurion sent more friends to tell Him not to come because he wasn't worthy to have Jesus enter his house. He told Jesus to just say the words and his servant would be healed: *"For I also am a man placed under authority, having under myself soldiers. I tell this one, 'Go!' and he goes; and to another, 'Come!' and he comes; and to my servant, 'Do this,' and he does it."* (Luke 7:8, WEB). The centurion had heard about the power of Jesus's words. He had faith that just the speaking of the words would bring healing. As a result of the centurion's faith, the servant was healed at that very moment.

The Bible tells us that God's Word is powerful: *"My words are a powerful fire; they are a hammer that shatters rocks"* (Jeremiah 23:29, CEV). The Word of God is your defence against evil. You wouldn't go to battle without a weapon. Don't try to live a Christian life without one either: *"We use God's mighty weapons, not worldly weapons, to knock down the strongholds of human reasoning and to destroy false arguments"* (2 Corinthians 10:4, NLT).

Father God, thank You for Your powerful Word. Your Word brings life where there is ruin. Help me to know more about Your Word and to use it every day as my weapon in this world. Amen.

NOVEMBER 5

"Put on the full armor of God, so that you can take your stand against the devil's schemes" (Ephesians 6:11).

"… take up the shield of faith, with which you can extinguish all the flaming arrows of the evil one" (Ephesians 6:16b).

"Take the helmet of salvation and the sword of the Spirit, which is the word of God" (Ephesians 6:17).

There he is again! That pesky fly! Where did he come from? It's November, for goodness' sake. Way past the time for house flies. Just when you think it's too cold for them now, one appears out of nowhere. All it takes is an unseasonably warm day and the window left open a crack and in he comes, buzzing around your head, the table, and anywhere he can just to annoy you. You can't let your guard down for a minute.

That's the way it is with sin, temptation, and Satan. You always need to be watching the conditions. Watch the temperature of your spiritual walk with Jesus. Don't leave any openings for a sin attack or for Satan to fly in. As soon as you see it happening, hit him hard with the biggest fly swatter you have. Hit him with the Word of God, with truth, with right living, with prayer, and with confidence that the Spirit of God living in you is greater than the evil one in the world. Jesus is the Son of God, and He has already conquered this pesky fly.

Now, where is that fly swatter?

Dear God, thank You for Your Spirit, Who is given to all believers. Thank You for helping us when the evil one attacks. Amen.

NOVEMBER 6

"You may be sure that wherever the good news is told all over the world, people will remember what she has done. And they will tell others" (Matthew 26:13, CEV).

Most of us have a hard time remembering, and forgetting seems to come easy. The older we get, the more we forget and the less we're able to remember. Why can we remember the tiniest detail of something that happened to us but not how many times we've told it to the same person? How many of us have walked into a room and then forgotten why we were there?

There are some things we should remember and some things we should forget. It's important to remember all of God's blessings to us so we can confidently look forward to the future. However, don't keep track of hurtful words or annoyances. Don't get stuck in the past. My sister says that's why God gave us two ears—what we hear goes in one ear and out the other, especially unkind words. Don't let it stick. Keep track of the good memories just like we keep photo albums of family celebrations, vacations, and other pleasant happenings. The Bible often tells us to remember God's love, faithfulness, and care.

God remembers us too. Psalm 115:12a says, *"The Lord remembers us and will bless us."* It's important to know that God remembers us, even when it seems everyone else has forgotten.

May you never forget what is worth remembering, and never remember what's best forgotten.

Father God, the unnamed woman in the verse above is remembered not for her name but for her act of kindness. Help me to focus on You and not on myself. Amen.

NOVEMBER 7

"A highway will be there, and a roadway; And it will be called the Holy Way" (Isaiah 35:8a, AMP).

You can get to the town of Chance Cove from the Trans-Canada Highway by either one of two turnoffs. One is marked Exit 210 and takes you to the town of Bellevue and a park campground. When you take this exit, follow the road down the hill and turn left at the bottom. Drive past the park and continue until you come to a crossroads, then turn right to Chance Cove.

The other way to Chance Cove is the turnoff by Gull Pond, Exit 210b, and it's marked as the Chance Cove turnoff. When you take this way, stay on the road (it's very winding) until you come to a stop sign at the crossroads. This is the same crossroads you reach coming the other way. Turn left and you're on the Chance Cove Road.

Although there are two separate exits, there's only one way to go through Chance Cove. There are many paths on our life journey, and we often find ourselves on secondary roads, not knowing where we are or how we got there. When we travel by road to new places, we use a GPS to ensure we stay on the right streets and highways. When we travelled in the United States, we used the GPS continuously to keep us on track. Only a few times did we take the wrong way.

For our Christian walk, we need to rely on our spiritual GPS to show us the way. Be attentive to God's leading and His Word, as only one road leads to Heaven. That road begins with belief in the Son of God. Now you're at the crossroads. Which way will you choose?

Father God, thank You that when I came to the crossroads, You helped me choose the right way. I pray for others who are reaching that crossroads right now. Please give them the encouragement they need to believe in You and to take the right road. From a thankful heart. Amen.

NOVEMBER 8

"Don't be afraid, for I have redeemed you. I have called you by your name. You are mine" (Isaiah 43:1b, WEB).

"Angel, come, your breakfast is ready. Angel, let's go for a walk. Angel, do you want a ride in the car?" My dog listens for her name. All I have to do to get her attention is say her name, and she's instantly alert and waiting for my next words. When I was a child playing outside with my friends, my mom would call us by name to come in for supper. The sound travelled around the cove, and it was no trouble to hear her call.

When we want to get someone's full attention, we say their name. Our ears are attuned to hearing our name, especially if we hear other people talking and then our name is mentioned. We immediately tune in and try to hear exactly what they're talking about.

The other night, I was in a deep sleep when I suddenly awoke after hearing my name being loudly called by Terry … or so I thought. I thought he was calling out to me because he was sick. Terry says he didn't call my name. Had I dreamt it?

There are many instances in the Bible where God called people to Him by using their name, for example, when Samuel was sleeping in the temple, God called out to him three separate times by name (1 Samuel 3:10). When Saul was on his way to Damascus to persecute Christians, he was blinded by a bright light and heard a voice say *"Saul, Saul, why do you persecute me?"* (Acts 26:14b).

Is God calling your name? How will you respond?

Father God, help me to be listening and attentive to You. I want to hear what You have to say to me in all circumstances. Amen.

NOVEMBER 9

"But if we walk in the light as he is in the light, we have fellowship with one another" (1 John 1:7a, WEB).

I stepped off the back steps and strolled down the lane. The full moon cast its light across the road and out over the bay. Without streetlights to light up the night, the moonlight helped me to see where I walked. I didn't have any trouble seeing the way to my friend's house.

On clear nights, we walked by the light of the moon, but on dark, cloudy nights, it was possible to walk off the road and into a ditch or off the bridge into the brook. On a dark night, only my brave friends walked past the graveyard alone. Still, there's nothing like a dark night to see the stars. They shine the brightest against the black sky.

Just think how many stars there must be! Too many to count, for sure. My friends and I would stare at the night sky and look for the patterns of the constellations. How many can you name? Did you ever make a wish on a falling star? They move fast, so you have to be quick. On very rare occasions, we saw the Northern Lights. The colours and patterns are like a symphony, creating a unique light show.

In the verse above, we're told that God is in the light and we should walk in that light. When we do this, we have fellowship with God. But just as I had fellowship with my friends when we walked by the moonlight, we also have fellowship with others who walk in God's light.

Father God in Heaven, thank You for the night lights: the moonlight, the starlight, the Northern Lights. Most of all, thank You for shining Your light on my life. Just as the stars are easy to see against the dark night sky, the proof of Your love is brightest in a dark world. Amen.

NOVEMBER 10

"With all your heart you must trust the Lord and not your own judgment. Always let him lead you, and he will clear the road for you to follow" (Proverbs 3:5–6, CEV).

Do you sometimes doubt? Are the things you always believed in now uncertain? Are there obstacles to overcome? Do you mutter to yourself, "There seem to be so many problems, this can't be the right way." One time a friend gave me a card that said, *Never doubt the path you've chosen*. I kept the card, and on difficult days, it's a constant reminder that I must keep on going and trusting that I'm on the right path.

We tend to live by sight and not by faith. The Bible tells us that we must trust in the Lord and not on what we see. This means that God will make a way for us if we let Him lead us.

When I was growing up in Chance Cove, road surfaces were unpaved gravel. Occasionally, the highway department sent a big yellow grader to smooth the road. The blade made a loud noise as it scraped the ground, filling in the potholes and removing large stones. I remember running to the window to see it coming down the road past the old Salvation Army church and school. I saw it coming with the big blade lowered to the ground. The scraping noise was so loud, I'm sure you could hear it a mile away. As the grader moved along, the blade scraped the gravel, widening the shoulders of the road. When it finished, we had a smooth road to walk and drive on.

When all you see are the obstacles, remember that God is working on your road. Trust in the Lord and let Him lead you.

Father in Heaven, sometimes there seem to be so many bumps in the road. Thank You for Your promise to make a way for me to follow You. Help me to trust You even when I don't understand. Amen.

NOVEMBER 11

"But those who came before us will teach you. They will teach you the wisdom of old" (Job 8:10, NLT).

It's important to remember the past so that we don't repeat our mistakes. It's important to remember the stories and courage of those who sacrificed their lives to preserve our freedom. Someone once said, "Those who can't remember the past are doomed to repeat it." I don't think any of us want to repeat those parts of our history.

Along with the past, we should remember the present. Remember, food and clothing aren't rationed, and we don't fear being bombed at night. Remember the men and women who currently are the protectors of the freedoms we enjoy today.

Lastly, we should remember the future. How do we do that? How do we best honour those who sacrificed their lives? We do it by living wisely in the present so that in the future we don't repeat the mistakes of the past.

Proverbs 26 has much to say about repeating folly: *"As a dog returns to its vomit, so fools repeat their folly"* (v. 11). Don't be someone who refuses to learn from the past. Ask God to show you the mistakes and help you learn from them so that you'll have a blessed future.

Deuteronomy 4:9 says, *"You must be very careful not to forget the things you have seen God do for you. Keep reminding yourselves, and tell your children and grandchildren as well"* (CEV).

Father God, thank You for the men and women who fought to give us the freedoms we have today. Bless our country, our leaders, and our military. Give them wisdom to not repeat the mistakes of the past. Raise up godly leaders who will look to You for guidance. Amen.

NOVEMBER 12

"I will not forget you! See, I have engraved you on the palms of my hands" (Isaiah 49:15b–16a).

When I want to remember something, I write notes. I write them on coloured sticky notes, sheets of lined paper, plain scraps of paper, and just about any kind of paper I find. Sometimes I write grocery lists and then go to the store without the list. Have you ever written a note for something and then forgotten where you put it?

Some people write notes to remember; some people tie strings on their fingers to remember; and some people put their ring on the wrong finger to remember. You can probably name a few other unique methods. Sometimes Terry says to me, "Remind me to do such and such tomorrow." Then I wonder who is going to remind me to remind him!

When I want to remember something really important, I write it on my hand. If I write a note on paper, I might lose it. But when I write it on my hand, I'm sure to see it. It's there as a constant reminder of something very important that I need to remember.

God has our name written on His hand. Wow! Not just written, but you might say He has our name tattooed on His hand. We are so important to God that He wants us to know that He could never forget us.

In Exodus 13:9a, we read, *"this observance will be for you like a sign on your hand ... that this law of the Lord is to be on your lips."* This means that we're not to forget what God has done for us, because we are unforgettable to Him.

Father God in Heaven, thank You for telling me that I am so important to You that You engraved my name on Your hand. I sometimes forget how much You love me. Please forgive me, and help me to remember that I am Yours for always. Amen.

NOVEMBER 13

"But the goat chosen by lot as the scapegoat shall be presented alive before the Lord to be used for making atonement by sending it into the wilderness as a scapegoat" (Leviticus 16:10).

"Who walked on the kitchen floor and left that dirt where I just cleaned?"

"Not me, Mom. I took my boots off in the porch. Maybe it was someone else."

Does this excuse sound familiar to you? Fearing punishment, I often blamed someone else. Many times, I wished for a scapegoat when I was in the wrong.

One day while reading the Bible, I came across the account in Leviticus that explained how when the priest put his hands on the head of the goat, he was putting all the people's sins on the goat. Then he sent the goat into the desert to perish, and their sins went with it. That's where the term "scapegoat" comes from. Have you ever let someone else take the blame for something that you did, or has someone ever blamed you for something you didn't do?

Maybe you were in the wrong place at the wrong time and got the blame and the undeserved punishment. It didn't feel good, did it? You didn't choose to be the scapegoat, did you? Just as the priest put the Israelites' sins on the head of the goat, Jesus took all of our sins upon Himself. When Jesus went to the cross to die, He chose to be our scapegoat, and our sins went with Him. Jesus was crucified for our sins—past, present, and future. In Romans 3:25a, Paul says, "*God presented Christ as a sacrifice of atonement.*"

Father God, thank You for giving us Your Son. I'm so glad that when I come to You and confess my wrongs, I know You forgive me. From a thankful heart, in Jesus's name. Amen.

NOVEMBER 14

"But when the king came in to see the guests, he noticed a man there who was not wearing wedding clothes" (Matthew 22:11).

I want to tell you a story about a wedding. This was no ordinary wedding. It was a wedding given by a king. Maybe you've read the story in Matthew 22 about the king giving a big wedding banquet for His son. The story goes on to say that the king invited guests who refused to come, so he invited other guests, who also refused to come. Finally, some people came, and the banquet hall was filled.

In today's passage, one of the guests isn't wearing wedding clothes. The king orders his aides to throw the man into the outer darkness. But when Jesus told this story, He wasn't speaking about what we wear physically but about being clothed in the righteousness of God.

In ancient times, it was a Jewish custom for the host of the wedding to give wedding clothes to all the invited guests. These garments were usually plain, so that they didn't distract from the bride. Rich and poor would look the same. It was improper to not wear a wedding garment, as it was a dishonour to the host. This is why the king in the story told the man he had to leave. Lacking a proper garment, he'd tried to gain entrance on his own terms. He wasn't there to honour the king.

Just as the king provided wedding garments for his guests, God provides our wedding garment—the righteousness of Christ. Unless we have it, we'll miss the wedding feast.

Put on your wedding clothes and come to the banquet!

Father God, help me to show others how to be clothed in Your righteousness. Amen.

NOVEMBER 15

"Jesus replied, 'All who love me will do what I say. My Father will love them, and we will come and make our home with each of them'" (John 14:23, NLT).

I had a friend once who decided that she and her family needed help with the weekly house cleaning and care of the home. With three busy school children and the parents' hectic work schedules, they all agreed that they needed assistance. She put the word out by advertising for help. Soon, someone was hired.

After a week or two, I asked her how the arrangement was going. She said it was wonderful to have help with the household chores, and it certainly freed up a lot of her valuable time. But do you know what she'd do the day before the house cleaner would arrive? She'd tidy and clean the whole house! Can you believe it? Would you hire someone to clean your house and then clean it yourself before they show up? I asked her why she did this, and she said she didn't want the house to look bad when the cleaner came.

When you come to Jesus, He doesn't require you to try cleaning yourself up first. Maybe you'd like to fix up the messes you've made, and correct your mistakes to prove your worth, but you can't. You can never do enough or change enough on your own. That's what got you where you are in the first place. If you want a clear conscience, ask Jesus to help you. The Bible says He is our redeemer. Not only does He forgive us, but He redeems (frees) us from our past sins. He wants you to trust Him.

Father in Heaven, thank You for loving me so much that You accept me just the way I am. Any fixing and changing that needs to be done with me, I leave to You. Amen.

NOVEMBER 16

"Therefore if any man be in Christ, he is a new creature"
(2 Corinthians 5:17a, KJV).

Theres an old saying that "The only thing constant in this world is change." The best example of this is the weather, especially in Newfoundland.

I'm not a person who looks for change, but I think that change looks for me. I actually like change most of the time. Change has been good to me. I've experienced significant change, especially in my career, which necessitated a move to a different town. To take the scary out of change, I just go with it, embrace it, own it, and get involved in it.

Change is a part of life, but sometimes it's scary because it means facing the unknown. I'm sure all of us have faced a significant change in our lives or circumstances, as there are many different types of change: changes in health, changes in where we live, changes in jobs, changes in finances, and changes in relationships. Change can make us feel stressed and anxious. We might feel that we can't cope with it and that we have no one to turn to. Whatever change you're facing, remember to face it with God in your life.

Let God transform your thoughts from anxiety and dread to calmness and confidence. Remember that *"... God causes everything to work together for the good of those who love God and are called according to his purpose for them"* (Romans 8:28, NLT).

Father God, I've had many changes in my life. But the biggest and most important change is when I gave my heart to You. Thank You for always being with me and for working out the changes for my good. Amen.

NOVEMBER 17

"And you should imitate me, just as I imitate Christ"
(1 Corinthians 11:1, NLT).

My brother-in-law, Chris, is very good at imitating other people's voices. When the family gets together, he provides hilarious entertainment and he keeps us laughing for hours. Of course, it's all done in a respectful, funny way and in fond memory of the people he imitates. When he speaks like them, using the same words and actions, we can picture the person in our mind. We hear their voice and see their actions. It keeps the memories of them alive.

All of us have seen comedians on television imitating movie stars, politicians, and other famous people. We can tell right away who it is. It's not easy to imitate people so well that others know without a doubt who's being imitated. To imitate others, you need to listen to their voice and their words, and watch their actions. You have to spend time with them and observe them closely. Some people have a knack (gift) for it. For most of us, it takes practice, practice, and more practice. With each try, we get better and better.

We become Christians by asking Jesus Christ into our hearts and lives. As Christians, we carry Christ's name. When others look at us, do they see Christ? Are we imitating Christ and His character? We need to spend a lot of time in His presence, observing His ways and listening to His voice. Then people will see Christ in us. In Ephesians 5:1, Paul says, *"Imitate God, therefore, in everything you do, because you are his dear children"* (NLT).

Father God, thank You for the people in our lives whom we fondly remember—sometimes with laughter and fun. Help us, Lord, to imitate You in our daily living so that others will see and know Christ through us. Amen.

NOVEMBER 18

"When a woman is about to give birth, she is in great pain. But after it is all over, she forgets the pain and is happy, because she has brought a child into the world" (John 16:21, CEV).

Some years ago, when one of my daughters was going through a difficult time, I wanted her to know how important her birth and life were to me and to God. So I wrote a little book about it for her.

In the book I talked about when I found out that I was pregnant. I told her about the pregnancy and what it felt like. I recounted her actual birth—the time, date, and what she looked like when she came into the world.

I told stories about her preschool years and her school years. I continued with some of her working years and adulthood. I included pictures to mark the highlights.

God tells us in Psalm 139 that He saw us before we were born and has written all of our days in His book. Imagine that! God has a book written about our birth and life. Although some births are unplanned by earthly parents, nobody is a surprise to God. Our birth is significant, and we are each special to God.

We remember and celebrate each other's birthdays because each of us is important to our families and to God. Jesus tells us in Matthew 10:30 that He even knows the number of hairs on our heads. How great is that? Remember, we are not a surprise to God. God bless you on your birthday.

Father God, Psalm 139 tells me that I am so important to You that You have a book written about my life. Help me to live my life so that I bring honour and glory to You. Amen.

NOVEMBER 19

"Don't copy the behavior and customs of this world, but let God transform you into a new person by changing the way you think" (Romans 12:2a, NLT).

I can't think of a better example of this verse than what my mother used to say to me: "If all of your friends wanted to jump over the cliff, would you want to do it too?" So often I tried to get permission to do something with my friends, only to be told that just because they were allowed didn't mean that I was. Usually, it was something questionable and not good for me. I probably told my mother that all my friends were allowed to do something or go somewhere when, in fact, they weren't.

Don't copy what the world does. The world will lead you to making wrong choices based on their standards, not God's. Spend time with Christian friends and talking with God in prayer. Spend time in church worshipping God, and fill your mind with the Word of God.

Whatever you put in your mind, stays with you. Be careful what information you allow to enter. Remember, we are God's temple. Don't allow evil and negative information to influence your thoughts. Protect your mind, and your heart will be healthy too.

Father God, we're often influenced by others to act a certain way or do a certain thing. Help me to recognize when these things have a negative impact on my mind and on my walk with You. Amen.

NOVEMBER 20

"He Himself will deliver you from the hunter's net, from the destructive plague" (Psalm 91:3, HCSB).

Life after the plague! It's been a few years since the plague of COVID swarmed our towns, province, country, and the world. The effects are still being felt and are far-reaching. Lives were changed forever by death, disease complications, job loss, inadequate health care, industry changes, food supply shortages, and countless other consequences. COVID took away our freedom to hug, to touch, and to have close contact.

Remember the old days, when you could hold hands with your friends? I remember holding hands with my friends while we walked to school. It was just the thing you did. Touch is important to humans. It's one of our most basic needs. The absence of touch can lead to depression and other health problems.

So how do we recover and rebuild after such devastation? Remember the song, "Put your hand in the hand". Even though we may not hold hands with our friends like we used to do, we can be assured that Jesus still holds our hand.

Maybe we have to start from the beginning again. Take an account of what is really important and build on that. Establish good relations with family and friends, practice healthy eating, get some kind of physical activity, reach out to neighbours and give what you can from your own resources to others.

Maybe we need to slow down and turn off the devices. The Bible tells us to return to the Lord and He will heal our land (2 Chronicles 7:14).

Father God in Heaven, "You made the earth shake and split wide open; now heal its wounds and stop its trembling" (Psalm 60:2, CEV). *Amen.*

NOVEMBER 21

"You are my hiding place; you will protect me from trouble and surround me with songs of deliverance" (Psalm 32:7).

Do you ever feel like hiding from the world? When cares, worries, and responsibilities become overwhelming, do you want to run away, or maybe just stay inside? I remember playing hide-and-seek with my friends. It was fun to find a spot where you could hide and not be found. Is there such a place today? The Bible says in Psalm 46:10a, *"Be still, and know that I am God"* (KJV).

Sometimes I just want to be in a quiet place to be still and not speak. I want to be closer to God and hear what He has to say to me. The world is full of false faces, hidden agendas, and self-seekers. There's an over abundance of negativity, sarcasm, and unkindness. It's too easy to get caught up in the world's view of things. When I feel this way, I remember Psalm 91:4 and ask God to hide me under His wing.

In Mark 4, we read the parable of the sower. The farmer sowed the seeds, which is the Word of God, to a variety of people. Some are like thorns along the path. Verse 18 and 19 (CEV) says that, *"The seeds that fell among the thornbushes are also people who hear the message. But they start worrying about the needs of this life. They are fooled by the desire to get rich and to have all kinds of other things. So the message gets choked out, and they never produce anything."*

Don't let the worries and cares of this world prevent you from receiving and following the Word of God. Be still before God and He will help you.

Father God, help me to be still and quiet before You so that I can receive Your strength and guidance for my life. I want to know You more and help others know You too. Amen.

NOVEMBER 22

"The thief only comes to steal, kill, and destroy. I came that they may have life, and may have it abundantly" (John 10:10, WEB).

I grew up living next door to my grandmother and grandfather. My grandparents owned and ran a general store across the road from their house. The shop was on the ocean side of the road, overlooking the bay. A lot of life happened between the house and the shop!

Nan was constantly going back and forth between the two buildings. When she went to the house to prepare meals or do chores, she locked the shop door. If you needed to buy something, you had to knock on the house door, and then she'd go to the shop and serve you. So a portion of her life was lived between the house and the shop.

Fishing nets were spread to dry on the grassy bank. Sometimes it was a gathering place, where fishermen stopped to chat with my grandfather. Sometimes they just stood by the shop and looked out over the ocean. There was a sawmill next to the shop, and my father spent many hours there sawing logs into lumber. There were horses inside the fenced garden and ducks quacking in the little manmade duck pond.

People walked by, and children played on the road. Sometimes even newly-built motorboats would be dragged by on the way to be launched. Orange Lodge parades and Easter Sunday morning marches went by between the house and the shop.

I really can't imagine a more abundant life on earth as this life between the house and the shop. But you know something? Heaven will be more, much more.

Father God, thank You for these memories and for the love that was shown in that place. Help me to live my life motivated by love, just as Your Son, Jesus, lived His life on earth. Amen.

NOVEMBER 23

"But when he, the Spirit of truth, comes, he will guide you into all truth" (John 16:13a).

"And with that he breathed on them and said, 'Receive the Holy Spirit'" (John 20:22).

When we were children, our parents taught us how to live in a family, how to ask for things, how to say sorry, how to behave properly with others, and so much more. They taught us how to love, how to treat others, and how to live in the world. They sent us to school and work. They helped us learn how to contribute to society.

The Holy Spirit living in the life of a Christian teaches us spiritual things and helps us live for God. You can tell if the Holy Spirit is present by the fruits of the Spirit in that person's life. The Bible lists them as love, joy, peace, patience, kindness, goodness, faithfulness, gentleness, and self-control (Galatians 5:22–23).

In Galatians 5:17, Paul tells us that *"The Spirit and your desires are enemies of each other. They are always fighting each other and keeping you from doing what you feel you should"* (CEV). But if you're led by the Spirit, you aren't left alone trying to obey the moral laws and the commandments.

When you have the Holy Spirit in you, you have the help of the Spirit. The Bible tells us that the Spirit comforts believers (John 14:16), fills us with peace (Acts 9:31), and helps us in our prayers (Romans 8:16).

Just writing this and relearning it again has given me peace and comfort. I'm so thankful for the gift of the Holy Spirit.

Father God, what a gift You have given us! Not only have You forgiven us and shown us Your love and grace, but You've also given us a Helper, Your Holy Spirit. May I know the power of Your Spirit in my life every single day. Amen.

NOVEMBER 24

"We know that God listens only to people who love and obey him. God doesn't listen to sinners" (John 9:31, CEV).

As a mother, I love my children more than my own life. I want them to have all the best of health and joy in their lives. More than anything, I want them to experience God's protection and provision.

When I first became aware of the above verse and read the story around it, I was more than a bit perturbed. I instantly realized that I probably fell into the category of sinner. "Is it possible," I asked myself, "that God doesn't hear my prayers for my beautiful daughters?" Who would pray for them if I didn't?

I wanted to be certain that my prayers were heard in Heaven. Maybe you've never noticed this verse either, or maybe you dispute the meaning of it. But do you want to take a chance that your prayers are unheard? I certainly didn't want to take that chance, so I asked for God's forgiveness, gave my heart to Him, and followed His leading to the best of my ability. I want Heaven to say, "There's that mother again on behalf of her children. Send out the angel armies; send down the healings; send down the provisions and prepare the table in the wilderness." I want God to say, "Let it be so."

Don't you want the assurance of Heaven's blessings for your children? Romans 3:23 tells us, *"For all have sinned, and come short of the glory of God"* (KJV). Won't you ask Jesus into your heart today?

Father God, thank You for opening my eyes with this piece of Scripture. I know that You love my children even more than I do. Surround them with Your protection from every kind of harm and evil. Heal their diseases and bless their hearts. Amen.

NOVEMBER 25

"Dear friends, although I was very eager to write to you about the salvation we share, I felt compelled to write and urge you to contend for the faith that was once for all entrusted to God's holy people" (Jude 1:3).

"To the only God our Savior be glory, majesty, power and authority, through Jesus Christ our Lord, before all ages, now and forevermore! Amen" (Jude 1:25).

In between these two verses—which are the first verse and the last verse—Jude, who was the half brother of Jesus, tells us to make sure we understand what we believe and why. He points out that godless people spread false teachings, and he gives examples. These false teachings can lead to murder, greed, and rebellion.

If you don't study and know the Scriptures, you're susceptible to false teachings. Some people are good at twisting the Scriptures around to suit any belief. It's important to understand the basic truths of the Bible to strengthen your faith and knowledge.

There will be ridiculers who will try to create division and conflict among believers. They believe there are many paths to God. But we are to stay firm on the foundation of God's Word and truth. Jesus said in John 14:6, *"… I am the way, the truth and the life. No one comes to the Father except through me"* (WEB). There is only one path to God, and that's through Jesus Christ and the cross.

Father God, help me to remember and understand the Scriptures so that I recognize false teachings. Help me to spread the truth about Your Word and the gospel. Amen.

NOVEMBER 26

"In the beginning God created ... " (Genesis 1:1, KJV)

When I read Genesis 1, a few words jumped out at me. When I wrote them down, other truths seemed to line up with the words. This is what I learned from the creation story in Genesis 1:1–28.

Verse 3 says, *"And God said, let there be light: and there was light"* (KJV). We are to create light and be the light to others, wherever we are. Let your light shine before others. God created light and He is light.

Verse 11 says, *"And God said, Let the earth bring forth grass, the herb yielding seed, and the fruit tree yielding fruit after his kind, whose seed is in itself, upon the earth: and it was so"* (KJV). Grow in your walk with God and produce fruit from a harvest of good works.

Verses 17–18 say, *"And God set them in the firmament of the heaven to give light upon the earth ... and to divide the light from the darkness ... "* (KJV). Be separate from the world, with all its ways and values. Be a beacon to those who live in the darkness.

Verse 28 says, *"... have dominion over the fish of the sea, and over the fowl of the air, and over every living thing that moveth upon the earth"* (KJV). Take care of what God has created and given to you. Be a caretaker of the world around you and the family you've been given.

Verse 27 says, *"So God created man in his own image, in the image of God created he him; male and female created he them"* (KJV). Remember who you are. You belong to God. You are made in His image.

Father God, thank You for this lesson from the story of creation. It reminds me that You have placed direction in Scripture for all of us. Amen.

NOVEMBER 27

"Even to your old age and gray hairs I am he, I am he who will sustain you. I have made you and I will carry you; I will sustain you and I will rescue you" (Isaiah 46:4).

Aging isn't always fun, but it is necessary. As the saying goes, "Sometimes we have to just embrace it." Several years ago, I decided to let my grey hair grow out. For most of my adult life, I coloured my hair with dye. My natural colour was sort of a medium to mousy brown. I thought it was dull, so I kept it lighter with dye. Finally, one day I just decided to let my grey hair grow out. I would have a lighter colour that was all natural.

Many changes come with growing older, especially as we enter what's considered *old age*. I don't know the number for that, and I think it's a matter of perspective and goes up as our age goes up. When you're younger, old age seems far away, but it comes upon us faster than we realize. Most of the changes seem to be with our physical bodies and our health.

As each new ailment settles into our bodies, we wonder where our youth has gone. When we were young, we took for granted the parts of us that don't work as well now. Proverbs 20:29 tells us, *"The glory of the young is their strength; the gray hair of experience is the splendor of the old"* (NLT). The young must use and take care of their strength wisely, and the old must use their experience wisely.

May this be our prayer today: *"Don't leave me when I am old and my hair turns gray. Let me tell future generations about your mighty power"* (Psalm 71:18, CEV). Rest assured, God promises to be with believers, to sustain us and carry us through our lives, even into old age.

Father God, even though my hair is grey and parts of me ache, I want to make the most of the time You've given me. I trust You to sustain me, even into old age. Amen.

NOVEMBER 28

"Dear friend, you have always been faithful in helping other followers of the Lord, even the ones you didn't know before"
(3 John 1:5, CEV).

Hospitality is so important that the apostle John wrote about it in a separate book (3 John, towards the end of the New Testament). He wrote it to Gaius, a dear friend in one of the churches known to John.

How often do we thank people for their hospitality to us? From a dinner invitation to an overnight stay, we should show our appreciation to the host/hostess. A note of thanks and a word of encouragement are good ways to convey our thanks.

Hospitality is a lost art in some social circles, as well as some churches. Sharing a meal is a good way to show friendship and kindness, and many people in our circle of influence would appreciate it. Many young people and seniors live alone.

Gaius practised hospitality with friendship and good deeds. Verse 5 tells us that he took care of the travelling teachers who were passing through, even though they were strangers. We could do a similar thing today. Do you know someone who needs a place to stay for a few nights? Why not offer your spare bed to someone in need?

Society today is more self-centred than ever, so it's important to practise hospitality. As Christians, we should be setting the example of serving others as Jesus did.

Father God, help me to practise this lost art. I want others to feel welcome in my home. Thank You for all Your gifts to us, and may I remember to share with those in need. Amen.

NOVEMBER 29

"Those who are wise will shine like the brightness of the heavens, and those who lead many to righteousness, like the stars for ever and ever" (Daniel 12:3).

"The fruit of the righteous is a tree of life; and he that winneth souls is wise" (Proverbs 11:30, KJV).

Who doesn't love tongue twisters? Do you remember this one: *Sally sells sea shells by the seashore?* What about this one: *How much wood could a woodchuck chuck, if a woodchuck could chuck wood?*

I came across this one from my Promise Box of Scripture verses: *If each saved one won one, and each one won, won one, what hosts would be won, when everyone won, had won one.* Don't you just love that one? I do. If you read it correctly, pausing at the commas, it makes sense, and it's quite fun to say out loud.

The Bible promises that those who lead others to Christ will shine like the stars forever: *"You can be sure that whoever brings the sinner back from wandering will save that person from death and bring about the forgiveness of many sins"* (James 5:20, NLT).

Once you become a follower of Christ, you're sent out to become a light to others and lead them to Jesus. However, not everyone can be a Billy Graham. But if you can make a difference to just one person, and that person makes a difference to one, then imagine how many will be won for Christ. Don't be discouraged if your influence is small. Anyone can be an influence for God.

Father God, help me to make a difference to as many people as possible. I want to help others find their way to You. In Jesus's name. Amen.

NOVEMBER 30

"You made summer and winter and gave them to the earth"
(Psalm 74:17, CEV).

Winter started early this year. We had a hot, dry summer, and the good weather extended into the fall. But one morning I woke up to the white stuff.

November was a cold, snowy month. I wondered how I'd get through the months until spring in April or May. *Will I be able to get outside? Will I have opportunities for walking the trails? Will I be able to continue helping with the snow clearing? How will I stay physically and mentally fit?*

As I reflected on the upcoming winter months, I looked up Scripture verses pertaining to winter. The above verse made me stop and consider the majesty and wisdom of God. Who am I to complain about what God has created? I'm thinking about winter all wrong. Winter was created and given to the earth—it is given to us.

It's up to me to make the most of this gift and to find something worthwhile in each cold day. Maybe it's a time of resting more from the summer gardening and travel. Maybe it's a time of reflection on my life, my walk with God, and how I can be a better person. Maybe it's a time to do the things inside that I neglected the rest of the year. Maybe I need to ask God what He wants me to do this winter.

As the days went by, the nudge and encouragement I received was to continue studying and writing. So instead of complaining about winter, I'm using the time to write these words. Maybe God has a special purpose for you this winter. Won't you ask Him?

Father God, thank You for this winter. Forgive me for complaining, and help me to use the time wisely in Your service. Amen.

DECEMBER 1

"... he led the flock to the far side of the wilderness and came to Horeb, the mountain of God" (Exodus 3:1).

Do you ever wonder why you're experiencing difficult circumstances? Every day, it seems like you're walking through a wilderness of dry, coarse ground. No one is around to help you. Your finances are getting scarce. Your health is failing. You feel like an emotional wreck. Are you in a wilderness experience right now? Sometimes going through this causes us to look to God and meet with Him. It causes us to depend on God. In fact, the road in the wilderness can lead you to God. There are many examples in the Bible of people who experienced wilderness situations.

Today's verse is about Moses, who was looking after his father-in-law's flock. He took them into the wilderness to the mountain of Horeb. There he saw the burning bush that didn't burn. God met and spoke with him there. God will go a long way to get someone's attention. God directed Moses to go to Egypt to bring out the Israelites from slavery. This is where Moses received his commission and purpose.

Because of their stubbornness, the Israelites were in the wilderness for forty years: *"Remember how the Lord your God led you all the way in the wilderness these forty years, to humble and test you in order to know what was in your heart, whether or not you would keep his commands"* (Deuteronomy 8:2). God sometimes sets you apart from the world so that you'll look to Him alone. God will meet you in the wilderness if you let Him be your guide, and He'll lead you out of the wilderness when you put your trust in Him. Whatever your wilderness situation, be assured that God is with you.

Father God, I'm so grateful that You promise to be with me in all my life experiences. I trust You to meet with me through the wilderness and valleys. Amen.

DECEMBER 2

"Therefore, be ye also ready: for in such an hour as ye think not the Son of man cometh" (Matthew 24:44, KJV).

Encouragement comes in many forms. But in this particular case, it came by Air Mail on December 2, 1950, from England to the town of Greenspond, Newfoundland. It was from a son to his mother after the death of his father:

My darling mother, here I am writing this letter hoping that God will help me to explain how I feel after the terrible shock about dear father. It was a shock in one way but not another.

I knew that something would happen because the week before, I dreamt that father died. I told Kathleen that something was wrong at home. I know it is hard for us to part but God's will must be done. Do we trust in Him to guide and help us?

Try and be brave mother. I know how you feel but I know God will take care of you. Cheer up. We will all meet some day and what a meeting that will be. I wish I could see you now mother but that little song says 'Thy way not mine O' Lord'. Keep praying mother. God will help you because He never leaves us alone.

It was a shock to me but the Bible says "In such a time as we think not the Son of Man cometh". So, cheer up mother and take care of yourself.

I have a little message from Kathleen. She says tell your mother "I am sharing your sorrows with you." That's all I can write now. Words can't explain what I have in mind. So, God bless you and take care of you. From your broken-hearted son, Frank.

We don't know when our hour will come. Are you ready to meet God?

Father God, I want all my family to be ready to meet You. Please help me to be a guide and encourager in that direction. Amen.

DECEMBER 3

"For God so loved the world that He gave His one and only Son ... to save the world through him" (John 3:16–17).

Some of the best gifts are surprises, especially if it's something you've always wanted. One Christmas, my sister gave me a beautiful writing pen. It was a slim, silver pen engraved with "Happy Writing Suzanne, Love Arlette." It was a special gift because it was a surprise from my sister. I love writing pens, and I'd never received a personalized pen before then.

Gift-giving doesn't need a special occasion. You can give gifts any time. I give gifts at various times throughout the year. Some I buy at a store, and some I make at home. I get the most pleasure from giving gifts that are unique finds or that I made myself (like a one-of-a-kind quilt). A gift can cost a lot of money, or it might cost no money. Sometimes it's a treasured possession to me but of no value to anyone else. What's important is that it's given from the heart.

At Christmas, we give gifts to others in recognition of God's gift to us. Even if we give a very special gift, none of our gifts can compare to the one God gave us. When God sent His Son to earth for us, He'd already planned it from before the creation of the world. What a gift! His Son was a gift from the heart of God. *"Thanks be unto God for his unspeakable gift!"* (2 Corinthians 9:15, KJV).

Father God, thank You for loving me so much that You gave me Your best—Your Son. From a thankful heart. Amen.

DECEMBER 4

"And I heard a sound from heaven like the roar of mighty ocean waves or the rolling of loud thunder. It was like the sound of many harpists playing together" (Revelation 14:2, NLT).

Remember the song from the 1960s, "Silence is Golden"? Well, maybe most of you don't remember. You should look it up, though, as it's a great song. It reminds me that I love quiet and solitude. I regain my energy from quiet times.

One day I was reading verses in Revelation (the last book in the Bible) when I came across the above verse. I suddenly realized that Heaven is not a quiet place. I was flabbergasted! How will I react to all the noise in Heaven? I read other verses on this topic and discovered that in Heaven, there is continual worship, with singing, praising, and celebrating. Some people don't like the sound of thunder. How will they feel when they hear the sound described in the above verse? I told my husband about this and he jokingly said, "I'll leave my hearing aids out." I said, "I'll wear my earplugs." All jokes aside, our human minds can't grasp the glory and majesty of Heaven. I'm certain we will be enthralled with the sights and sounds, so much that we'll be part of the worshiping throng.

Revelation 8:1 tells us that there will be a time of silence in Heaven: *"When he opened the seventh seal, there was silence in heaven for about half an hour"* (WEB). Some think that's when all of Heaven will show awe and respect for the Judge of all the earth.

If you want to experience the sights and sounds of Heaven, make sure your heart is right with God. Whether it's quiet or noisy, I am positively looking forward to Heaven.

Father God, Thank You for Your promise of Heaven. Thank You for forgiving my sins and making me a child of God. I even look forward to the noise of Heaven. Amen.

DECEMBER 5

"But when they cried out to the Lord, he raised up for them a deliverer ... who saved them" (Judges 3:9).

I have a childhood memory of playing at the beach by our house with a couple of friends and two of my sisters. This particular memory stands out because at that time, the ocean was teeming with jellyfish of all sizes. The water was thick with them. We were amazed at this spectacle, so we stood on the long rock and reached into the ocean to scoop them up in our buckets. We were having great fun.

Suddenly, my sister Arlette was in the water, over her head. She had long, blonde hair, and each time she went under the surface, her hair floated on the water. I reached but couldn't get a hold of her. As she went down the third time, I grabbed her hair and pulled until she was out of the water. My biggest worry was that she was wet and Mom was going to be angry, because Arlette was frail and got sick often. But I lived to tell the story, as did my sister.

Salvation can be described as snatching someone from serious danger. Dictionary.com says it's the act of saving or protecting from harm, loss, risk, etc. There are many accounts in the Bible of God sending deliverers to rescue people. The word *salvation* in Scripture refers to God's deliverance, specifically His deliverance from sin.

In the book of Acts, a jailer asks Paul, *"'Sirs, what must I do to be saved?' They replied, 'Believe in the Lord Jesus, and you will be saved—you and your household'"* (Acts 16:30b–31).

Do you want to be snatched from the danger of losing your soul?

Father God in Heaven, thank You for Your plan of salvation. I'm grateful I was there to snatch my sister from the water, and I'm thankful You saved me. Amen.

DECEMBER 6

"He summoned the Twelve and began to send them out in pairs ... He instructed them to take nothing for the road except a walking stick: no bread, no traveling bag, no money in their belts" (Mark 6:7–8, HCSB).

What a day that was for the disciples! They were called to a meeting with the CEO and given more authority and power—with extra responsibility but no extra staff. They were sent out into what could be hostile and sometimes unknown territory. They were instructed to speak to everyone about Jesus and the Kingdom of Heaven. They didn't have notes, and there were no phones, radios, cameras, or social media.

He told them to heal the sick, even though they had no training, no medical books, and no supplies. They weren't to take any personal items or food. This gives the term *travelling light* a new meaning for me. There were no prearranged accommodations, no calling ahead to book a room at the local hotel or Airbnb. No change of clothes, no deodorant, and no razors.

They didn't have to worry about purchasing travel tickets or buying gas. They had to go everywhere on foot. Would we even think about such a thing? Christianity is a travelling religion. It started with Jesus going from place to place and then commissioning His disciples to go into all the world. They just went where Jesus sent them, without even an overnight bag.

Today we spend more time and energy getting our stuff ready and getting to a place than actually doing anything for God. There are a lot of distractions today to take away from God's work. What can we do about it? We can spend less time and energy on things and just go where He sends us.

Father God, there are so many things that take our attention away from You. Please help us to go, just as the first disciples did. Amen.

DECEMBER 7

"So he stood at the entrance to the camp and shouted, 'All of you who are on the Lord's side, come here and join me'"
(Exodus 32:26a, NLT).

We are faced with a multitude of choices every day, and the world would have us choose their way. The world says, "Try this drug. Smoke this, or have a drink. Join us at this open party. Look at this X-rated movie. Take this—the store won't miss it. Experiment with different partners. Complain about your neighbour or friend. Don't go to church or give to charity. Buy something for yourself instead." Gone are the carefree days of childhood when all we had to do was choose which team we wanted to be on in our games.

Sometimes it's easy to give in to the world and choose that way, but the consequences are harsh. After the Israelites had abandoned God and chosen the way of the world by worshipping a man-made golden calf, Moses asked them to make a choice. They had abandoned themselves to immorality and forgotten about God and what He had done for them: Jeremiah 2:12 declares, *"'The heavens are shocked at such a thing and shrink back in horror and dismay,' says the Lord"* (NLT).

For those who didn't choose the Lord's side, the penalty was death by the sword. Three thousand died, and the rest of the camp faced a severe plague. We may not be killed by the sword, but we've certainly faced a plague in these recent years.

Today, do we choose the Lord's side or the world's side?

Father God, have mercy on us and forgive us when we put worldly idols ahead of You. Please continue to guide us and be with us in this life's journey. Amen.

DECEMBER 8

"They gave up the truth about God for a lie, and they worshiped God's creation instead of God, who will be praised forever. Amen" (Romans 1:25, CEV).

Can we grasp the greatness of our Creator? Just think about it. The Creator wasn't born, because He always existed. He has no ending and will not die. He's the Creator of all the earth and all the heavenly bodies that have ever, or will ever, exist.

How can we doubt the existence of an architect and master builder who designed creation? If you know anything about nature and life on earth, you know that all of life exists together and is interdependent. Is one created object better than any other created object? Someone once asked, "Is the quilt block better than the quilt, or the quilt better than the quilter?"

Why would you worship a created object, such as a rock or a piece of wood, instead of the Creator? They are dead objects incapable of any living reaction. Why would you worship a god who isn't alive? It certainly can't forgive your sin, hear your prayers, or heal your problems. Only a living God can do that. Even the earliest people believed in a Creator God.

When you give up the truth about God, you're in danger of God removing His blessing from your life. In Romans 1:28, Paul says, *"Since these people refused even to think about God, he let their useless minds rule over them. That's why they do all sorts of indecent things"* (CEV).

Be careful what and who you believe, because it has an eternal impact on your destiny.

Father God, please forgive me when I veer away from Your truth. Help me to never forget that You are the Creator. I worship You and praise You. Amen.

DECEMBER 9

"To appoint unto them that mourn in Zion, to give unto them beauty for ashes, the oil of joy for mourning, the garment of praise for the spirit of heaviness" (Isaiah 61:3a, KJV).

People grieve for different reasons. When we talk about grief, we're usually referring to the death of a loved one. Some people grieve over the loss of a friendship, or the loss of material things, or the loss of health. Then there are people who grieve over past mistakes. Whatever the reason for grief, we need this promise from God.

Today's verse gives us a picture of someone in deep distress. We can imagine what they look like. Maybe their clothing is drab and stained; their hair is uncombed; and their eyes are red from tears. Their whole face conveys nothing but gloom. But Jesus came to change all that. He tenderly wipes our dirty hair; He dresses us in a beautiful garment; and He replaces our tears with joy. One day, we'll be able to say, *"I am overwhelmed with joy in the Lord my God! For he has dressed me with the clothing of salvation and draped me in a robe of righteousness."* (Isaiah 61:10, NLT).

God sees us in our grieving, and He walks with us. At times, He carries us. He also sends people to help us: *"He has sent me to comfort the broken-hearted"* (Isaiah 61:1b, NLT). He sent His Son, Jesus, to bring us comfort, joy, freedom, victory, and salvation.

Read God's promises and be encouraged today. God sees you where you are. When you don't know how to get up in the morning, or how to go about your day and converse with others, be assured that one day God will replace all your pain, if you trust in Him.

Father God, thank You for Your Son, Jesus. Thank You for the comfort and peace that only You can give. Please comfort the person reading this today and meet them right where they are. Amen.

DECEMBER 10

"Let them praise your great and awesome name. Your name is holy!"
(Psalm 99:3, NLT)

When I was growing up, family names had geographic significance around Newfoundland. Back then, you could tell what part of the province someone came from by their family name. As people immigrated from other areas and countries, their family names were attached to the places where they settled, and they might even have a reputation attached to it. It could be respectable or not so respectable.

Sometimes you could even say what type of work people did for a living based on their name. Perhaps they were fishermen, worked in the woods, were merchants, were crafty, were hardworking, or maybe you might say they were a rough bunch.

Most Newfoundlanders are proud of their family name and try to live up to the positive aspects associated with it. Some can say their ancestors came from Ireland, England, or some other part of Europe. Some descended from Native peoples and proudly display their heritage.

When we become Christians, we acquire a heavenly family name. When people look at us, they should be able to see something positive. Our reputation should honour the Christian family name. Our lives should bring glory to our heavenly Father.

Are we living like that? Can people say they know where we're from based on our family name?

Father God, thank You for my family name. I want to bring honour to Your name in all that I am and in all that I do. Amen.

DECEMBER 11

"So when they continued asking him, he lifted up himself, and said unto them, He that is without sin among you, let him first cast a stone at her" (John 8:7, KJV).

This is the story of the sinful woman whom the scribes and Pharisees brought before Jesus to be condemned and stoned. The only one there without sin was Jesus. At that moment, He could have brought to light the sins of all the people there, but He didn't. Jesus didn't throw a stone at any of them, and He didn't condemn the woman caught in adultery.

The world says, "Nothing in this world is free" and "If it sounds too good to be true, then it probably is." People who believe this don't know about grace. In the story referenced above, everyone condemned the woman except Jesus.

Think about your own life and the times you've messed up. Were you always forgiven and restored, or were you made to feel guilty? Be assured that God forgives, restores, and cancels the guilt. This is grace. Sometimes we find grace in others, and sometimes we don't. How have you shown grace to someone who wronged you? Do you forgive but continue to rub it in to make them feel guilty? Do you feel that they must make amends for the wrong, or beg for your forgiveness? This is not grace.

Just like the woman who was accused, when we're accused by everyone else, Jesus won't throw stones at us. He is a forgiving God, not a condemning God. When we ask for forgiveness and mercy, Jesus is quick to give it to us. But we must be quick to forgive others as Jesus has forgiven us.

Father God, what would I do without Your grace? I know that even if others don't forgive, I have Your forgiveness and righteousness. I have the promise of eternal life in Heaven. Help me to forgive just the same as I have been forgiven. Amen.

DECEMBER 12

"I am overwhelmed with joy in the Lord my God! For he has dressed me with the clothing of salvation and draped me in a robe of righteousness" (Isaiah 61:10a, NLT).

Remember, there's no such thing as bad weather, only bad clothing. It is so true. There is bad weather and then there is really bad weather. Seems like no matter what you put on, it's still cold. I've noticed that as I've gotten older, I've been buying more appropriate clothing for winter, and it does help. Invest in a really warm winter coat, and that will help tremendously when you have to be outside. I like the fashionable cute jackets as much as anyone, but let's face it, they are not warm.

Here's a list of some of your winter-weather clothing essentials: When you're getting ready to go outside, wear a super warm jacket, hat, scarf, gloves, wool socks, and warm boots. For inside the house, wear fleece-lined leggings/cozy sweatpants, oversized cozy sweaters, comfy sweatshirts, and, of course, the coziest pajamas.

In order to have a place in Heaven, we have to be wearing special clothing. When we become believers and followers of Jesus Christ, God clothes us in salvation and offers us a robe of righteousness. When God looks at us, He sees the righteousness of Christ. We can say that we are the righteousness of Christ. Therefore, we are now dressed appropriately for Heaven.

Through this journey of life and through the storms, don't forget the clothing that God gave you. You can face many tempests clothed with the righteousness of Christ.

Father God, thank You for salvation and right standing with You. Thank You for giving me the clothing I need for Heaven. Amen.

DECEMBER 13

"Suddenly a great company of the heavenly host appeared with the angel, praising God ... " (Luke 2:13)

We met together outside the little house that was on the turn to the store. It was an overcast night, but the snow sparkled from the house lights. I put my music book in the clip attached to my new, shiny brass coronet and prepared to play the carol. The mouthpiece was cold on my lips as I blew into it. I was only a beginner player, but I put my best effort into it.

Our little band was comprised of only five or six members—nothing like the size of the mega-bands in the big churches, and certainly not like the heavenly host the shepherds saw when the angel gave them the good news. I was excited and a little proud to be able to play with the band. Christmas was a special event, and the Salvation Army band went caroling to bring music, song, and cheer to the older residents who were unable to get out.

I remember it made me feel happy to be in the band and play all the beautiful Christmas songs. I can't imagine what it would be like to be part of the heavenly host singing that night in the sky over the shepherds. I think they must have been very happy about Christmas when Jesus was born.

Are we as excited today to celebrate the original and real reason for the holiday we call Christmas? This year, focus on the birth of Jesus and the reason why He came. Spread the good news and be joyful.

Father God, we set aside a time of the year to celebrate the birth of Your Son, Jesus. But we fill it with busyness, shopping, parties, and stress. Forgive us, Lord, for focusing on things instead of giving our thoughts to You. Amen.

DECEMBER 14

"But because of the crowd, they could not get him to Jesus. So they went up on the roof, where they removed some tiles and let the mat down in the middle of the room" (Luke 5:19, CEV).

Imagine the scene. Crowds of people (including Pharisees and teachers of the religious law) were gathered outside and inside the house. It was so crowded that no one could push through the tightly packed group. Some were standing as tall as they could to see over the people in front of them. They'd heard that Jesus was in there, and they all wanted to get closer to hear what He was saying.

Suddenly, some men tried to push through the crowds. They were carrying a man on a mat. Of course, they couldn't get a clear path to the door to get inside the house. Then they sized up the situation and took another course. They climbed onto the roof, removed part of it, and lowered their friend through the opening. Their friend was paralyzed, and they wanted Jesus to heal him, so they lowered him down right in front of Jesus!

Aren't you amazed at the ingenuity of these people? They were determined to get their friend to Jesus. They used their physical strength to carry him, and their minds to think of a solution. They exercised their faith to help him. Never doubt the faith and strength of friends to help you in your time of need. Jesus recognized their faith and healed their friend.

These friends were worth their weight in gold. Are we friends like that? Will we do anything to get the people we love to Jesus?

Father God, help me to be a friend like these men. Help me to do everything I can to influence others and lead them to You. Amen.

DECEMBER 15

"We have come to know [by personal observation and experience], and have believed [with deep, consistent faith] the love which God has for us. God is love, and the one who abides in love abides in God, and God abides continually in him" (1 John 4:16, AMP).

"Jesus loves me this I know, for the Bible tells me so." I learned this hymn when I was a child going to church and Sunday school. Today, we often take the lines in our hymns for granted. Do we really know in our hearts that we're loved by God? This children's hymn tells us it is so, but do we believe it? The Bible says, *"For God so loved the world … "* (John 3:16, KJV).

One time on a drive to my mom's house, I poured out my heart to God, as I was feeling exhausted and tired. In my mind, I knew that He did love me, and I remembered several Bible verses that tell me this. But I was fatigued, and my heart was weary. I wanted affirmation of His love for me. I was feeling low and needed to hear from God.

As soon as I voiced this to God, I heard a song on the radio that confirmed that I am loved by God. Even Judas, who betrayed Jesus, was loved. It was a new song that I'd never heard before, and I loved it. Its meaning was clear to me—Jesus is the forgiver. He forgave the man who gave Him to the Romans to be crucified. *Jesus loves me, this I know.*

You may have doubts about other people loving you, but never doubt God's love for you. Jesus Himself is close to you and telling you, "I love you." All we have to do is believe. I'd never felt more loved by God than on that day.

Father God, I believe that You love me more than anyone else could ever love me. You see me as I am, and You still love me. Help me to never forget or doubt Your love. Amen.

DECEMBER 16

"I have told you these things, so that in me you may have peace. In this world you will have trouble. But take heart! I have overcome the world" (John 16:33).

God doesn't want us to live stressful lives. He wants us to feel peace no matter what our circumstances.

"But God, you know what's happening in my life. How can I have peace?"

"But God, my family member is very ill. How can I have peace?"

"But God, the price of everything has doubled. How can I have peace?"

What about my relative who's an addict? What about my responsibility to look after my elderly parent? What about my tiredness and my aching back? We worry over things, from the biggest to the smallest. How can we have peace?

At Christmas time, some people experience high anxiety, and many people stress over shopping, cleaning, and baking. The kids want things you can't afford. You don't know how you'll get everything done. The pressures are high at this time of year. But you know what? That is not God's plan.

In Matthew 11:28, Jesus says, *"Come to me, all of you who are weary and carry heavy burdens, and I will give you rest"* (NLT). There is a gospel song that says, "Take your burden to the Lord and leave it there." But how do we do that? First, ask God to give you the proper focus and perspective on your circumstances. Ask for His peace to fill your mind and heart. As you do this, take one step at a time, one day at a time, and just do the next thing. Jesus tells us to take heart, because He has overcome the world with all of its trials and troubles.

Father God, forgive me when I worry to the point where it affects my peace. I know that You alone have the peace I need. I want to give all my troubles to You and leave them there. Amen.

DECEMBER 17

"John spoke about him and shouted, 'This is the one I told you would come! He is greater than I am, because he was alive before I was born'" (John 1:15, CEV).

When I was young, the times I looked forward to almost as much as Christmas Day were the trips I took with my parents and my grandmother to St. John's to buy Christmas supplies and gift items for Nan's shop. It was so exciting to go to the department stores on Water Street. There was Ayre and Sons, Parker and Monroe, and I can't forget Bowring Brothers. We always had lunch at a restaurant there that overlooked the harbourfront. Most times, it was dark before we left. I slept contentedly all the way home.

The next few days and weeks would be spent unpacking things and putting them on display in Nan's shop. I thought the store was as close to Santa's workshop as you could get. To me, it was a wonderful place of new things that kids dream about. All the children around loved to look at the toys and things she had there. I loved to open the display cases and gaze at all the new items. My friends and I anticipated the joy of Christmas Day and awaited the gifts we would receive on Christmas morning.

I can imagine now the exhilaration of John the Baptist when he realized that the Messiah who'd been talked about and foretold in Scripture had finally arrived. Talk about excitement! He said, "This is the one I told you about." What a gift to the world!

Father God, thank You for all Your gifts. Just as I anticipated receiving toys at Christmas time, I now anticipate celebrating the gift of Your Son, Jesus. Amen.

DECEMBER 18

"Jesus said to them, 'Very truly I tell you, it is not Moses who has given you the bread from heaven, but it is my Father who gives you the true bread from Heaven'" (John 6:32).

Baking sweet goodies for Christmas is a tradition not only in Newfoundland, but around the world. In Newfoundland, we like sweet raisin bread and fruit cake. There's something special about the flavours that form a Christmas fruit cake: spices, citrus, and soaked fruit.

All over the world, people bake and share special treats to remember the Christmas season. In Germany, they enjoy a type of sweet bread called Christollen that is dusted with icing sugar. People in the United Kingdom eat Christmas cake and gingerbread cookies. Many parts of the world enjoy a Christmas pudding. The people in Iceland make pepper cookies similar to ginger snaps. In Australia and New Zealand, they make pavlova, which is made with sugar and egg whites and baked like a meringue.

Maybe you know someone who bakes special treats like these from other countries. One of our European friends made delicate pastries. The tradition of baking special things for Christmas to share with family and friends goes back a long way and is time-honoured.

In the verse above, Jesus tells us that He is the Bread from Heaven and that the manna that the Israelites received in the wilderness came from Heaven as well. As you enjoy baking and eating your Christmas goodies this year, remember that this is when we celebrate Jesus, who is the true and lasting Bread from Heaven.

Father in Heaven, thank You for your Son, Jesus, the reason for the season. Help us to remember that only Jesus can satisfy the hunger and emptiness in our souls. Amen.

DECEMBER 19

"He directs the snow to fall on the earth" (Job 37:6a, NLT).

"The windstorms of winter strike" (Job 37:9, CEV).

I finished work early because there was a snowstorm forecast, and the snow had been coming down heavy all morning. I had a long drive from the centre of the city where I worked to the rural farm area where I lived.

The city streets were snow-covered but passable, as the snowplows were out in force. When I arrived at the turnoff to the road leading out of the city, I knew I was in trouble. The snow was much deeper, and I didn't know how I'd get through the drifts. I kept going, afraid to slow down in case I got stuck.

I arrived at the turnoff to our road and could finally see my house in the distance. But when I reached our road, I saw that it hadn't been plowed. I hit the gas and forced my car to go a bit farther, but the snowdrifts were too deep. I put on my hat and gloves, abandoned my vehicle, and walked through the thigh-high snow to my house. That winter was the winteriest winter I'd ever experienced. It seemed we were in a giant snow globe that was being shaken around.

Job 37:5 says, *"God's voice thunders in marvelous ways; he does great things beyond our understanding."* Who can know the mind of God? Why does He allow the storms in our lives? Is it to teach us to look for refuge in Him?

All nature looks for shelter during a storm. We should follow nature's example. Be prepared for the storms and the wrath of the last days. Listen to the voice of God and accept His offer of salvation by believing in His Son, Jesus Christ.

Father God, thank You for Your plan of salvation. When that day comes, I want to have my refuge in You. Help me extend this message to others. Amen.

DECEMBER 20

"The trees of the Lord are well watered, the cedars of Lebanon that he planted" (Psalm 104:16).

"I'd like you to send your workers to cut down cedar trees in Lebanon for me" (1 Kings 5:6a, CEV).

When I was a child, I went Christmas tree hunting with my dad. The snow was deep as we carefully made our way through the side garden and into the tree line. Some years, it was hard to see what the tree looked like, because the branches were weighed down with snow. We'd bring home several trees for Mom to choose from. I admit that sometimes they were kind of pitiful. But she'd always pick one out and decorate it as best she could.

In later years, my husband and I cut down Christmas trees as well. One year we walked the path behind our house into the woods. Not far along the way, we spotted the perfect tree by the side of the path. It would look beautiful in our home.

According to historical records, the cedars of Lebanon were the grandest trees known to the people of that day. It was felt that these magnificent trees could only have been planted by the Lord, and that they had everything they needed from the Lord for growth. They surpassed any plantings done by humans.

These trees were valued and highly prized for all kinds of building projects. So naturally when King Solomon planned to build a temple for the Lord, he wanted to use these cedars. Only the best materials would be used for the house of God.

Father God, thank You for all the wonderful trees of the world. As King Solomon demonstrated, anything we do for You deserves our best care and effort. Amen.

DECEMBER 21

"'To what can I compare the people of this generation?' Jesus asked. 'How can I describe them?'" (Luke 7:31, NLT)

It seems that down through the ages, we tend to put generations into different categories. I'm from the Baby Boomer generation. I was born after WWII (1946–1964), when the birth rate spiked. Baby boomers are said to have focus and a strong work ethic.

Before me, there were the Traditionalists, who were born before 1946. They're called the silent generation. If you were born between 1965 and 1980, you're known as Generation X. Those born between 1981 and 1996 are known as Millennials. These people are said to be confident and tech savvy.

The words in today's verses come from Jesus. He was wondering how to describe the generation of His day. We say the same thing today: "What's this generation coming to?"

In these Bible passages, we learn that the Pharisees and teachers of the Law of Moses looked at John the Baptist and thought he was crazy. He didn't drink wine, and he fasted. They looked at Jesus and called Him a drunkard because He drank wine and feasted. Even though the Scriptures foretold the coming of them both, many people of His generation didn't believe. There was no way to please them. That generation saw the Messiah born among them, but most didn't accept it.

Whatever characteristics make up your generation, be sure that you believe in the message Jesus and John the Baptist both preached: repent of your sin and believe in the one that God sent—His Son, Jesus Christ.

Father God, thank You for Your Son, Jesus, who died for my sins. Help me to influence this generation to believe in You. Amen.

DECEMBER 22

"Our lives are a Christ-like fragrance rising up to God. But this fragrance is perceived differently by those who are being saved and by those who are perishing" (2 Corinthians 2:15, NLT).

My favourite perfume was always Chanel No. 5. It's a light fragrance that's not overwhelming, but gently scents the air as the wearer passes by. Unlike some perfumes, whose aroma is overpowering and repugnant, leaving a sickening smell around the person, Chanel No. 5 leaves a subtle, sweet aroma.

Diffusers are a popular item in the marketplace today. People put fragrance in them, and the diffuser lightly sends the aroma around the room. There are many different scents available; however, what's pleasant to one person may be overpowering to someone else. One time I was in someone's house where the diffuser scent made me sneeze and cough. It was definitely too strong for me. It was a scent that I didn't prefer.

Just like good and bad perfumes, we leave an aroma wherever we go. Are we a pleasant aroma, or an offensive one? Are those around us saying—as a Newfoundlander would say—"What a hum off that person." Christians living holy lives may be the aroma of life to people who are being saved. But people whose hearts are hard and who reject God don't want to be reminded of their sin and where it will lead. Song of Solomon 1:3a says, *"Pleasing is the fragrance of your perfumes; your name is like perfume poured out."*

Father God, help me to be a good and pleasing fragrance for You to whomever I meet. Amen.

DECEMBER 23

"God has given each of you a gift from his great variety of spiritual gifts. Use them well to serve one another" (1 Peter 4:10, NLT).

Is it still a tablecloth if it's stored in a drawer and never used? When does it stop being a tablecloth and become a piece of material taking up space?

A fancy tablecloth is a beautiful way to dress up your table. I remember long ago when women made tablecloths with crocheted edges and needlework designs placed throughout the material. They lovingly displayed them on the table for special events and special guests. These days, it's hard to find one of those tablecloths. Most of us use placemats, plastic tablecloths, or an occasional cloth tablecloth. However, I do have a few nice linen and cotton tablecloths for Christmas time.

I was thinking about this the other day when I packed up my mother-in-law's tablecloths that she had for years. There were a couple of the old square ones with the crocheted edges and needlework patterns in the corners. I'd never seen them before and wondered why she'd never used them.

When you become a believer in Christ, you're given special gifts and abilities, as well as your natural talents, to help you serve God and others. God expects us to use our gifts and not waste or hide them. Everyone is good at something. Take your gift out of the drawer and let it fulfill its purpose.

Father God, thank You for the reminder to use the gifts You've given me. Help me to apply them wisely in the work You have for me to do. Amen.

DECEMBER 24

"That night in the fields near Bethlehem some shepherds were guarding their sheep" (Luke 2:8, CEV).

It was 3:00 p.m. Christmas Eve, and I was stuck at the office. We were supposed to be driving to my parents' house for Christmas, but I still had to stop at the mall on my way, pack our bags, wrap gifts, and get the girls ready. Terry got off work early and was at home waiting for me. At the last minute, the Assistant Deputy Minister gave me dictation, and I couldn't leave until I typed the letter for him to sign. Where did he think it would go today? It wasn't a letter to Santa.

I was so stressed, I felt like crying. These were busy days, and the office was short-staffed. Finally, I finished the letter and was allowed to leave. I stopped at the mall and bought what I needed. It wouldn't be too late for us to get on the road.

I thought about the eve of Jesus's birth and what people were doing then. I'm sure they were going about their business, working and caring for their family and homes. They had no idea that the very next day, the Saviour they had waited for and heard about from the old prophets would be born.

The lowly shepherds were doing what they'd always done—looking after the sheep in their care. They moved them to the best pasture. They found water for them. They cooked their own meals. They looked up at the sky and rested. Suddenly, an angel stood with them, and heavenly beings surrounded them. On that first Christmas Eve, the shepherds were the first ones to witness the arrival of the Messiah. What started as a normal workday turned out to be one of the most significant events in the Bible.

Father God, when I'm busy rushing here and there, help me to remember the meaning of Christmas. Help me to remember to welcome You into my heart and life. Amen.

DECEMBER 25

"She wrapped him in cloths and placed him in a manger, because there was no guest room available for them" (Luke 2:7b).

Many times while I was growing up, I'd go on a little trip to visit cousins in St. John's. I'd spend a week or two at their house enjoying their company and having fun together. Sometimes my parents drove me there, and sometimes I got a ride with someone else. I was always welcome to visit, and no one ever told me not to come. I can't even imagine how I would feel if I was turned away.

When Joseph and Mary arrived at Bethlehem, they had nowhere to stay. Imagine, no one had room for them in their homes. No one had room for God's Son! The King of Heaven, Creator of our world, sent His Son to earth, and no one had room for Him! God's Son was born in a stable carved out of the rocky ground.

Can you imagine what it would be like to arrive at a relative's house and be told, "Sorry, you can't stay here because we don't have any room for you." Would you put a visitor, especially a woman ready to give birth, in your shed? Have you put Jesus in the shed, with all the other seldom-used or rarely-needed items?

This year as you remember the day Jesus was born and the circumstances around His birth, ask Him to come and stay in your heart. Make room for Him and let Him take up residence in your life. Jesus told us that He has room for us: *"There are many rooms in my Father's house. I wouldn't tell you this, unless it was true. I am going there to prepare a place for each of you"* (John 14:2, CEV).

Father God, I'm so thankful that You didn't turn me away. Thank You for Your promise that You have a place for all who believe in You. Amen.

DECEMBER 26

"But Mary treasured up all these things and pondered them in her heart" (Luke 2:19).

Did you ever hear something that seemed so impossible, you didn't even talk about it but instead kept it in your mind and on your heart? That was Mary when the shepherds told her what the angel had said: *"For there is born to you today, in David's city, a Savior, who is Christ the Lord"* (Luke 2:11, WEB).

Imagine the news and the feeling! Someone tells you something so incredible that you don't know what to say about it. It could be unbelievably good or incredibly bad. This was the case in Genesis 37:11, when Joseph told his family about a dream he'd had. His brothers became jealous, but his father kept in mind what he had said. Daniel experienced something similar: *"That was the end of the vision. I, Daniel, was terrified by my thoughts and my face was pale with fear, but I kept these things to myself"* (Daniel 7:28, NLT).

I'm sure Mary pondered the words told to her but didn't quite know what to do with them. Her role was to be a mother to the Son of God. For the next few years she would raise the child and care for Him as any mother would do. When Jesus started His ministry, I'm sure that Mary recalled the words of long ago. Maybe she hoped there would be more time and He would remain her beloved son for a while longer. Nevertheless, she supported Him and followed Him to the cross. She knew that His purpose was to save humanity, but her heart broke just the same.

Father God, what a story of love we read about with Jesus and His mother, Mary. Thank You for Your plan of salvation for the world. May we be quick to tell others about Your Son, and may they treasure the words in their hearts. Amen.

DECEMBER 27

"This truth gives them confidence that they have eternal life, which God—who does not lie—promised them before the world began" (Titus 1:2, NLT).

"And he who is the Glory of Israel will not lie, nor will he change his mind, for he is not human that he should change his mind!" (1 Samuel 15:29, NLT)

Do you know someone with exemplary character? The Merriam-Webster dictionary defines "exemplary" as "deserving imitation because of excellence." How many people do we know like that? Maybe we know some people with good character. When someone has good character, you can usually trust that what they promise will happen. Still, they may not be exemplary. Be assured, God's character is without blemish or spot. His character is the standard we use and the one we want to imitate in our own Christian walk. God is faithful: *"If we are unfaithful, he remains faithful, for he cannot deny who he is"* (2 Timothy 2:13, NLT). We can be confident in the steadfastness of God's character.

In the book of Titus, Paul gives direction on how to choose godly leaders and elders for the church. They must be above reproach in their example to others, displaying the highest standard of character and godly living. We'd be hard-pressed today to find a leader with all of these traits. But I think the intention is to strive towards these. Sometimes things happen in our lives over which we have no control, but our witness and character should still be trustworthy.

We live in an impure world, but we must do our best with God's help and example to live pure lives with commitment, discipline, self-control, and solid relationships.

Father God, I know Your character is perfect, and I can trust in Your words and promises. Help me to live the best Christian life I can. I want to be a trustworthy person who keeps promises. Amen.

DECEMBER 28

"After agreeing with the workers on one denarius for the day, he sent them into his vineyard" (Matthew 20:2, HCSB).

The owner of the vineyard hired workers in the early morning and agreed to pay them the normal daily wage. Next, he hired workers at 9:00 a.m., and then at noon, he hired more. Finally, at 5:00 p.m., he hired even more workers. In the evening, he called them into the office to pay them. First, he called in the last workers who'd been hired, and then on down the line until he got to the workers who'd been hired early in the morning.

The workers who'd been hired at 5:00 received a full day's wage, so those hired earlier expected to be paid more than a full day's wage, but they were not. All of them received the same wage—a full day's pay. All of them received the same benefit and reward.

It doesn't seem fair, does it? But that's the way of grace. We receive grace even though we didn't work for it; in fact, we can't work for it. When you answer the call of the vineyard owner (no matter when), you'll receive the full benefit of eternal life in Heaven. If you get saved at ninety years old, you'll receive the same wage as someone saved at twelve years old—eternal life. This is the opposite of the world system, where you're paid according to the time put in.

When I worked for the government back in the 1980s, they introduced a temporary benefit whereby employees could buy unworked service for pension benefits. Grace is like that, except you don't pay for it. Jesus purchased it for you. He paid the price for your full benefits—salvation and eternal life in Heaven. Your part is to answer the call of the vineyard owner and believe in God's Son, Jesus.

Father God, your grace is so amazing that I can hardly describe it. Thank You for the story of the vineyard owner as an example to us of Your grace. Amen.

DECEMBER 29

"You prepare a table before me in the presence of my enemies. You anoint my head with oil; my cup overflows" (Psalm 23:5).

Oh, the stories a table could tell. Have you ever thought of the importance and many uses of a table? It's a place to prepare food, serve food, and share food. It's a gathering place to play games, study schoolbooks, complete assignments, and work on art projects and sewing projects. It's a gathering place for Bible study, important meetings, discussions, and business.

I had a dining table for years that we moved around with us from house to house. One day, my husband said we should get a new table, because ours was worn and showing its age. So we looked around for a while and finally bought a brand-new dining table.

I hated to part with the old table, with its dents, scratches, and loose legs. A lot of living happened at that table. A lot of memories were made there. I felt that I was giving up on the memories that it had helped to make for my family. Of course, I eventually realized I still had the memories, and it helped to know that my table went to a new home to help make memories somewhere else. It was a dining table, conference table, homework table, sewing table, and prayer table.

In Psalm 23, the writer gives us a picture of the shepherd providing sanctuary and preparing a meal for us when we're in the dark valley and surrounded by enemies. The shepherd's tent was a place of safety for all weary travellers.

Just like my table had many uses, God says, "Come to my table, and I will provide what you need."

Father God, You are my Shepherd. Thank You for being my refuge and for supplying all that I need through the difficult days. Amen.

DECEMBER 30

"Then Jesus came with them to a place called Gethsemane, and said to his disciples, 'Sit here, while I go there and pray'"
(Matthew 26:36, WEB).

One of my favourite hymns is, "Sweet Hour of Prayer." But how often do we pray for sixty whole minutes? It seems like a long time when you're kneeling by the bed. Do you run out of things to say? Even the disciples didn't stay awake when Jesus asked them to.

If it's so sweet to spend time with God in prayer, why do we go through our day neglecting to pray? I've asked myself the same question. Why do we wait until bedtime and then try to placate God by naming all the people we know and asking for His blessings? From an early age, we were taught to pray this way. We quickly say amen and then go off to sleep.

I like to think of prayer as being in group chat with my family. Every morning since the pandemic began, and still continuing, my four sisters, our mom, and I connect on Messenger Video to talk. We talk about our children, our extended family, and ourselves. We update everyone on our activities, health concerns, and needs. We talk about things happening in the world. We discuss plans for get-togethers and special occasions. We listen to each other and offer advice. Sometimes we disagree, but always out of love.

This is the way prayer should be with our heavenly Father. Prayer is a two-way conversation. But most of us have trouble listening, and when there is silence, we try to fill it with something. The Bible tells us in Colossians 4:2 to *"Devote yourselves to prayer with an alert mind and a thankful heart"* (NLT). Take prayer seriously, approach it boldly, be specific in your requests, and expect God to move.

Father God, sometimes my prayers are rushed. Please forgive me. I know that You're always available for a chat. Help me to take advantage of every opportunity to talk with You. Amen.

DECEMBER 31

"Every word of God is tested and refined [like silver]; He is a shield to those who trust and take refuge in Him" (Proverbs 30:5, AMP).

I just want to sit for a few minutes and listen to the clock ticking. The sound reminds me that time is passing. Soon a new year will begin. Life for me and all creation is marked by the hands of the clock. God's hands started everything and set everything in motion towards a final end. Only God has the stopwatch. Only He can stop the motion of time.

I like to hear the clock ticking. The sound tells me that another day is done, and it reminds me that all things pass and change. On some days, I don't want time to stop. You know the days I mean—the really hard days. I love to hear the clock ticking. It helps me to relax, think, and listen. It helps me listen for God.

I'm grateful for this day that will soon be yesterday. If I see a new day in the morning, I'll be thankful for that. Lamentations 3:23 says, *"Great is his faithfulness; his mercies begin afresh each morning"* (NLT).

This past year, as we visited the promises that He gave us in ages past, old promises became new again. God's Word fills me with fresh hope and stronger faith. I don't know about you, but I'm grateful for this past year, and I look forward to the new. God is with me through every moment.

Father God, thank You for the year that has just ended. Whatever it was, it was. There were joys and celebrations, and there was sadness and times of reflection. I'm so glad that You were with me through each day. Every morning, I was assured of Your continued grace and mercy, because it is new every morning. Amen.

"He was fully convinced that God is able to do whatever he promises"
(Romans 4:21, NLT).

ABOUT THE AUTHOR

Are you one of those people who can't go anywhere without a pen and paper? Suzanne Wheeler is one, and even though she has a background in technology, she still enjoys the simple pen-on-paper method to capture her thoughts. In this regard, she's kept a journal throughout most of her life.

Suzanne comes from the small fishing community of Chance Cove on the Island of Newfoundland. She has a strong love for everything attached to the sea, and many of her devotions reflect that influence and culture. She had a solid Christian upbringing and influence from her family and especially her grandmother, who lived next door, and later from Christian women God placed in her path. From living by the ocean to living in a city, her life experiences are multifaceted, and this has shaped her writings.

Blessed with a love of reading and a very active imagination, she dabbled at writing during high school with poems and essays. As she matured, she often reflected on childhood memories. This led her to write down these reflections as a gift to family under the title *First Encounter*. This was her first published work in 2007, and in 2013, she published *Wooden Ships & Iron Men: The Story of the Schooner* Fronie Myrtle. Suzanne continues to write, and her latest adventure is a collection of stories and reflections she has compiled into a new work, *The Promise Box*.

Suzanne lives in Grand Falls-Windsor, Newfoundland, with her husband, Terry, and her Pomeranian dog, Angel. Besides writing, Suzanne loves cooking, piecing a quilt in the winter months, and collecting driftwood on the beach in summer.

www.ingramcontent.com/pod-product-compliance
Lightning Source LLC
Chambersburg PA
CBHW071313150426
43191CB00007B/603